PROPER ENGLISH?

Debates about the state and status of the English language are rarely debates about language alone. Closely linked to the question, what is proper English? is another, more significant social question: who are the proper English?

The texts in this book have been selected to illustrate the process by which particular forms of English usage are erected and validated as correct and standard. At the same time, the texts demonstrate how a certain group of people, and certain sets of cultural practices are privileged as correct, standard and central.

Covering a period of three hundred years, these writers, who include Locke, Swift, Webster, James, Newbolt and Marenbon, wrestle with questions of language change and decay, correct and incorrect usage, what to prescribe and proscribe. Reread in the light of recent debates about cultural identity – how is it constructed and maintained? what are its effects? – these texts clearly demonstrate the formative roles of race, class and gender in the construction of 'proper Englishness'.

Tony Crowley's introductory material breaks new ground in rescuing these texts from the academic backwater of the 'history of the language' and in reasserting the central role of language in history.

Tony Crowley is a lecturer in the English Department at the University of Southampton, and has taught at the universities of Oxford and Rutgers. He has published widely in the area of language and cultural theory, including *The Politics of Discourse: The Standard Language Question in British Cultural Debates* (1989).

The Politics of Language series is edited by Tony Crowley and Talbot J. Taylor.

THE POLITICS OF LANGUAGE SERIES

In the lives of individuals and societies, language is a factor of greater importance than any other. For the study of language to remain solely the business of a handful of specialists would be a quite unacceptable state of affairs.

(Ferdinand de Saussure)

The Politics of Language Series covers the field of language and cultural theory and will publish radical and innovative texts in this area. In recent years the developments and advances in the study of language and cultural criticism have brought to the fore a new set of questions. The shift from purely formal, analytical approaches has created an interest in the role of language in the social, political and ideological realms and the series will seek to address these new problems with a clear and informed approach. The intention is to gain recognition for the central role of language in individual and public life.

Tony Crowley, University of Southampton
Talbot J. Taylor, College of William and Mary, Virginia

PROPER ENGLISH?

Readings in Language, History and Cultural Identity

Tony Crowley

London and New York

First published 1991
by Routledge
11 New Fetter Lane, London EC4P 4EE

Simultaneously published in the USA and Canada
by Routledge
a division of Routledge, Chapman and Hall, Inc.
29 West 35th Street, New York, NY 10001

Set in 10/12pt Baskerville by
Hope Services (Abingdon) Ltd, Oxon.
Printed in Great Britain by
T. J. Press (Padstow) Ltd, Padstow, Cornwall

British Library Cataloguing in Publication Data
Crowley, Tony
Proper English?: readings in language, history and
cultural identity. – (Politics of language series).
1. English language. Historical linguistics
I. Title   II. Series
420

Library of Congress Cataloging-in-Publication Data
Crowley, Tony.
Proper English?: readings in language, history, and cultural
identity / Tony Crowley.
p.   cm. – (Politics of language)
Includes bibliographical references and index.
1. English language – Great Britain – Standardization – History
– Sources.   2. English language – Social aspects – Great
Britain – History – Sources.   3. Speech and social status –
Great Britain – History – Sources.   4. Language and culture –
Great Britain – History – Sources.   5. Standard language
– History – Sources.   I. Title.   II. Series.
PE1074.7.C7   1991
420.9′41 – dc20   91–9656

ISBN 0–415–04678–5
ISBN 0–415–04679–3 pbk

For
Cornelius and Ellen Crowley
Annie and Tony Fyldes

Contents

Preface   ix

Acknowledgements   x

Introduction: Language, History and the Formation of
Cultural Identity   1

1 John Locke   13
   Extracts from *An Essay Concerning Human Understanding*
   (1690)

2 Jonathan Swift   28
   Extracts from *A Proposal For Correcting, Improving and
   Ascertaining The English Language* (1712)

3 Samuel Johnson   42
   Extract from *The Plan of A Dictionary Of the English
   Language* (1747)

4 Thomas Sheridan   63
   Extracts from *A Course of Lectures on Elocution* (1762)

5 James Buchanan   73
   Extract from *An Essay Towards Establishing A Standard
   For An Elegant and Uniform Pronunciation Of the English
   Language* (1764)

6 Noah Webster   81
   Extract from *Dissertations on the English Language*
   (1789)

7 John Walker   94
   Extracts from *A Critical Pronouncing Dictionary And
   Expositor Of the English Language* (1791)

CONTENTS

8 John Pickering 111
Extract from *A Vocabulary or Collection of Words and Phrases* (1816)

9 T. Watts 123
'On the Probable Future Position Of the English Language' (1850)

10 Archbishop R.C. Trench 136
Extracts from *On the Study of Words* (1851)

11 *Proposal for the Publication Of A New English Dictionary* 150
(1858)

12 G.F. Graham 159
Extracts from *A Book About Words* (1869)

13 Henry Alford 171
Extracts from *The Queen's English* (1864; 3rd edn 1870)

14 Henry James 181
Extract from 'The Speech of American Women' (1905)

15 Henry Newbolt 193
Extracts from *The Teaching of English in England* (1921)

16 Henry Wyld 207
Extracts from 'The Best English: A Claim for the Superiority of Received Standard English' (1934)

17 A.S.C. Ross 219
Extracts from 'Linguistic Class-Indicators In Present-Day English' (1954)

18 Alison Assiter 229
Extracts from 'Did Man Make Language?' (1983)

19 John Marenbon 243
Extracts from *English Our English: The New Orthodoxy Examined* (1987)

Select bibliography 261
Index 265

Preface

The texts collected here constitute an attempt to gather together an overview of an enormous body of work stretching back over three hundred years. They do not tell the whole story. In fact it may be one of the merits of the selection to suggest that there are a number of different stories and histories into which these pieces fit. There are texts which have been missed out and others which have been included which may cause surprise to the reader. However, I have chosen major and minor texts with the aim of both demonstrating the diversity and complexity of the field, and indicating its significance.

Any success in fulfilling these intentions is at least partly thanks to the support and help of a number of people. First I offer my belated thanks and love to Micheline Ishay. To the colleagues and students with whom I have worked over recent years I owe a particular debt; in this regard I am of course very grateful to the present and former members of the Department of English at the University of Southampton. But perhaps my greatest debt is to my family. I would particularly like to mention Seán Joseph Cornelius Gannon, Ellen Roisín Gannon and Ruairí Daniel Crowley Linton, my nephews and nieces, and my grandparents to whom this book is dedicated.

Finally I want to offer my special thanks to Ursula for her strength and love: Is ar scáth a chéile a mhaireann na daoine.

Acknowledgements

The author and publishers would like to thank the following copyright holders for permission to reprint material:

Harper's Bazaar for 'The Speech of American Women' by Henry James; The Oxford University Press for 'The Best English: A Claim for the Superiority of Received Standard English' by Henry Wyld; *Neuphilologische Mitteilungen* for 'Linguistic Class-Indicators in Present-Day English' by A.S.C. Ross; *Radical Philosophy* and Alison Assiter for 'Did Man Make Language' by Alison Assiter; and the Centre for Policy Studies and John Marenbon for *English Our English: The New Orthodoxy Examined* by John Marenbon.

Introduction
Language, history and the formation of cultural identity

A definition of language is always implicitly or explicitly, a definition of human beings in the world.
(Raymond Williams, *Marxism and Literature*, Oxford, Oxford University Press, p. 21)

The aim of this collection is to present a selection of texts which concern themselves with the question of 'proper English'. At first sight such a collection might seem anachronistic for the theoretical changes in disciplines as diverse as English studies, linguistics and the social sciences more generally, might appear to make the question irrelevant. Have not these disciplines developed in ways such that the question itself sounds as though it belongs to a former era? An era in which the answer to such a question took the form of a collection of exemplary texts by the major English stylists? It will be the contention of this introduction that not only is the topic not anachronistic, but that it has become of central importance in debates in many fields precisely because of the recent theoretical advances. Following from this, it is argued that the utility of a collection such as this lies in its provision of the material with which the question can be re-addressed.

The collection is not a selection of the 'major writers' of 'intrinsic merit'. The reader will find that many of the writers are not 'major' and that the worth of their writing is contestable rather than intrinsic. The significance of the collection, however, lies in the fact that the texts gathered here enable us to view the process by which a particularly important theoretical construction is put in place and consolidated. That theoretical construction, postulated and put into practice in a number of distinct historical contexts and in a variety of different discourses, is what is loosely described by the phrase 'proper

1

English'. Yet this phrase has to be analysed if we are to see the full potential of the selection of texts which follows. On one level the meaning of the phrase is fairly narrow: 'proper English' refers to a particular form of English linguistic usage which is erected and validated as correct, standard and central. The texts below have been selected in order to illustrate the development of the process by which this takes place. On another level, however, the phrase has a fairly wide meaning: 'proper English' here refers both to a group of people and to certain sets of cultural practices which are also privileged as correct, standard and central. It is intended that the same texts will also demonstrate this process taking place.

To put the point more clearly, the texts do not simply address the problem of delineating what is to count as 'proper English' in the realm of language. They are also linked to what are, although related, more significant social questions such as, 'who are the proper English?', or 'what are the criteria for proper Englishness in a number of different areas of social and cultural life?' It is this stress which gives these texts their relevance since recent developments across a variety of disciplines have addressed themselves precisely to questions of this sort.[1] Questions, that is, which revolve around the problem of cultural identity: how is it constructed, how is it maintained, what are its effects and what are the advantages and disadvantages of any particular form of cultural identity in a given context.

Before turning to the question of cultural identity it seems pertinent to say something more on the difficulties of presenting the texts which follow. There are two critical difficulties, both of which are traceable to different ways in which language studies have developed in the modern period. The first difficulty stems from the fact that many of the texts assembled below would traditionally have belonged to an established sub-branch within the field of language study (particularly in English studies), 'the history of the language'. I have written elsewhere on the origin and historical development of this area of study, in particular its tendency towards a seamless narrative, its deployment for nationalist purposes and its curious division between 'internal' and 'external' history.[2] The interest of this field for present purposes, however, lies in the way in which it has placed such texts firmly within certain parameters and thus has ascribed to them a set of familiar characteristics by which we recognise them and evaluate their significance. That this *is* a difficulty only becomes apparent when we try to do more with these texts, to read them in different ways, than is allowed for by the limits imposed by the field. For example, it is only when we want to suggest more than that Swift's *Proposal For Correcting, Improving and Ascertaining The English Language* is a prime example of eighteenth-century prescriptivism (of which, the familiar refrain might follow, Johnson's Preface to his *Dictionary* is another example, but Priestley's *Course of Lectures on the Theory of Language and Universal Grammar* is not) that the problem becomes evident. For it is when we read these texts not simply in order to illustrate a linguistic practice whose history might seem familiar but to demonstrate the complex relations which hold between a text which treats of language and the history with which it is enmeshed and in which it is an intervention, that the difficulties arise. To argue that any particular text is an instance of a general practice such as prescriptivism creates a dual problem. On the one hand it reduces the specificity of the text in its context; and on the other hand it brings about a reductive account of the long, varied and historically differentiated set of practices covered by the term prescriptivism.

The first difficulty then is to escape from the familiar boundaries set by 'the history of the language' as we read these texts. Boundaries whose effects can be noted both in academic accounts of *the* English language (in itself already a theoretical construct) and what are termed 'folk-linguistic' versions of the history. The first necessary step away from this difficulty is to acknowledge the intimate relations of these texts with attempts to forge cultural identity in specific historical contexts. That is, to see these texts as belonging not to a continuous tradition but as interventions in debates and historical conjunctures designed to bring about certain effects. The advantage of taking this step is that it frees us from the notion that the texts were all in some sense doing the same thing; and it demands from us that if we are to use the term prescriptivism, we have to recognise that it takes a multiplicity of forms, practices and purposes. Indeed the diversity of the texts gathered here might even force a revision of the call for an examination of the history of prescriptivism, to an appeal for analyses of the histories of prescriptivisms.

There is, however, a more powerful difficulty to be faced when attempting to present these texts for re-consideration, and one which comes from what may appear a strange quarter. 'The history of the language' causes problems by dint of its established and rather conservative limitations (though the field itself is ripe with opportunity for radical analysis). The other field which causes problems,

3

however, is the discipline of linguistics and its more radical effects across the arts and humanities.

For the purposes of this argument we may for the moment take modern linguistics, and more specifically General Linguistics, to be the discipline which made use of a number of pioneering theoretical distinctions formulated by Saussure in his *Course in General Linguistics*. Of course this should not be taken to mean that the *Course* was an originating moment for linguistics since accounts that specify Saussure as the creator of 'the science of language' are at best simplified and at worst misleading. Yet the *Course* did consolidate and give enormous impetus to the tendencies towards abstraction, formalisation and systematisation within the study of language. And the effects of the theoretical developments were explosive, not just within the study of language, but across the whole range of the social sciences. It is certainly the case that as a result of Saussure's thought, the study of language increasingly sought recognition as a pure science: as an abstract, objective study concerned with the rational and all-inclusive rules and relations which govern the system of language.[3]

The problem that Saussure's influence poses is that the revolution in linguistic thought consequent upon it made other approaches appear secondary and in many ways unscientific. Compared with the abstract work of post-Saussurean linguistics, other branches of language study were open to the charge of lacking rigour or theoretical sophistication. Thus given that the texts gathered here do not deal with language in the terms of scientific linguistics, must they be deemed unscientific? Or perhaps to be charitable, pre-scientific? Moreover, in view of the fact that these texts actually talk about language in relation to history, are they not, in the context of Saussure's alleged absolute rejection of history, to be banished as mere un- or pre-scientific chit-chat? The ponderings of benighted minds unfortunate enough not to be able to take advantage of the most important breakthrough in linguistic thought? It would not in fact be surprising to find such texts described in this way and because it is at this point that the difficulty becomes most pressing it will be necessary to explore briefly Saussure's attitude to language and history.

We can begin by considering the following declarations by a twentieth-century linguist on the topic of what he calls 'important matters' which 'demand attention when one approaches the study of language'. First, he claims,

4

there are all the respects in which linguistics links up with ethnology. There are all the relations which may exist between the history of a race or a civilisation. The two histories intermingle and are related one to another. . . . A nation's way of life has an effect upon its language. At the same time it is in great part the language which makes the nation.

A second important consideration is articulated by this linguist when he argues that,

mention must be made of the relations between languages and political history. Major historical events such as the Roman Conquest are of incalculable linguistic importance in all kinds of ways. Colonisation, which is simply one form of conquest, transports a language into new environments, and this brings changes in the language. A great variety of examples could be cited in this connexion. Norway, for instance, adopted Danish on becoming politically united to Denmark, although today Norwegians are trying to shake off this linguistic influence. The internal politics of a country is of no less importance for the life of a language.

And a third matter:

A language has connexions with institutions of every sort: church, school, etc. These institutions in turn are intimately bound up with the literary development of a language. This is a phenomenon of general importance, since it is inseparable from political history. A literary language is by no means confined to the limits apparently imposed upon it by literature. One has only to think of the influence of salons, of the court, and of academies. In connexion with a literary language, there arises the important question of conflict with local dialects.[4]

Evidently this stress on the historical dimension in the study of language could be read as the record of the dying moments of an outmoded approach (the words were first published in 1916). It may be surprising for some readers, particularly those familiar with the more popular accounts of the history of modern linguistic ideas, to discover that these are the words of Saussure. Moreover, it may be even more of a revelation to find that these words are not tucked away in some obscure manuscripts but in fact appear in chapter five of the 'Introduction' to the *Course in General Linguistics*.

Of course readers conversant with the *Course* will know that Saussure mentions these factors precisely in order to relegate them to the realm of 'external linguistics' rather than to include them within the scientific gaze of his theoretical study ('internal linguistics'). However, it is worth noting for the moment that the founder of General Linguistics viewed the topics outlined above as not only significant for linguists, but important in a more general sense. For Saussure this is the case because, he asserts, 'in practice the study of language is in some degree or other the concern of everyone'. He also makes the forceful contention that,

> In the lives of individuals and societies, language is a factor of greater importance than any other. For the study of language to remain solely the business of a handful of specialists would be a quite unacceptable state of affairs.[5]

Arguing against the prevailing trend in linguistic thought in the twentieth century, and indeed the trend which his own thought engendered, Saussure argues that it should not be a sealed and impenetrable field for specialists alone but a discipline whose significance is general precisely because its object is of singular importance in social life. Already in such declarations we can find a clear recognition that Saussure is aware of the importance of language in history; that is, he recognises the relevance of thinking about language not only in relation to 'political history' but also with regard to the importance of the study of language for its users in the historical present. I have argued elsewhere in detail against the reading of Saussure which takes him to be not only unconcerned with, but positively antagonistic to, the connections which hold between language and history.[6] The essential argument is that the rejection, or better the relegation, of the diachronic viewpoint is not a denial of the historical perspective. Rather, what appears in Saussure's account, though it is hardly developed, is the field of external linguistics which takes as its object of study the role of language in history, or more precisely of the relations between language and political history. There is no absolute rejection of history then, but a new positioning of the historical viewpoint in the field of linguistic study. There is even evidence that it is a viewpoint which Saussure might have favoured once the arduous task of clearing the ground for the science of language had been completed.[7]

The difficulty mentioned earlier in regard to the presentation of the sort of texts which follow (that is that post-Saussurean linguistics in its anti-historical stance has made them appear outdated) can now be re-addressed. For if the argument that Saussure does not in fact reject history but merely re-locates it in linguistic study is accurate, then the difficulty becomes less significant. Indeed we can claim that the texts and their presentation below are a contribution to a field which is signalled by Saussure in his work but hardly detailed. It may be called language and history (to differentiate it from historical linguistics), or language and its political history; the name is as yet not so important.[8] The emergence of the field, however, does have enormous implications: first, it brings history back and gives it a long-delayed relevance in linguistic study. And second, it makes us re-consider the stance taken towards language and history in the sub-branch of English studies, 'the history of the language'. For the new attitude to language and history embodied in the field to which Saussure alludes, is not one which takes history to be an empty category, or linguistic history to be a mere succession of facts, but one which sees linguistic history to be a varying, conflictual and power-laden set of relations concerned with the intertwining of language and race, language and nationality, language and colonisation, language and institutions and so on. In its broadest scope it can be taken as the history of the role of language in the construction of forms of cultural identity.

This returns us to the collection below. The texts themselves are documents which may allow the reader to see the myriad ways in which language and political history are interlinked. They are not a gathering of curiosities or obsolete ways of thinking about language, but a guide to the processes by which certain powerful constructions are instituted and take effect in the social order. It was argued earlier that these texts present, in different forms, at different times, for different audiences, the question of what and who is to count as 'proper English'. In that sense they can be taken as one element of a social group's self-understanding, a part of the process in and by which it represents to itself and to others what it considers to be correct and incorrect patterns of belief, value and identity. They set out in various ways patterns of prescription (guidance for those included) and proscription (banishment for the others). At this important level then the texts offer just a glimpse of an enormous, active and still continuing project of self-definition within particular communities.

The texts are varied and span the period 1690 to the present. Three hundred years in which the social orders in which these texts are set – Britain and America – have changed beyond recognition. Yet what we return to time and again in these texts is the intermingling of language and political history, and the crucial role which language has in determining definitions of the social realm and its constituent limits. The texts range from the attempt made by the major English philosopher John Locke to offer a theory of language which would give it semantic stability and therefore enable it to become 'the common Tye of Society', to a contemporary feminist account which attempts to stabilise signification in order to pinpoint sexism more accurately in language and thus to highlight one of the major conflictual tendencies in contemporary social life. There are evident common themes which run through these texts; but there are also great differences as we note at distinct conjunctures the emergence of language and class, language and the writing of history, language and colonialism and language and gender, among other topics, as major issues to be debated. What these texts demonstrate is just the historically varying attempts to define who is to be included and who excluded, on what grounds, in what forms, within or without the prevailing social order. Among them all, however, we can see the constant theme which gives validity to the claim made by Williams and recalled at the head of this essay: 'a definition of language is always implicitly or explicitly, a definition of human beings in the world'.

The differing definitions of language which are set out below are markers in the formation of cultural identity. It is of course an identity which shifts historically and which has no essence to it, as we can see evinced in the changing patterns and beliefs recorded here. In moments of particular crisis the criteria change: what counts as 'proper English' in the realm of language is as likely to vary as what counts as 'proper English' behaviour, or who count as 'proper English' people. There is no essential continuity in the detailed forms of cultural identity, only in the constantly shifting reassertions of a need for it. Thus it is the aim of this selection to allow the reader access to these shifts, reversals and occasional continuities. But it is also hoped that such access may warn us against contemporary efforts to pre- or pro- scribe 'proper English' language, behaviour and people. This is unfortunately necessary since such attempts to produce narrow delimitations of cultural identity are not confined to the past but continue to play a role in the present. It is perhaps one of the major advantages of the study of language and political history to put such endeavours in a perspective where they can be seen to be what they are: thinly veiled attempts to legitimate patterns of exclusion and hierarchy by reference to discourses which have long lost their validity or coherence.

It may be useful to end this introduction with a couple of examples which may serve to show the necessity of studying language in relation to political history with a critical stance. They are both taken from contemporary British social life but could no doubt be compared to similar examples elsewhere. The first is a commentary on the revision of two of the Anglican Church's central texts and takes the form of an attack by no less than the heir to the British throne who speaks as an apparent expert on standards of contemporary English usage:

> Looking at the way English is used in our popular newspapers, our radio and television programmes, even in our schools and theatres, they [a great many people] wonder what it is about our country and our society that our language has become so impoverished, so sloppy and so limited – that we have arrived at such a dismal wasteland of banality, cliché and casual obscenity.[9]

The next head of the Church of England continues by comparing the golden age of the language (a common reflex as the reader will find) with its present degenerate state:

> If English is spoken in Heaven (as the spread of English as a world language makes more likely each year) God undoubtedly employs Cranmer as his speechwriter. The angels of the lesser ministries probably use the language of the New English Bible and the Alternative Service Book for internal memos.

In one sense the substance here makes a familiar refrain, but it is only by considering the history of such complaints that we can see it in a proper perspective in all its vacuity and irrelevance. For rather than noting, as is claimed in the speech, 'a calamitous decline in literacy and the quality of English' (decline since when we may ask, given that literacy has never been higher?), what is in fact at stake here is the interpretation of continuing processes and changes within the social order. It is not only 'proper English' language which is being debated here, but 'proper English' values, modes of behaviour and patterns of belief, which are presented as 'the more eternal values and principles which run like a thread through the whole tapestry of human existence'. It is an attempt to validate a particular viewpoint as enshrined in the eternal past of human history, in order to achieve specific effects in the present.

If this is the familiar plaint of the old guard in a changing social order and as such not so alarming, there are more sinister figures on the horizon. One lesson that the following selection of texts can serve to teach is that the language is often used as a cipher to include or exclude on the grounds of race – inclusions or exclusions whose terms are of course inextricably linked to the formations of cultural identity. The second contemporary example is precisely of this order and is taken from a British parliamentary debate on the question of permitting the settlement in Britain of a number of Hong Kong Chinese. During the debate a Conservative member declared his opposition in these terms:

> We should debate the extent to which our multicultural experiment has succeeded before deciding whether it is prudent to extend it. . . . Vast areas of our inner-cities have already been colonised by alien peoples with little commitment to our society or our way of life.[10]

These are sentiments taken from the discourse of 'proper English' which holds that there is indeed a given, settled and inflexible cultural identity in which language has a crucial determining role and to which 'aliens' simply do not belong. This belief is contradicted by the evidence set out in the texts below. For not only does the evidence demonstrate that the criteria by which the language is evaluated change, so that what counts as 'proper English' usage at one time is rapidly superseded, it also shows that what counts as 'proper English' society or 'way of life', is also historically shifting, mobile and indeterminate. Indeed we could claim that the language offers us a model of social and cultural identity. For by a neat irony, if the argument of the linguistic nationalists is correct, that the language is a rich, flexible and glorious instrument attesting to the nation's cultural ascendancy, then it is so precisely by dint of its history of linguistic and cultural 'bastardisation', 'miscegenation' and 'promiscuous' intercourse with other languages and cultures. Despite all the attempts to delimit the language, to restrict it, to force it to serve only specific functions, it carries on changing, developing and meeting the needs of its speakers. To the dominant and hierarchical forces it is as slippery as the texts below demonstrate it to be; open to use by anyone certainly, but by that very fact thus undermining efforts to make it serve the crude interests of only a few. To those opposed to such forces it shows itself to be as flexible as any useful description of cultural identity itself might be.

10

Against the narrowness of the conservative view of 'proper English' language, culture and history, we can pose a text which dates from the historical moment at which this collection begins. And we discover there an account of the way in which attempts to pre- or pro- scribe a linguistic or cultural identity, to posit a longed for purity, are undermined by the very language in which they are written. If we return to Defoe's satire on 'The True-Born Englishman' (1703) we find:

> The wonder which remains is at our pride
> To value that which all men else deride.
> For Englishmen to boast of generation
> Cancels their knowledge and lampoons the nation.
> A true-born Englishman's a contradiction,
> In speech an irony, in fact a fiction;
> A banter made to be a test to fools,
> Which those that use it justly ridicules;
> A metaphor invented to express
> A man akin to all the universe.

It is the aim of this collection to demonstrate the ways in which the 'fiction' of 'true', 'real', 'proper' English has been constructed; and to enable the reader to see the effects it has produced.

NOTES

1 Examples of such work are R. Colls and P. Dodd (eds) *Englishness* (London: Croom Helm, 1986) and B. Doyle, *English and Englishness* (London: Routledge, 1989) . Perhaps the best is P. Gilroy, *There Ain't No Black in the Union Jack* (London: Hutchinson, 1987). A collection of essays around this theme is included in Homi K. Bhabha (ed.), *Nation and Narration* (London: Routledge, 1990).

2 Tony Crowley, *The Politics of Discourse* (London: Macmillan, 1989) and 'Bakhtin and the History of the Language' in *Bakhtin and Cultural Theory*, ed. D. Shepherd and K. Hirschkop (Manchester: Manchester University Press, 1989).

3 For an account of the difficulties that the new 'science of language' had in sustaining its scientificity, see T. Crowley, 'That Obscure Object of Desire: A Science of Language' in *Ideologies of Language*, ed. J. E. Joseph and T. J. Taylor (London: Routledge, 1990). For another account of the way in which the *Course* has difficulty maintaining its theoretical and methodological distinctions, see S. Weber, 'Saussure and the Apparition of Language: The Critical Perspective', *Modern Language Notes*, 91 (1976), 913–38. An interesting discussion of Saussure's attitude to language and

history (though from a different perspective than that employed here) is
D. Attridge, 'Language as History/History as Language: Saussure and
the Romance of Etymology', in *Peculiar Language* (London: Methuen,
1988).

4 Ferdinand de Saussure, *Course in General Linguistics*, trans. R. Harris
(London: Duckworth, 1983), pp. 21–2. There is also a fourth point
mentioned by Saussure which is concerned with 'everything which relates
to the geographical extension of languages and to their fragmentation into
dialects'.

5 ibid., p. 7.

6 See Tony Crowley, 'The Return of the Repressed: Swift and Saussure on
Language and History' in *New Departures in Linguistics*, ed. G. Woolf (New
York: Garland, 1991).

7 In a now famous letter to Meillet, Saussure claimed

In the last analysis, only the picturesque side of a language still
holds my interest, what makes it different from all others insofar as
it belongs to a particular people with a particular origin, the almost
ethnographic side of language. . . . The utter ineptness of current
terminology, the need for reform, and to show what kind of an
object language is in general – these things over and over again spoil
whatever pleasure I can take in historical studies, even though I
have no greater wish than not to have to bother myself with these
general linguistic considerations.

(*Cahiers Ferdinand de Saussure*, 21 (1964), 93)

8 Another possibility is 'The Social History of Language', the title of a
recent book edited by Peter Burke and Roy Porter (Cambridge: Cambridge
University Press, 1987). The introduction to this text offers a useful
overview of developments in the field. The special issue of *History Workshop
Journal*, 27 (1989), dedicated to the topic of 'Language and History', is also
very illuminating.

9 The Prince of Wales, Address at the Church of St James Garlickhythe in
the City, December 19th 1989, quoted in *Daily Telegraph*, December 29th
1989. The address was ostensibly concerned with the revisions which have
recently been made to the Authorised Version of the Bible and the Book of
Common Prayer.

10 Report on Parliamentary debate held on December 11th 1989, *Guardian*,
December 12th 1989.

1

John Locke

Locke's *Essay* is one of the main works in the English philosophical tradition and one which had a wide-ranging influence in Europe. The historical context of the *Essay* is significant for it can be read as an attempt to give a theoretical account of social unity at a time when the society in which its author lived was recovering from a major set of cultural and political upheavals. Written during the period in which the bourgeoisie had negotiated a powerful position for itself within a new social order, the piece is marked by a concern with one of the fundamental underlying problems of the day: how to reconcile the liberty of the individual on the one hand with the demands of social cohesion on the other. Locke's theoretical account attempts to posit language as the location in which this conflict was to be resolved. The place where we are able at one and the same time to be absolutely individual while at the same time being necessarily social.

Locke's philosophy is empiricist in that it holds knowledge to be based in experience. There are two sources of knowledge in his account: sensation and reflection. The senses are the primary source of knowledge since it is by these means that we acquire our 'simple ideas', such as the ideas of 'cold', 'hard', 'yellow' and so on. The second source of our knowledge is the act of reflection by the mind upon its own operations, which produces ideas not derived from external objects but from mental activities. Examples of such ideas are those of 'perception', 'thinking', 'reasoning', 'knowing', 'willing' and so on. These two means then are the foundations of our knowledge and as we make our way in the world we gradually store up a collection of the various types of ideas. Thus Locke's is an aggregational theory of knowledge in that it argues that we start from the very simplest base (experience of external objects resulting in ideas) and then work our way up to very complex forms of knowledge. So for example, when Locke defines the word 'gold' he says that it stands for the 'complex idea' which is made up of an aggregation of 'simple ideas'; in this case they are the 'simple ideas' of 'a body', 'bright', 'yellow', 'fusible', 'heavy' and 'malleable'. Therefore when we come across words which stand for 'complex ideas' which we do not understand we have to seek to analyse them into their component 'simple ideas' in order to ascertain their reference. Locke's theory of ideas is important because it underpins his theory of language; but as the reader will find, it is a support which has the effect of rendering the task which Locke allots to language a theoretical impossibility.

Locke's theory of knowledge is radically individual since it posits that our own experience is the source of our ideas and that no two people can have the same experience. Yet the theory of language which he builds upon this foundation is intended to indicate how it is that we can come together in society. It is a paradox that needs to be explored in order to perceive the difficulties which it creates. Locke says that words 'stand for nothing, but the Ideas in the mind of him that uses them'. Therefore, he argues in the extract below, words are arbitrary (in that there is no natural connection between a word and an idea), voluntary (the result of an act of willed imposition of a link between a sound and an idea) and individual (in that they can only refer to an idea in the mind of the speaker). Our words then, just as much as our ideas, are radically private and individual. The problem that follows is this: if language is radically private and individual then how can it also be, as is claimed in the *Essay*, 'the great Instrument, and common Tye of Society'? In a sense this is the deep problem which Book III of the *Essay* faces and it can properly be read as rooted in the difficulty of reconciling an individualist account of knowledge and language with the need for a common means of social bonding.

I speak, according to Locke, in order to convey my ideas to my hearers and of course the only way of doing so is the use of words. Yet since the words which I use are arbitrary, voluntary and individual it means that when I talk I cannot be sure that my hearers understand me. For not only do my words signify nothing but the ideas in my head, it is also the case that my words will signify to my hearers nothing but the ideas in their own heads. What cannot be guaranteed is that we both have the same ideas fixed to the same words and that is the central problem. Of course this then opens up the problem of what has been called communicational scepticism, against which Locke fights a rearguard action throughout his text. Communicational scepticism postulates that since I cannot be sure that you understand

14

by my words what I intend you to understand then there can be no certainty that communication has taken place. But if this is the case, then how are we to be reassured that we are not, as Locke says, like parrots, able 'to make articulate sounds distinct enough, which yet, by no means, are capable of language'? If we are, like the later Lockean Humpty Dumpty, able to make words mean just what we want them to mean, then are we not doomed to an individual existence, vainly uttering sounds which refer to our ideas but which give us no reliable contact with anybody else?

It is Locke's task to demonstrate that such is not our fate and this can be taken as the aim of the extract below. The remedies for the 'imperfections and abuses' of words are the summation of his attempt to ensure that individuals can be brought together socially whilst guaranteeing both individuals and the social realm their proper rights. Whether Locke is successful in his attempt to marry radical individualism with the demands of social life is for the reader to decide. It may be worth questioning, however, whether the effort is not doomed from the start. For as Locke points out, 'so hard it is, to show the various meanings and imperfections of Words, when we have nothing else but Words to do it by'. That is, if there is an imperfect language then the only medium in which we can attempt to alter it is that of an imperfect language. The circle is closed. Theories of radical individualism at the level of knowledge and language may mean that the leap to the level of the social order can never be made. The implications of that for a theory of community would be profound.

AN ESSAY CONCERNING HUMAN UNDERSTANDING

Book III
Chapter II
Of the Signification of Words

1. Man, though he have great variety of Thoughts, and such, from which others, as well as himself, might receive Profit and Delight; yet they are all within his own Breast, invisible, and hidden from others, nor can of themselves be made to appear. The Comfort, and Advantage of Society, not being to be had without Communication of Thoughts, it was necessary, that Man should find out some external sensible Signs, whereby those invisible *Ideas*, which his thoughts are made up of, might be made known to others. For this purpose, nothing was so

fit, either for Plenty or Quickness, as those articulate Sounds, which with so much Ease and Variety, he found himself able to make. Thus we may conceive how *Words*, which were by Nature so well adapted to that purpose, come to be made use of by Men, as *the Signs of* their *Ideas*; not by any natural connexion, that there is between particular articulate Sounds and certain *Ideas*, for then there would be but one language amongst all Men; but by a voluntary Imposition, whereby such a Word is made arbitrarily the Mark of such an *Idea*. The use then of Words, is to be sensible Marks of *Ideas*; and the *Ideas* they stand for, are their proper and immediate signification.

2. The use Men have of these Marks, being either to record their own Thoughts for the Assistance of their own Memory; or as it were, to bring out their *Ideas*, and lay them before the view of others: *Words in their primary or immediate Signification, stand for nothing, but the IDEAS in the Mind of him that uses them*, how imperfectly soever, or carelessly those *Ideas* are collected from the Things which they are supposed to represent. When a Man speaks to another, it is, that he may be understood; and the end of Speech is, that those Sounds, as Marks, may make known his *Ideas* to the Hearer. That then which Words are the Marks of, are the *Ideas* of the speaker: Nor can any one apply them, as Marks, immediately to anything else, but the Ideas, that he himself hath: For this would be to make them Signs of his own Conceptions, and yet apply them to other *Ideas*; which would be to make them Signs, and not Signs of his *Ideas* at the same time; and so in effect, to have no signification at all. Words being voluntary Signs, they cannot be voluntary Signs imposed by him on Things he knows not. That would be to make them Signs of nothing, Sounds without Signification. A Man cannot make his Words the Signs either of Qualities in Things, or of Conceptions in the Mind of another, whereof he has none in his own. Till he has some *Ideas* of his own, he cannot suppose them to correspond with the Conceptions of another Man; nor can he use any Signs for them; For thus they would be Signs of he knows not what, which is in Truth to be Signs of nothing. But when he represents to himself other Men's *Ideas*, by some of his own, if he consent to give them the same names, that other Men do, 'tis still to his own *Ideas*; to *Ideas* that he has, and not to *Ideas* that he has not.

3. This is so necessary in the use of Language, that in this respect, the Knowing, and the Ignorant; the Learned, and Unlearned, use the *Words* they speak (with any meaning) all alike. They, *in every Man's mouth, stand for the IDEAS he has*, and which he would express by them. A child having taken notice of nothing in the Metal he hears called

Gold, but the bright shining yellow colour, he applies the Word Gold only to his own *Idea* of that Colour, and nothing else; and therefore calls the same colour in a Peacock's Tail, Gold. Another that hath better observed, adds to shining yellow, great Weight: And then the Sound Gold, when he uses it, stands for a Complex *Idea* of a shining Yellow and very weighty Substance. Another adds to those Qualities, Fusibility: and then the Word Gold to him signifies a Body, bright, yellow, fusible, and very heavy. Another adds Malleability. Each of these uses equally the Word Gold, when they have Occasion to express the *Idea*, which they have apply'd it to: But it is evident, that each can apply it only to his own *Idea*; nor can he make it stand, as a Sign of such a complex *Idea*, as he has not.

4. But though Words, as they are used by Men, can properly and immediately signify nothing but the *Ideas*, that are in the Mind of the Speaker; yet they in their thoughts give them a secret reference to two other things.

First, they suppose their Words to be the Marks of the IDEAS in the Minds also of other Men, with whom they communicate: For else they should talk in vain, and could not be understood, if the sounds they applied to one *Idea*, were such, as by the Hearer, were applied to another, which is to speak two Languages. But in this, Men stand usually not to examine, whether the *Idea* they, and those they discourse with have in their Minds, be the same: But think it enough, that they use the Word, as they imagine, in the common Acceptation of that Language; in which case they suppose, that the *Idea*, they make it a Sign of, is precisely the same, to which the Understanding Men of that country apply that name.

5. *Secondly*, Because Men would not be thought to talk *barely* of their own Imaginations, but of Things as they really are; therefore they *often suppose their Words to stand for the reality of Things*. But this relating more particularly to Substances, and their Names, as perhaps the former does to simple *Ideas* and Modes, we shall speak of these two different ways of applying Words more at large, when we come to treat of the Names of mixed Modes, and Substances, in particular: Though give me leave here to say, that it is a perverting the use of Words, and brings unavoidable Obscurity and Confusion into their Signification, whenever we make them stand for any thing, but those *Ideas* we have in our own minds.

6. Considering Words also it is farther to be considered. *First*, That they being immediately the Signs of Men's *Ideas*; and, by that means, the Instruments whereby Men communicate their Conceptions, and

express to one another those Thoughts and Imaginations, they have within their own Breasts, *there comes by constant use*, to be such *a connexion between certain sounds and the IDEAS they stand for*, that the Names heard, almost as readily excite certain *Ideas*, as if the Objects themselves, which are apt to produce them, did actually affect the senses. Which is manifestly so in all obvious sensible Qualities; and in all Substances, that frequently, and familiarly occur to us.

7. *Secondly*, That though the proper and immediate Signification of Words, are *Ideas* in the Mind of the Speaker; yet because by familiar use from our Cradles, we come to learn certain articulate Sounds very perfectly, and have them readily on our Tongues, and always at hand in our Memories; but yet are not always careful to examine, or settle their Significations perfectly, it *often* happens that *Men*, even when they would apply themselves to an attentive Consideration, do *set their Thoughts more on Words than on Things*. Nay, because Words are many of them learn'd, before the *Ideas* are known for which they stand; Therefore some, not only Children, but Men, speak several words, no otherwise than Parrots do, only because they have learn'd them, and have been accustomed to those Sounds. But so far as Words are of Use and Signification, so far is there a constant connexion between the Sound and the *Idea*; and a Designation, that the one stand for the other: without which Application of them, they are nothing but so much insignificant Noise.

8. *Words*, by long and familiar use, as has been said, come to excite in Men certain *Ideas*, so constantly and readily, that they are apt to suppose a natural connexion between them. But that they *signify* only Men's peculiar *Ideas*, and that *by a perfectly arbitrary Imposition*, is evident, in that they often fail to excite in others (even that use the same language) the same *Ideas*, we take them to be the Signs of: And every Man has so inviolable a liberty, to make Words stand for what *Ideas* he pleases, that no one hath the Power to make others have the same *Ideas* in their Minds, that he has, when they use the same Words, that he does. And therefore the great *Augustus* himself, in the Possession of that Power which ruled the World, acknowledged that he could not make a new Latin Word: which was as much to say, that he could not arbitrarily appoint, what *Idea* any Sound should be a Sign of, in the Mouths and common Language of his Subjects. 'Tis true, common use, by a tacit Consent, appropriates certain Sounds to certain *Ideas* in all Languages, which so far limits the signification of that Sound, that unless a Man applies it to the same *Idea*, he does not speak properly: And let me add, that unless a Man's Words excite the same *Ideas* in

the Hearer, which he makes them stand for in speaking, he does not speak intelligibly. But whatever be the consequence of any Man's using of Words differently, either from their general Meaning, or the particular Sense of the Person to whom he addresses them, this is certain, their signification, in his use of them, is limited to his *Ideas*, and they can be Signs of nothing else.

Chapter XI
Of the Remedies of the Foregoing Imperfections and Abuses

1. The natural and improved Imperfections of Language, we have seen above at large: and Speech being the great Bond that holds Society together, and the common Conduit, whereby the Improvements of Knowledge are conveyed from one Man, and one Generation to another, it would well deserve our most serious Thoughts, to consider what *Remedies* are to be found for *these Inconveniences* abovementioned.

2. I am not so vain to think, that anyone can pretend to *Reforming* the *Languages* of the World, no not so much as that of his own Country, without rendering himself ridiculous. To require that Men should use their words constantly in the same sense, and for none but determined and uniform *Ideas*, would be to think, that all Men should have the same Notions, and should talk of nothing but what they have clear and distinct *Ideas* of. Which is not to be expected by anyone, who hath not vanity enough to imagine he can prevail with Men, to be very knowing, or very silent. And he must be very little skill'd in the world, who thinks that a voluble Tongue, shall accompany only a good Understanding; or that Men's talking much or little, shall hold proportion only to their Knowledge.

3. But though the Market and Exchange must be left to their own ways of Talking, and Gossipings not to be robb'd of their ancient Privilege: though the Schools, and Men of Argument would perhaps take it amiss to have anything offered, to abate the length, or lessen the number of their Disputes; yet, methinks those, *who* pretend *seriously* to *search after*, or maintain *Truth*, should think themselves obliged to study how they might deliver themselves without Obscurity, Doubtfulness, or Equivocation, to which Men's Words are naturally liable, if care be not taken.

4. For he that shall well consider the *Errors* and Obscurity, the Mistakes and Confusion, that is *spread in the World by an ill use of Words*, will find some reason to doubt, whether Language, as it has been

employ'd, has contributed more to the improvement or hindrance of Knowledge amongst Mankind. How many are there, that when they would think on Things, fix their Thoughts only on Words, especially when they would apply their Minds to Moral matters? And who can then wonder, if the result of such Contemplations and Reasonings, about little more than Sounds, whilst the *Ideas* they annexed to them, are very confused, or very unsteady, or perhaps none at all; who can wonder, I say, that such Thoughts and Reasonings, end in nothing but Obscurity and Mistake, without any clear Judgment or Knowledge?

5. This Inconvenience, in an ill use of Words, Men suffer in their own private Meditations: but much more manifest are the Disorders which follow from it, in Conversation, Discourse and Arguings with others. For Language being the great Conduit, whereby Men convey their Discoveries, Reasonings, and Knowledge, from one to another, he that makes an ill use of it, though he does not corrupt the Fountains of Knowledge, which are in Things themselves; yet he does, as much as in him lies, break or stop the Pipes, whereby it is distributed to the publick use and advantage of Mankind. He that uses Words without any clear and steady meaning, What does he but lead himself and others into Errors? And he that designedly does it, ought to be looked on as an Enemy to Truth and Knowledge. And yet, who can wonder, that all the Sciences and Parts of Knowledge, have been so over-charged with obscure and equivocal terms, and insignificant and doubtful Expressions, capable to make the most attentive or quick-sighted, very little, or not at all the more Knowing or Orthodox; since Subtility, in those who make a Profession to teach or defend Truth, hath passed so much for a vertue: A Vertue, indeed, which consisting, for the most part, in nothing but the fallacious and illusory use of *obscure* or *deceitful Terms*, is only fit to *make Men* more *conceited* in their Ignorance, and *obstinate* in their Errors.

6. Let us look into Books of Controversy of any kind, there we shall see, that the effect of obscure, unsteady, or equivocal Terms, is nothing but noise and wrangling about Sounds, without convincing or bettring a Man's Understanding. For if the *Idea* be not agreed on, betwixt the Speaker and Hearer, for which the Words stand, the Argument is not about Things, but Names. As often as such a Word, whose Signification is not ascertained between them, comes in use, their Understandings have no other Object wherein they agree, but barely the Sound, the Things, that they think on at that time as expressed by that Word, being quite different.

7. Whether a *Bat* be a *Bird*, or no, is not a question, whether a Bat be

another Thing than indeed it is, or have other Qualities than indeed it has, for that would be extremely absurd to doubt of: But the question is, 1. Either between those that acknowledged themselves to have but imperfect *Ideas* of one or both of those sorts of Things, for which these Names are supposed to stand; and then it is a real Enquiry, concerning the nature of a *Bird*, or a *Bat*, to make their yet imperfect *Ideas* of it more complete, by examining, whether all the simple *Ideas*, to which combined together, they both give the name *Bird*, be all to be found in a *Bat*: But this is a question only of Enquirers, (not Disputers,) who neither affirm, nor deny, but examine: Or, 2. It is a question between Disputants; whereof the one affirms, and the other denies, that a *Bat* is a *Bird*. And then the question is barely about the signification of one, or both these Words; in that they not having both the same complex *Ideas*, to which they give these two Names, one hold, and t'other denies, that these two names may be affirmed one of another. Were they agreed in the signification of these two Names, it were impossible they should dispute about them. For they would presently and clearly see, (were that adjusted between them,) whether all the simple *Ideas*, of the more general name *Bird*, were found in the complex *Idea* of a *Bat*, or no; and so there could be no doubt, whether a *Bat* were a *Bird*, or no. And here I desire it may be considered, and carefully examined, whether the greatest part of the Disputes in the World, are not meerly Verbal, and about the signification of Words; and whether if the terms they are made in, were defined, and reduced in their Signification (as they must be, were they to signify anything) to determined Collections of the simple *Ideas* they do or should stand for, those Disputes would not end of themselves, and immediately vanish. I leave it then to be considered, what the learning of Disputation is, and how well they are employed for the advantage of themselves, or others, whose business is only the vain ostentation of Sounds; *i.e.* those who spend their lives in Disputes and Controversies. When I shall see any of these Combatants, strip all his Terms of Ambiguity and Obscurity, (which everyone may do in the Words he uses himself) I shall think him a Champion for Knowledge, Truth, and Peace, and not the Slave of Vain-Glory, Ambition, or a Party.

8. *To remedy the Defects of Speech* before mentioned, to some degree, and to prevent the Inconveniences that follow from them, I imagine, the observation of these following Rules may be of use, till some body better able to judge it worth his while, to think more maturely on this Matter, and oblige the World with his Thoughts on it.

First, A Man should take care *to use no word without a signification*, no

Name without an *Idea* for which he makes it stand. This rule will not seem altogether needless, to any one who shall take the pains to recollect how often he has met such Words; as *Instinct*, *Sympathy*, and *Antipathy*, etc. in the Discourse of others, so made use of, as he might easily conclude, that those that used them, had no *Ideas* in their Minds to which they applied them; but spoke them only as Sounds, which usually served instead of Reasons, on the like occasions. Not but that these Words, and the like, have very proper Significations in which they may be used; but there being no natural connexion between any Words, and any *Ideas*, these, and any other, may be learn'd by rote, and pronounced or writ by Men, who have no *Ideas* in their Minds, to which they have annexed them, and for which they make them stand; which is necessary they should, if Men would speak intelligibly even to themselves alone.

9. *Secondly*, 'Tis not enough a Man *uses* his *Words as signs of* some *Ideas*; those *Ideas* he annexes them to, if they be *simple* must be clear and distinct; if *complex* must be *determinate*, *i.e.* the precise Collection of simple *Ideas* settled in the Mind, with that Sound annexed to it, as the sign of that precise determined Collection, and no other. This is very necessary in Names of Modes, and especially Moral Words; which having no settled Objects in Nature, from whence their *Ideas* are taken, as from their Original, are apt to be very confused. *Justice* is a Word in every Man's Mouth, but most commonly with a very undetermined loose signification: Which will always be so, unless a Man has in his Mind a distinct comprehension of the component parts, that complex *Idea* consists of; and if it be compounded, must be able to resolve it still on, till he at last comes to the simple *Ideas*, that make it up: And unless this be done, a Man makes an ill use of a Word, let it be *Justice*, for example, or any other. I do not say, a Man needs stand to recollect, and make this Analysis at large, every time the Word *Justice* comes in his way: But this, at least, is necessary, that he have so examined the signification of that Name, and settled the *Idea* of all its Parts in his Mind, that he can do it when he pleases. If one, who makes his complex *Idea* of *Justice*, to be such a treatment of the Person or Goods of another, as is according to Law, hath not a clear and distinct *Idea* what *Law* is, which makes part of his complex *Idea* of Justice, 'tis plain, his *Idea* of Justice it self, will be confused and imperfect. This exactness will, perhaps, be judged very troublesome: and therefore most Men will think, they may be excused from settling the complex *Ideas* of mixed Modes so precisely in their Minds. But yet I must say, till this be done, it must not be wondred, that they have a

22

great deal of Obscurity and Confusion in their own Minds, and a great deal of wrangling in their Discourses with others.

10. In the Names of *Substances*, something more is required than barely *determined Ideas*; In these *the Names must also be conformable to Things*, as they exist: But of this, I shall have occasion to speak more at large by and by. This Exactness is absolutely necessary in Enquiries after philosophical Knowledge, and in Conversations about Truth. And though it would be well too, if it extended it self to common Conversation, and the ordinary Affairs of Life; yet I think, that is scarce to be expected. Vulgar Notions suit vulgar Discourses: and both, though confused enough, yet serve pretty well the Market, and the Wake. Merchants and Lovers, Cooks and Taylors, have Words wherewithal to dispatch their ordinary Affairs; and so, I think, might Philosophers and Disputants too, if they had a Mind to understand, and to be clearly understood.

11. *Thirdly*, 'Tis not enough that Men have *Ideas*, determined *Ideas*, for which they make these signs stand; but they *must* also take care to *apply their Words*, as near as may be, *to such IDEAS as common use has annexed them to*. For Words, especially of Languages already framed, being no Man's private possession, but the common measure of Commerce and Communication, 'tis not for any one, at pleasure, to change the stamp they are current in; nor alter the *Ideas* they are affixed to; or at least when there is a necessity to do so, he is bound to give notice of it. Men's Intentions in speaking are, or at least should be, to be understood; which cannot be without frequent Explanations, Demands, and other the like incommodious Interruptions, where Men do not follow common use. Propriety of Speech, is that which gives our Thoughts entrance into other Men's Minds with the greatest ease and advantage: and therefore deserves some part of our Care and Study, especially in the names of moral Words. The proper signification and use of Terms is best to be learned from those who, in their writings and Discourses, appear to have the clearest Notions, and apply'd to them their Terms with the exactest choice and fitness. This way of using a Man's Words, according to the Propriety of the Language, though it have not always the good Fortune to be understood: Yet most commonly leaves the blame of it on him, who is so unskilful in the Language he speaks, as not to understand it, when made use of, as it ought to be.

12. *Fourthly*, But because common use has not so visibly annexed any signification to Words, as to make Men know always certainly what they precisely stand for: And because Men in the Improvement of

their Knowledge, come to have *Ideas* different from the vulgar and ordinarily received ones, for which they must either make new Words, (which Men seldom venture to do, for fear of being thought guilty of Affectation, or Novelty,) or else *must* use old ones, in a new signification. Therefore after the Observation of the foregoing Rules, it is sometimes necessary for the ascertaining the signification of Words, to *declare their Meaning*; where either common use has left it uncertain and loose; (as it has in most Names of very complex *Ideas*) or where a Man uses them in a sense any way peculiar to himself; or where the Term, being very material in the Discourse, and that upon which it chiefly turns, is liable to any Doubtfulness, or Mistake.

13. As the *Ideas*, Men's Words stand for, are of different sorts: so the way of making known the *Ideas*, they stand for, when there is Occasion, is also different. For though defining be thought the proper *way, to make known the proper signification of words*; yet there be some Words, that will not be defined, as there be others, whose precise meaning cannot be made known, but by Definition: and, perhaps, a third, which partake somewhat of both the other, as we shall see in the names of simple *Ideas*, Modes, and Substances. . . .

24. But though Definitions will serve to explain the Names of Substances, as they stand for our *Ideas*; yet they leave them not without great imperfection, as they stand for Things. For our Names of Substances being not put barely for our *Ideas*, but being made use of ultimately to represent Things, and so are put in their place, their signification must agree with the Truth of Things, as well as with Men's *Ideas*. And therefore in Substances, we are not always to rest in the ordinary complex *Idea*, commonly received as the signification of that Word, but must go a little farther, and enquire into the Nature and Properties of the Things themselves, and thereby perfect, as much as we can, our *Ideas* of their distinct Species; or else learn them from such as are used to that sort of Things, and are experienced in them. For since 'tis intended their Names should stand for such Collections of simple *Ideas*, as do really exist in Things themselves, as well as for the complex *Idea* in other Men's Minds, which in their ordinary acceptation they stand for: therefore *to define their Names right, Natural History is to be enquired into*; and their Properties are, with care and examination, to be found out. For it is not enough, for the avoiding Inconveniencies in Discourses and Arguings about natural Bodies and substantial Things, to have learned, from the Propriety of the Language, the common but confused, or very imperfect *Idea*, to which each Word is applied, and to keep them to that *Idea* in our use of

them: but we must, by acquainting our selves with the History of that sort of Things, rectify and settle our complex *Idea*, belonging to each specifick Name; and in Discourse with others, (if we find them mistake us) we ought to tell, what the complex *Idea* is, that we make such a Name stand for. This is the more necessary to be done by all those, who search after Knowledge, and philosophical Verity, in that Children being taught Words whilst they have but imperfect Notions of Things, apply them at random, and without much thinking, and seldom frame determined *Ideas* to be signified by them. Which Custom, (it being easy, and serving well enough for the ordinary Affairs of Life and Conversation) they are apt to continue, when they are Men: And so begin at the wrong end, learning Words first, and perfectly, but make the Notions, to which they apply those words afterwards, very overtly. By this means it comes to pass, that Men speaking the proper Language of their Country, *i.e.* according to Grammar-Rules of that Language, do yet speak very improperly of Things themselves; and by their arguing one with another, make but small progress in the discoveries of useful Truths, and the Knowledge of Things, as they are to be found in themselves, and not in our Imaginations; and it matters not much, for the improvement of our Knowledge, how they are call'd.

25. It were therefore to be wished, that Men, versed in physical Enquiries, and acquainted with the several sorts of natural Bodies, would set down those simple *Ideas*, wherein they observe the individuals of each sort constantly to agree. This would remedy a great deal of that confusion, which comes from several persons, applying the same Name to a Collection of a smaller, or greater number of sensible Qualities, proportionately as they have been more or less acquainted with, or accurate in examining the Qualities of any sort of Things, which come under one denomination. But a Dictionary of this sort, containing, as it were, a Natural History, requires too many hands, as well as too much time, cost, pains, and sagacity, ever to be hoped for; and till that be done, we must content ourselves with such Definitions of the Names of Substances, as explain the sense Men use them in. And 'twould be well, where there is occasion, if they would afford us so much. This is yet not usually done; but Men talk to one another, and dispute in Words, whose meaning is not agreed between them out of a mistake, that the signification of common Words, are certainly established, and the precise *Ideas*, they stand for, perfectly known; and that it is a shame to be ignorant of them. Both which suppositions are false: no Names of complex *Ideas* having so settled determined

Significations, that they are constantly used for the same precise *Ideas*.
Nor is it a shame for a Man not to have a certain Knowledge of any
thing, but by the necessary ways of attaining it; and so it is no
discredit not to know, what precise *Idea* any Sound stands for in
another Man's Mind, without he declare it to me, by some other way
than barely using that Sound, there being no other way, without such
a Declaration, certainly to know it. Indeed, the necessity of communication by Language, brings Men to an agreement in the signification of common Words, within some tolerable latitude, that may
serve for ordinary Conversation: and so a Man cannot be supposed
wholly ignorant of the *Ideas*, which are annexed to Words by common
Use, in a Language familiar to him. But common Use, being but a
very uncertain Rule, which reduces it self at last to the *Ideas* of
particular Men, proves often but a very variable Standard. But
though such a Dictionary, as I have above mentioned, will require too
much time, cost, and pains to be hoped for in this Age; yet, methinks,
it is not unreasonable to propose, that Words standing for Things,
which are known and distinguished by their outward shapes, should
be expressed by little Draughts and Prints made of them. A Vocabulary made after this fashion, would, perhaps with more ease, and in
less time, teach the true signification of many Terms, especially
in Languages of remote Countries or Ages, and settle truer *Ideas* in
Men's Minds of several Things, whereof we read the Names in
ancient Authors, than all the large and laborious Comments of
learned Criticks. Naturalists, that treat of Plants and Animals, have
found the benefit of this way: And he that has had occasion to consult
them, will have reason to confess, that he has a clearer *Idea* of *Apium*,
or *Ibex* from a little Print of that Herb, or Beast, than he could have
from a long Definition of the Names of either of them. And so, no
doubt, he would have of *Strigil* and *Sistrum*, if instead of a *Curry-Comb*,
and *Cymbal*, which are the English Names Dictionaries render them
by, he could see stamp'd in the Margin, small Pictures of these
Instruments, as they were in use amongst the Ancients. *Toga, Tunica,
Pallium*, are Words easily translated by *Gown, Coat*, and *Cloak*: but we
have thereby no more true *Ideas* of the Fashion of those Habits
amongst the *Romans*, than we have of the Faces of the Taylors who
made them. Such things as these, which the Eye distinguishes by their
shapes, would be best let into the Mind by Draughts made of them,
and more determine the signification of such Words, than any other
Words set for them or made use of to define them. But this is only by
the bye.

26. *Fifthly*, If Men will not be at pains to declare the meaning of their Words, and Definitions of their Terms are not to be had; yet this is the least that can be expected, that in all Discourses, wherein one Man pretends to instruct or convince another, he should *use the same Word constantly in the same sense*: If this were done, (which no body can refuse, without great disingenuity) many of the books extant might be spared; many of the Controversies in Dispute would be at an end; several of those great Volumes, swollen with ambiguous Words, now used in one sense, and by and by in another, would shrink into a very narrow compass; and many of the Philosophers (to mention no other,) as well as Poets Works, might be contained in a Nut-shell.

27. But after all, the provision of Words is so scanty in respect of that infinite variety of Thoughts, that Men, wanting Terms to suit their precise Notions, will, notwithstanding their utmost caution, be forced often to use the same Word in somewhat different Senses. And though in the continuation of a Discourse, or the pursuit of an Argument, there be hardly room to digress into a particular Definition, as often as a Man varies the signification of any Term; yet the import of the Discourse will, for the most part, if there is no designed fallacy, sufficiently lead candid and intelligent Readers, into the true meaning of it: but where that is not sufficient to guide the Reader, there it concerns the Writer to explain his meaning, and show in what sense he there uses that Term.

TEXT AND SELECTED READING

Locke's *Essay* was originally published in December 1689 but the present text is taken from the fourth edition (1700). Interesting discussions of Locke's philosophy of language are contained in chapter nine of R. Harris and T.J. Taylor's *Landmarks in Linguistic Thought* (London: Routledge, 1989) and chapter two of S.K. Land's *The Philosophy of Language in Britain* (New York: AMS Press, 1986). The general philosophical background is examined in E. Cassirer, *The Philosophy of Symbolic Forms, Vol. 1: Language* (London: Yale University Press, 1953). Locke's influence in subsequent centuries is discussed in H. Aarsleff's *The Study of Language in England 1780–1860* (Princeton: Princeton University Press, 1967) and *From Locke to Saussure* (London: Athlone Press, 1983). The political significance of Locke's thought is evaluated in N. Wood's *The Politics of Locke's Philosophy* (Berkeley: University of California Press, 1983).

2

Jonathan Swift

The political aftermath of the English Revolution and the settlement which followed it provides the historical context of Swift's *Proposal*. In particular the emergence of a newly powerful bourgeoisie and its effect in public life are concerns with which Swift is engaged in the form of attempting to correct the language. As a major Tory pamphleteer Swift was radically opposed to the liberalising tendencies of the emergent class and it is this which leads him to treat linguistic change as a cipher for historical change. In both cases he is implacably at odds with novelty and innovation, seeing such developments as signs merely of degeneracy and a falling off from the standards of a golden age.

The *Proposal* can be read as expressing a number of anxieties about history, in several different senses of that term. There is, for example, Swift's argument that language itself, or at least the reform of language, is as important historically as a number of other pressing political questions (such as the state of the constitution, or the national debt). That the reform of language should be ranked along-side these matters is clear evidence of Swift's evaluation of its import-ance in cultural and political affairs. It is not that he was the only figure to see the importance of the prescription of 'proper English' in the rapidly developing 'public sphere' of the eighteenth century, but it is certainly the case that he articulates what were already, and what later in the century were to become more so, significant worries about language and social life.

Another way in which Swift engages with history lies in his brief survey of the historical vicissitudes of the languages used in Britain. Again though not the first to do so (his history like many others in the eighteenth century is clearly influenced by Wallis' *Grammatica Lingua Anglicanae*, 1653), Swift is an important figure in the process of recalling the nation's past and linking it to the language. This rapidly becomes an attempt to intervene in history since the history of the language develops into an account of the golden age, 'the period wherein the English tongue received most improvement'. That this Tory reading of linguistic and literary history is an historical intervention can be noted from the dates specified for its duration: from the reign of Elizabeth the First to the English Revolution in 1642. The 'great Rebellion', the 'Usurpation', and the Restoration are all historical events to which Swift was opposed for various reasons. His opposition is signalled by his assertion that they were each accompanied by degeneracy in language.

The most important sense, however, in which the *Proposal* articulates worries about language and history is given by Swift's long treatment of the danger of linguistic mutability. At first sight this may appear to be no more than the familiar cry of writers concerned with the fact that historical change in language will limit their fame. Waller, for example, had written some fifty years earlier in *Of English Verse*:

> But who can hope his lines should long
> Last, in a daily changing tongue?
> . . .
> Poets that lasting Marble seek,
> Must write in Latin or in Greek;
> We write in Sand . . .

This fear would have been compounded in the eighteenth century as the reading-public grew, though in fact it is true that this expansion itself helped to stabilise the language. Yet Swift's problem is a deeper one than the search for literary fame, for in his view language was both an historical and political problem in a different sense.

He argues that the correcting, and more specifically the stabilising of the language at a permanent level, would 'very much contribute to the Glory of Her Majesty's [Queen Anne] Reign'. That is, that the successful completion of the project would be a credit to the Queen and therefore be an act of patriotism. However, the task is even more important than a contribution to the reputation of the Queen; for if the task is not completed, according to Swift, then it is possible that future readers may not be able to know of the Queen's glory (nor that of her Prime Minister to whom the letter is addressed), since the texts which record history will have become undecipherable by dint of linguistic change. In short, if history is not recorded 'in Words more durable than Brass, and such as Posterity may read a thousand years hence', then it cannot be guaranteed that 'Memory shall be preserved above an Hundred Years, further than by imperfect Tradition'. If the language is not fixed unalterably then the narratives of history, our 'memories' of the past, will not be able to be communicated successfully to the future. Thus it was not simply Swift's desire to be the historiographer royal which led him to worry about the role of language in history-making. For cultural and political reasons he was acutely aware of the importance of ensuring that language and historiography played their role in the construction of tradition. The values to be handed down from the present were to be encased in a language which would ensure their effective transmission to the future. It is an attempt to fix not just language but the future forms of social life.

A PROPOSAL FOR CORRECTING, IMPROVING AND ASCERTAINING THE ENGLISH LANGUAGE

To the Most Honourable Robert Earl of Oxford
My Lord,

What I had the Honour of mentioning to your Lordship some Time ago in Conversation, was not a new Thought, just then started by Accident or Occasion, but the Result of long Reflection; and I have been confirmed in my Sentiments by the Opinion of some very judicious Persons, with whom I consulted. They all agreed, That nothing would be of greater Use towards the Improvement of Knowledge and Politeness, than some effectual Method for *Correcting*, *Enlarging*, and *Ascertaining*, our Language; and they think it a Work very possible to be compassed, under the Protection of a Prince, the Countenance and Encouragement of a Ministry, and the Care of proper Persons, chosen for such an Undertaking. I was glad to find your Lordship's Answer in so different a Style, from what hath commonly been made use of on such like occasions, for some years past; *That all such Thoughts must be deferred to a Time of Peace*: A Topick which some have carried so far, that they would not have us by any Means think of preserving our Civil or Religious Constitution, because we are engaged in a War abroad. It will be among the distinguishing Marks of your Ministry, My Lord, that you had a Genius above all such Regards; and that no reasonable Proposal for the Honour, the Advantage, or the Ornament of your Country, however foreign to your immediate Office, was ever neglected by you. I confess, the

Merit of this Candour and Condescension is very much lessened; because your Lordship hardly leaves us Room to offer our good wishes; removing all our Difficulties, and supplying our Wants, faster than the most visionary Projector can adjust his Schemes. And therfore, my Lord, the Design of this Paper is not so much to offer you *Ways and Means*, as to complain of a *Grievance*, the Redressing of which is to be your own Work, as much as that of paying the *Nation's Debts*, or opening a Trade into the *South-Sea*; and although not of such immediate Benefit, as either of these, or any other of your glorious Actions, yet perhaps in future Ages not less to your Honour.

My Lord, I do here, in the Name of all the learned and polite Persons of the Nation, complain to your Lordship as *First Minister*, that our Language is extremely imperfect; that its daily Improvements are by no Means in proportion to its daily Corruptions; that the Pretenders to polish and refine it, have chiefly multiplied Abuses and Absurdities; and, that in many Instances, it offends against every Part of Grammar. But lest your Lordship should think my Censure too severe, I shall take leave to be more particular.

I believe your Lordship will agree with me in the Reason, why our Language is less refined than those of *Italy*, *Spain*, or *France*. It is plain, that the *Latin* Tongue in its Purity was never in this Island; towards the Conquest of which, few or no Attempts were made till the Time of *Claudius*. Neither was that Language ever so vulgar in *Britain*, as it is known to have been in *Gaul* and *Spain*. Further, we find that the *Roman* Legions here, were at length all recalled to help their Country against the *Goths*, and other barbarous Invaders. Mean time, the *Britons* left to shift for themselves, and daily harassed by cruel Inroads from the *Picts*, were forced to call in the *Saxons* for their Defence; who consequently reduced the greatest Part of the Island to their own Power, drove the *Britons* into the most remote and mountainous Parts; and the Rest of the Country in Customs, Religion, and Language, became wholly *Saxon*. This I take to be the Reason why there are more *Latin* Words remaining in the *British* Tongue than in the old *Saxon*; which, excepting some few variations in the Orthography, is the same in most original Words with our present *English*, as well as with the *German* and other *Northern* Dialects.

Edward *the Confessor* having lived long in *France*, appears to be the first, who introduced any Mixture of the *French* Tongue with the Saxon; the Court affecting what the Prince was fond of, and others taking it up for a Fashion, as it is now with us. *William the Conqueror* proceeded much further; bringing over with him vast Numbers of that

Nation, scattering them in every Monastery, giving them great Quantities of Land, directing all Pleadings to be in that Language, and endeavouring to make it universal in the Kingdom. This, at least, is the Opinion generally received: But your Lordship hath fully convinced me, that the *French* Tongue made a greater Progress here under *Harry* the Second, who had large territories on that Continent, both from his Father and his Wife; made frequent Journeys and Expeditions thither, and was always attended with a Number of his Countrymen, Retainers at his Court. For some Centuries after, there was a Constant Intercourse between *France* and *England*, by the Dominions we possessed there, and the Conquests we made: So that our Language, between two and three hundred Years ago, seems to have had a greater Mixture with the *French* than at present; many Words having been afterwards rejected, and some since the Time of *Spencer*; although we have still retained not a few, which have long been antiquated in *France*. I could produce several Instances of both Kinds, if it were of any Use or Entertainment.

To examine into the several Circumstances by which the Language of a Country may be altered, would force me to enter into a wide Field. I shall only observe, that the *Latin*, the *French*, and the *English*, seem to have undergone the same Fortune. The first, from the days of *Romulus* to those of *Julius Caesar*, suffered perpetual changes; and by what we meet in those Authors who occasionally speak on that Subject, as well as from certain Fragments of old Laws; it is manifest that the *Latin*, three hundred years before *Tully*, was as unintelligible in his Time, as the *English* and *French* of the same period are now. And these two have changed as much since *William the Conqueror*, (which is but little less than seven Hundred Years) as the *Latin* appears to have done in the like Term. Whether our Language, or the *French*, will decline as fast as the *Roman* did, is a Question that would perhaps admit more Debate than it is worth. There were many Reasons for Corruption of the last: As the Change of their Government into a Tyranny, which ruined the Study of Eloquence; there being no further Use or Encouragement for popular Orators: Their giving not only the Freedom of the City, but Capacity for Employments, to several Towns in *Gaul*, *Spain*, and *Germany*, and other distant Parts, as far as Asia; which brought a great number of Foreign Pretenders into *Rome*: The slavish Disposition of the Senate and People; by which the Wit and Eloquence of the Age were wholly turned into Panegyrick, the most barren of all Subjects; The great Corruption of Manners, and Introduction of foreign Luxury, with foreign Terms to express it: With several others that might be assigned: Not to mention those Invasions from the *Goths* and *Vandals*, which are too obvious to insist on.

The *Roman* Language arrived at great Perfection before it began to decay: The *French*, for these last fifty years, hath been polishing as much as it will bear; and appears to be declining by the natural Inconstancy of that People, as well as the Affectation of some late authors, to introduce and multiply *Cant* Words, which is the most ruinous Corruption in any Language. *La Bruyère*, a late celebrated Writer among them, makes use of many new Terms which are not to be found in any of the common Dictionaries before his Time. But the *English* Tongue is not arrived to such a Degree of Perfection, as, upon that Account, to make us Apprehend any Thoughts of its Decay: And if it were once refined to a certain Standard, perhaps there might be Ways to fix it for ever, or at least till we are invaded, and made a Conquest by some other State: And even then, our best Writings might probably be preserved with Care, and grow into Esteem, and the Authors have a chance for Immortality.

But without such great Revolutions as these, (to which we are, I think, less subject than Kingdoms on the Continent,) I see no absolute Necessity why any Language should be perpetually changing; for we find many Examples to the contrary. From *Homer* to *Plutarch*, are above a thousand years; so long, at least, the Purity of the Greek Tongue may be allowed to last; and we know not how far before. The *Grecians* spread all their Colonies round all the Coasts of *Asia Minor*, even to the Northern Parts, lying towards the *Euxine*; in every Island of the *Aegean Sea*, and several in the *Mediterranean*; where the Language was preserved entire for many Ages, after they themselves became Colonies to *Rome*, and till they were overrun by the barbarous Nations, upon the Fall of that Empire. The *Chinese* have books in their Language above two Thousand Years old; neither have the frequent Conquests of the *Tartars* been able to enter it. The *German, Spanish*, and *Italian*, have admitted few or no changes for some Ages past. The other Languages of *Europe* I know nothing of; neither is there any Occasion to consider them.

Having taken this Compass, I return to those Considerations upon our own Language, which I would humbly offer to your Lordship. The Period wherein the *English* Tongue received most Improvement, I take to commence with the Beginning of Queen *Elizabeth's* Reign, and to conclude with the great Rebellion in Forty-Two. It is true, there was a very ill taste both of Style and Wit, which prevailed under King *James* the First; but that seems to have been corrected in the first

Years of his Successor; who, among many other Qualifications of an excellent Prince, was a great Patron of Learning. From that great Rebellion to this present Time, I am apt to doubt whether the Corruptions in our Language have not, at least, equalled the Refinements of it; and these Corruptions very few of the best Authors in our Age have wholly escaped. During the Usurpation, such an Infusion of Enthusiastick Jargon prevailed in every Writing, as was not shaken off in many Years after. To this succeeded that Licentiousness which entered with the *Restoration*; and from infecting our Religion and Morals, fell to corrupt our Language: Which last, was not like to be much improved by those, who, at that Time, made up the Court of King *Charles* the Second; either such who had followed him in his Banishment, or who had been altogether conversant in the Dialect of those *Fanatick Times*; or young Men, who had been educated in the same Company; so that the *Court*, which used to be the Standard of Propriety, and Correctness of Speech, was then, and I think hath ever since continued the worst School in *England*, for that Accomplishment; and will so remain, till better Care be taken in the Education of our young Nobility; that they may set out into the World with some Foundation of Literature, in order to qualify them for Patterns of Politeness. The Consequence of this Defect upon our Language may appear from the Plays, and other Compositions, written for Entertainment, within fifty Years past; filled with a Succession of affected Phrases, and new conceited Words, either borrowed from the current Style of the Court, or from those, who, under the Character of Men of Wit and Pleasure, pretended to give the Law. Many of these Refinements have already been long antiquated, and are now hardly intelligible; which is no Wonder, when they were the Product only of Ignorance and Caprice.

I have never known this great Town without one or more *Dunces* of Figure, who had Credit enough to give Rise to some new Word, and propagate it in most Conversations; although it had neither Humour nor Significancy. If it struck the present Taste, it was soon transferred into the Plays, and current Scribbles of the Week, and became an Addition to our Language; while the Men of Wit and Learning, instead of early obviating such Corruptions, were too often seduced to imitate and comply with them.

There is another set of Men, who have contributed very much to the spoiling of the *English* Tongue; I mean the Poets from the Time of the Restoration. These Gentlemen, although they could not be sensible how much our Language was already overstocked with

Monosyllables, yet to save Time and Pains, introduced that barbarous Custom of abbreviating Words, to fit them to the Measure of their Verses; and this they have frequently done, so very injudiciously, as to form such harsh unharmonious Sounds, that none but a *Northern* Ear could endure. They have joined the most obdurate Consonants, without one intervening Vowel, only to shorten a Syllable: And their Taste in time became so depraved, that what was at first a poetical Licence, not to be justified, they made their choice; alledging, that the Words pronounced at length, sounded faint and languid. This was a Pretence to take up the same Custom in Prose; so that most of the Books we see now-a-days, are full of those Manglings and Abbreviations. Instances of this Abuse are innumerable: What does your Lordship think of the Words, *Drudg'd, Disturb'd, Rebuk'd, Fledg'd*, and a Thousand others, every where to be met in Prose, as well as Verse? Where, by leaving out a Vowel to save a Syllable, we form so jarring a Sound, and so difficult to utter, that I have often wondered, how it could ever obtain.

Another Cause (and perhaps borrowed from the former) which hath contributed not a little to the maiming of our Language, is a foolish Opinion, advanced of late Years, that we ought to spell exactly as we speak; which beside the obvious Inconvenience of utterly destroying our Etymology, would be a Thing we should never see an End of. Not only the several Towns and Counties of *England*, have a different Way of pronouncing; but even here in *London*, they clip their Words after one Manner about the Court, another in the city, and a third in the Suburbs; and in a few Years, it is probable will all differ from themselves, as Fancy or Fashion shall direct: All which reduced to Writing, would entirely confound Orthography. [It would be just as wise to shape our Bodies to our Cloathes and not our Cloaths to our bodyes.] Yet many People are so fond of this Conceit, that it is sometimes a difficult Matter to read modern Books and Pamphlets; where the Words are so curtailed, and varied from their original Spelling, that whoever hath been used to plain *English*, will hardly know them by Sight.

Several young Men at the Universities, terribly possessed with the Fear of Pedantry, run into a worse Extream; and think all Politeness in reading the daily Trash sent down to them from hence: This they call *knowing the World*, and *reading Men and Manners*. Thus furnished, they come up to Town; reckon all their Errors for Accomplishments, borrow the newest Set of Phrases; and if they take a Pen into their Hands, all the odd Words they have picked up in a Coffee House, or a Gaming Ordinary, are produced as Flowers of Style, and the Orthography refined to the utmost. To this we owe those monstrous Productions which under the Names of *Trips*, *Spies*, *Amusements*, and other conceited Appellations, have over-run us for some Years past. To this we owe that strange Race of Wits, who tell us they write to the *Humour of the Age*. And I wish I could say, these quaint Fopperies were wholly absent from graver Subjects. In short, I would undertake to shew your Lordship several Pieces, where the Beauties of this Kind are so predominant, that with all your Skill in Languages, you could never be able either to read or understand them.

But I am very much mistaken, if many of these false Refinements among us, do not arise from a Principle which would quite destroy their Credit, if it were well understood and considered. For I am afraid, my Lord, that with all the real good Qualities of our Country, we are naturally not very polite. This perpetual Disposition to shorten our Words, by retrenching the Vowels, is nothing else but a Tendency to lapse into the barbarity of those *Northern* Nations from whom we are descended, and whose Languages labour all under the same Defect. For it is worthy our Observation, that the *Spaniards*, the French, and the *Italians*, although derived from the same *Northern* Ancestors with ourselves, are, with the utmost Difficulty taught to pronounce our Words; which the *Swedes* and the *Danes*, as well as the *Germans* and the *Dutch*, attain to with Ease, because our Syllables resemble theirs, in the Roughness and Frequency of Consonants. Now, as we struggle with an ill Climate to improve the Nobler Kinds of Fruits; are at the Expence of Walls to receive and reverberate the faint Rays of the Sun, and fence against the *Northern* Blasts; we sometimes by the Help of a good Soil equal the Productions of warmer Countries, who have no need to be at so much Cost or Care: It is the same Thing with respect to the politer Arts among us; and the same Defect of Heat which gives a Fierceness to our Natures, may contribute to that Roughness of our Language, which bears some Analogy to the harsh Fruit of colder Countries. For I do not reckon, that we want a *Genius* more than the rest of our Neighbours: But your Lordship will be of my Opinion, that we ought to struggle with these natural Disadvantages as much as we can; and be careful whom we employ, whenever we design to correct them; which is a Work that hath hitherto been assumed by the least qualified Hands: So that if the Choice had been left to me, I would rather have trusted the Refinement of our Language, as far as it relates to Sound, to the Judgment of the Women, than of illiterate Court-Fops, half-witted Poets, and University Boys. For, it is plain, that Women in their Manner of corrupting Words, do naturally discard the Consonants, as we do the Vowels. What I am going to tell your Lordship, appears very trifling; that more than once, where some of both Sexes were in Company, I have persuaded two or three of each to take a Pen, and write down a Number of Letters joined together, just as it came into their Heads; and upon reading this Gibberish we have found that which the men had writ, by the frequent encountering of rough Consonants, to sound like *High-Dutch*; and the other by the women, like *Italian*, abounding in Vowels and Liquids. Now, although I would by no Means give Ladies the Trouble of advising us in the Reformation of our Language; yet I cannot help Thinking, that since they have been left out of all Meetings, except Parties at Play, or where worse Designs are carried on, our Conversation hath very much degenerated.

In order to reform our Language; I conceive, my Lord, that a free judicious Choice should be made of such Persons, as are generally allowed to be best qualified for such a Work, without any regard to Quality, Party, or Profession. These to a certain Number, at least, should assemble at some appointed Time and Place, and fix on Rules by which they design to proceed. What methods they will take, is not for me to prescribe. Your Lordship and other Persons in great Employment, might please to be of the Number: And I am afraid, such a Society would want your Instruction and Example, as much as your Protection: For I have, not without a little Envy, observed of late the Style of some great Ministers very much to exceed that of any other Productions.

The Persons who are to undertake this Work, will have the Example of the *French* before them, to imitate where these have proceeded right, and to avoid their mistakes. Besides the Grammar-Part, wherein we are allowed to be very defective, they will observe many gross Improprieties, which however authorised by Practice, and grown familiar, ought to be discarded. They will find many Words that deserve to be utterly thrown out of our Language; many more to be corrected, and perhaps not a few, long since antiquated, which ought to be restored, on Account of their Energy and Sound.

But what I have most at heart, is that some Method should be thought on for *Ascertaining* and *Fixing* our Language for ever, after such alterations are made in it as shall be thought requisite. For I am of Opinion, that it is better a Language should not be wholly perfect, than that it should be perpetually changing; and we must give over at one Time or other, or at length infallibly change for the worse: As the

37

Romans did, when they began to quit their simplicity of Style for affected Refinements; such as we meet in *Tacitus* and other Authors, which ended in Degrees in many Barbarities, even before the *Goths* had invaded *Italy.*

The Fame of our Writers is usually confined to these two Islands; and it is hard it should be limited in *Time* as much as *Place*, by the perpetual Variations of our Speech. It is your Lordship's Observation, that if it were not for the *Bible* and *Common Prayer-Book* in the Vulgar Tongue, we should hardly be able to understand anything that was written among us an Hundred Years ago; which is certainly true: For those Books being perpetually read in Churches, have proved a Kind of Standard for Language, especially to the common People. And I doubt whether the Alterations since introduced, have added much to the Beauty or Strength of the *English* Tongue, although they have taken off a great deal from that *Simplicity*, which is one of the greatest perfections in any Language. You, my Lord, who are so conversant in the sacred Writings, and so great a Judge of them in their Originals, will agree, that no Translation our Country ever yet produced, hath come up to that of the *Old* and *New Testament*: And by the many beautiful Passages which I have often had the Honour to hear your Lordship cite from thence, I am persuaded that the Translators of the Bible were Masters of an *English* Stile much fitter for that Work, than any we see in our present Writings; which I take to be owing to the *Simplicity* which runs through the Whole. Then, as to the greatest Part of our *Liturgy*, compiled long before the Translation of the *Bible* now in use, and little altered since; there seem to be in it as great Strains of true sublime Eloquence, as are any where to be found in our Language; which every Man of good Taste will observe in the *Communion-Service*, that of *Burial*, and other Parts.

But where I say that I would have our Language, after it is duly correct, always to last; I do not mean that it should never be enlarged; Provided, that no Word, which a Society shall give a Sanction to, be afterwards antiquated and exploded, they may have Liberty to receive whatever new ones they shall find Occasion for: Because then the old Books will yet be always valuable according to their intrinsick Worth, and not thrown aside on Account of unintelligible Words and Phrases, which appear harsh and uncouth, only because they are out of Fashion. Had the *Roman* Tongue continued vulgar in that City till this Time, it would have been absolutely necessary, from the mighty Changes that have been made in Law and Religion; from the many Terms of Art required in Trade and War; from the new Inventions that have happened in the World; from the vast spreading of Navigation and Commerce; with many other obvious Circumstances, to have made great Additions to that Language; yet the Antients would still have been read, and understood with Pleasure and Ease. The *Greek* Tongue received many Enlargements between the time of *Homer*, and that of *Plutarch*; yet the former Author was probably as well understood in *Trajan's* Time, as the latter. What *Horace* says of *Words going off, and perishing like Leaves, and new ones coming in their Place*, is a misfortune he laments, rather than a Thing he approves: But I cannot see why this should be absolutely necessary, or if it were, what would have become of his *Monumentum aere perennis*.

Writing by Memory only, as I do at the present, I would gladly keep within my Depth; and therefore shall not enter into further Particulars. Neither do I pretend more than to shew the Usefulness of this Design, and to make some general Observations; leaving the rest to that Society, which I hope will owe its Institution and Patronage to your Lordship. Besides, I would willingly avoid Repetition; having about a Year ago communicated to the Publick, much of what I had to offer on this Subject, by the Hands of an ingenious Gentleman, who for a long time did thrice a Week divert or instruct the Kingdom by his Papers, and is supposed to pursue the same Design at present, under the Title of *Spectator*. [In a Conversation some Time ago with a person to whom these Productions are ascribed, I happened to mention the Proposal I have here made to your Lordship; and in a few dayes thereafter I observed that the Author had taken the Hint and treated the same matter in one of his Papers, and with much Judgement, except where he is pleased to put so great a Compliment on me, as I can never pretend to Deserve.] This Author, who hath tried the Force and Compass of our Language with so much Success, agrees entirely with me in most of my Sentiments relating to it: So do the greatest part of the Men of Wit and Learning, whom I have had the Happiness to converse with: And therefore I imagine, that such a Society would be pretty unanimous in the main points.

Your Lordship must allow, that such a work as this, brought to perfection, would very much contribute to the Glory of Her Majesty's Reign; which ought to be recorded in Words more durable than Brass, and such as our Posterity may read a thousand Years hence, with Pleasure as well as Admiration. I have always disapproved that false Compliment to Princes: That the most lasting Monument they can have, is the Hearts of their Subjects. It is indeed their greatest present Felicity to reign in their Subjects Hearts; but these are too perishable to preserve their Memories, which can only be done by the Pens of able and faithful Historians. And I take it to be your Lordship's Duty, as *prime Minister*, to give Order for inspecting our Language, and rendering it fit to record the History of so great and good a Princess. Besides, my Lord, as disinterested as you appear to the World, I am convinced, that no Man is more in the Power of a prevailing favourite Passion than your self; I mean, that Desire of true and lasting Honour, which you have born along with you through every Stage of your Life. To this you have often sacrificed your Interest, your Ease, and your Health: For preserving and encreasing this, you have exposed your Person to secret Treachery, and open Violence. There is not perhaps an Example in History of any Minister, who in so short a Time hath performed so many great Things, and overcome so many great Difficulties. Now, although I am fully convinced, that you fear God, honour your Queen, and love your Country, as much as any of your Fellow-Subjects; yet I must believe, that the Desire of Fame hath been no inconsiderable Motive to quicken you in the Pursuit of those Actions which will best deserve it. But, at the same Time, I must be so plain as to tell your Lordship, that if you will not take some Care to Settle our Language, and put it into a State of Continuance, I cannot promise that your Memory shall be preserved above an Hundred Years, further than by imperfect Tradition.

As barbarous and ignorant as we were in former Centuries, there was more effectual Care taken by our Ancestors, to preserve the Memory of Times and Persons, than we find in this Age of Learning and Politeness, as we are pleased to call it. The rude *Latin* of the *Monks* is still very intelligible; whereas, had their Records been delivered down only in the vulgar Tongue, so barren and so barbarous, so subject to continual succeeding Changes, they could not now be understood, unless by Antiquaries, who made it their Study to expound them: And we must, at this Day, have been content with such poor Abstracts of our *English* Story, as laborious Men of low Genius would think fit to give us: And even these, in the next Age, would be likewise swallowed up in succeeding Collections. If things go on at this Rate; all I can promise your Lordship, is that about two Hundred Years hence, some painful compiler, who will be at the Trouble of studying old Language, may inform the World, that in the Reign of *Queen Anne*, *Robert* Earl of *Oxford*, a very wise and excellent Man, was made *High-Treasurer*, and saved his Country, which in those Days was almost ruined by a *foreign War*, and a *domestick Faction*. Thus much he may be able to pick out, and willing to transfer into his new History; but the rest of your Character, which I, or any other Writer, may now value our selves by drawing; and the particular Account of the great Things done under your Ministry, for which you are already celebrated in most Parts of *Europe*, will probably be dropt, on Account of the antiquated Style, and the Manner they are delivered in.

How then shall any Man, who hath a Genius for History, equal to the best of the Antients, be able to undertake such a Work with Spirit and Chearfulness, when he considers, that he will be read with Pleasure but a very few Years, and in Age or two shall hardly be understood without an Interpreter? This is like employing an excellent Statuary to work upon mouldring Stone. Those who apply their Studies to preserve the Memory of others, will always have some Concern for their own. And I believe it is for this Reason, that so few Writers among us, of any Distinction, have turned their Thoughts to such a discouraging Employment. For the best *English* Historian must lie under this Mortification, that when his Style grows antiquated, he will be only considered as a tedious Relater of Facts; and perhaps consulted in his Turn, among other neglected Authors, to furnish Materials for some future Collector.

TEXT AND SELECTED READING

The text is that of Swift's letter to the Earl of Oxford, published in 1712. Swift's influence on linguistic and political debates in the eighteenth century is explored in J. Barrell's 'The Language Properly So-Called' in *English Literature in History 1730-80* (London: Hutchinson, 1983). The linguistic and educational context is discussed in M. Cohen's *Sensible Words* (Baltimore: Johns Hopkins University Press, 1977), S.K. Land, *From Signs to Propositions* (London: Longman, 1974) and A.P.R. Howatt, *A History of English Language Teaching* (Oxford: Oxford University Press, 1984). A.C. Kelly's *Swift and the English Language* (Philadelphia: University of Pennsylvania Press, 1988) is an account of the centrality of linguistic thought to Swift's work in general.

3

Samuel Johnson

Although Johnson begins his *Plan* with a self-deprecating evaluation of the role of the lexicographer, it is not a declaration which can be taken too seriously. For like Swift, Johnson links the concern with language to matters of state; or at least he claims that his patron, the Earl of Chesterfield, has made this connection by sharing his attention to language 'with treaties and wars'. It is a trope which indicates the importance attached to language as it became the focus for a number of important political and cultural anxieties, the ground upon which all sorts of social values and differences are debated. Johnson himself posits the relation between the linguistic and political realms in the Preface to the *Dictionary* when he asserts: 'tongues, like governments, have a natural tendency to degeneration, we have long preserved our constitution, let us make some struggles for our language'.

Having noted the importance of his work, Johnson declares its intent. He aims to compose 'a dictionary by which the pronunciation of our language may be fixed, and its attainment facilitated; by which its purity may be preserved, its use ascertained, and its duration lengthened'. The echoes of Swift's *Proposal* are clear here and it is a connection which is strengthened by Johnson's opposition to innovation and change. In relation to orthography, for example, he declares that 'all change is of itself an evil'. However, if there are common links with Swift's tract there are also major differences, the principal being Johnson's explication of his methodology. Whereas in Swift the points are simply asserted, in Johnson's text there is a reasoned statement of his principles which are worthy of consideration.

The two major decisions discussed by Johnson are the delimitation of the *Dictionary*, what to put in and what to leave out, and that of the authority by which such decisions are made. The problem of delimitation is interesting in that it prefigures many of the debates around the language with particular regard to the inclusion or exclusion of foreign words, scientific terms, the lexicon of law and so on. This is a significant problem because it entails the imposition of limits, the necessity of including or excluding, validating or rejecting, particular lexical items. However, the real interest here is the language which Johnson uses to discuss this problem for it is a vocabulary which later shifts and is attached not merely to the question of 'proper English' words, but to the question of who are the 'proper English' people. The vocabulary which Johnson uses to describe these dubious terms is that of citizenship.

The problem Johnson sets himself is to 'preserve the purity and ascertain the meaning of the English idiom; and this seems to require nothing more than that our language be considered in so far as it is our own.' It is clearly a question of delimitation, of deciding what is 'our own' and what not. Of disputed terms such as those of 'foreign extraction' he says: 'all are not equally to be considered as parts of our language, for some of them are naturalised and incorporated, but others still continue aliens, and are rather auxiliaries than subjects.' Comparing his own method to that of the French Academicians who faced a similar problem with specialist words, he notes, 'tho' they would not naturalise them at once by a single act, [they] permitted them by degrees to settle themselves among the natives, with little opposition.' In fact Johnson's own position is that such words should be included within a definition of the language in so far as they are 'useful in the occurrences of common life'; however, it is not this which is of significance here, but his use of the language of citizenship to describe these terms. For 'naturalisation', 'native', 'incorporation', 'aliens', 'auxiliaries' and 'subjects' are all terms which are to apply not only to words but to people. And the same concern with 'purity' as the basis for deciding what or who is to be included and who or what excluded, will later manifest itself in debates around nationality and citizenship in which language will play an important role.

Johnson's second important question is that of authority and concerns the basis on which his decisions are made. He cites literary figures as the standards by which he evaluates and this is evidence of that shift in the signification of the word in which literature narrows from meaning all writing to a specific sort of writing with elevated status. His use of literature as a source of authority is interesting in that he uses it to suggest that rather than analogy (the articulation of rules based on the similarity of forms) being the basis of good grammar, we should turn instead to the 'proper authorities', 'the best authors'. In an argument that has implications across a number of distinct social discourses, he claims that we should not be 'taught by general rules, but by special precedents'. Against the French Academy's attempt to regulate usage by means of rational principles, Johnson in his Preface pits 'the spirit of English liberty' which is based on the works of great minds expressing the nation's genius.

In fact on consideration the argument for literary authority turns out to be fairly vacuous and though conducted at length can hardly be considered rigorous. It is tantamount to saying that 'writers of the first reputation' are to be the authoritative basis for the dictionary, but only those judged so by Johnson can qualify for the role. As though expecting some challenge to this basis he seeks to obviate the problem 'by declaring that many of the writers whose testimonies will be alleged, were selected by Mr. Pope'. The argument amounts to this: if it is not to be Johnson, then it is to be Pope; either way the selection of the authorities is not open to serious challenge. Yet as he pertinently asks, 'who shall judge the judges?' It is an important question when we consider the extent to which the language itself is judged in the *Dictionary* and the ways in which it is delimited, divided and evaluated. Foreign words may be 'naturalized', the legal lexicon may be incorporated, the terms of science may become subjects enjoying the rights of the citizen of language; but there are terms which are not included, words which are not to be given membership of the nation. These are the words belonging to those whose dis-enfranchisement is not merely linguistic; for these are the words of the practitioners of 'art and manufacture', the miners, sailors, labourers and merchants. The Preface develops the point clearly:

> Nor are all the words which are not found in the vocabulary, to be lamented as omissions. Of the laborious and mercantile part of the people, the diction is in a great measure casual and mutable; many of their terms are formed for some temporary or local convenience, and though current at certain times and places, are in others utterly unknown. This fugitive cant, which is always in a state of increase or decay, cannot be regarded as any part of the durable materials of a language, and therefore must be suffered to perish with other things unworthy of preservation.

This is a division of the language which recalls the division of the nation and it is one which will reappear.

THE PLAN OF A DICTIONARY OF THE ENGLISH LANGUAGE

My Lord,

When I first undertook to write an English Dictionary, I had no expectation of any higher patronage than that of the proprietors of the copy, nor prospect of any other advantage than the price of my labour; I knew that the work in which I engaged is generally considered as drudgery for the blind, as the proper toil of artless industry, a task that requires neither the light of learning, nor the activity of genius, but may be successfully performed without any higher quality than that of bearing burthens with dull patience, and beating the track of the alphabet with sluggish resolution.

Whether this opinion, so long transmitted and so widely propagated, had its beginnings from truth and nature, or from accident and prejudice, whether it be decreed by the authority of reason, or the tyranny of ignorance, that of all the candidates for literary praise, the unhappy lexicographer holds the lowest place, neither vanity nor interest incited me to enquire. It appeared that the province allotted to me was of all the regions of learning generally confessed to be the least delightful, that it was believed to produce neither fruits nor flowers, and that after a long and laborious cultivation, not even the barren laurel had been found upon it.

Yet on this province, my Lord, I enter'd with the pleasing hope, that as it was low, it likewise would be safe. I was drawn forward with the prospect of employment, which, tho' not splendid, would be useful, and which tho' it could not make my life envied, would keep it innocent, which would awaken no passion, engage me in no contention, nor throw in my way any temptation to disturb the quiet of others by censure, or by my own flattery.

I had read indeed of times, in which princes and statesmen thought it part of their honour to promote the improvement of their native tongues, and in which dictionaries were written under the protection of greatness. To the patrons of such undertakings, I willingly paid the homage of believing that they, who were thus solicitous for the perpetuity of their language, had reason to expect that their actions would be celebrated by posterity, and that the eloquence which they promoted would be employed in their praise. But I considered such acts of beneficence as prodigies, recorded rather to raise wonder rather than expectation; and content with the terms that I had stipulated, had not suffr'd my imagination to flatter me with any other encouragement, when I found that my design had been thought by your Lordship of importance sufficient to attract your favour.

How far this unexpected distinction can be rated among the happy incidents of life, I am not yet able to determine. Its first effect has been to make me anxious lest it should fix the attention of the public too much upon me, and as it once happened to an epic poet of France, by raising the reputation of the attempt, obstruct the reception of the work. I imagine what the world will expect from a scheme, prosecuted under your Lordship's influence, and I know that expectation, when her wings are once expanded, easily reaches heights which performance never will attain, and when she has mounted the summit of perfection, derides her follower, who dies in the pursuit.

Not therefore, to raise expectation, but to repress it, I here lay before your Lordship the plan of my undertaking, that more may not be demanded than I intend, and that before it is too far advanced to be thrown into a new method, I may be advertised of its defects or superfluities. Such informations I may justly hope from the emulation with which those who desire the praise of elegance or discernment must contend in the promotion of a design which you, my Lord, have not thought unworthy to share your attention with treaties and with wars.

In the first attempt to methodise my ideas, I found a difficulty which extended itself to the whole work. It was not easy to determine by what rule of distinction the words of this dictionary were to be chosen. The chief intent of it is to preserve the purity and ascertain the meaning of our English idiom; and this seems to require nothing more than that our language be considered so far as it is our own; that the words and phrases used in the general intercourse of life, or found in the works of those we commonly stile polite writers, be selected, without including the terms of particular professions, since, with the arts to which they relate, they are generally derived from other nations, and are very often the same in all the languages of this part of the world. This is perhaps the exact and pure idea of a grammatical dictionary; but in lexicography, as in other arts, naked science is too delicate for the purposes of life. The value of a work must be estimated by its use: It is not enough that a dictionary delights the critic, unless at the same time it instructs the learner; as it is to little purpose, that an engine amuses the philosopher by the subtilty of its mechanism, if it requires so much knowledge in its application, as to be of no advantage to the common workman.

The title which I prefix to my work has long conveyed a miscellaneous idea, and they that take a dictionary into their hands have been expected to expect from it, a solution of almost every difficulty. If foreign words therefore were rejected, it could be little regarded, except by critics, or those who aspire to criticism; and however it might enlighten those that write, would be all darkness to those that only read. The unlearned much oftner consult their dictionaries, for the meaning of words, than for their structures or formations; and the words that most want explanation, are generally terms of art, which therefore experience has taught my predecessors to spread with a kind of pompous luxuriance over their productions.

The academicians of France, indeed, rejected terms of science in their first essay, but found afterwards a necessity of relaxing the rigour of their determination; and tho' they would not naturalise them at once by a single act, permitted themselves by degrees to settle themselves among the natives, with little opposition, and it would surely be no proof of judgment to imitate them in an error which they have now retracted, and deprive the book of its chief use by scrupulous distinctions.

Of such words, however, all are not equally to be considered as parts of our language, for some of them are naturalised and incorporated, but others still continue aliens, and are rather auxiliaries than subjects. This naturalisation is produced either by an admission into common speech in some metaphorical signification, which is the acquisition of a kind of property among us, as we say the *zenith* of advancement, the *meridian* of life, the *cynosure* of neighbouring eyes; or it is the consequence of long intermixture and frequent use, by which the ear is accustomed to the sound of words till their original is forgotten, as in *equator, satellites*; or of the change of a foreign to an English termination, and a conformity to the laws of speech into which they are adopted, as in *category, cachexy, peripneumony*.

Of those which yet continue in the state of aliens, and have made no approaches towards assimilation, some seem necessary to be retained, because the purchasers of the dictionary expect to find them. Such are many words in the common law, as *capias, habeas corpus, praemunire, nisi prius*: such are some terms of controversial divinity, as *hypostasis*; and of physick, as the names of diseases; and in general all terms which can be found in books not written professedly upon particular arts, or can be supposed necessary to those who regularly study them. Thus when a reader not skilled in physick happens in Milton upon this line,

. . . pining atrophy,
Marasmus, and wide-wasting pestilence,

47

he will with equal expectation look into his dictionary for the word *marasmus*, as for *atrophy*, or *pestilence*, and will have reason to complain if he does not find it.

It seems necessary to the completion of a dictionary design'd not merely for critics but for popular use, that it should comprise, in some degree, the peculiar words of every profession; that the terms of war and navigation should be inserted so far as they can be required by readers of travels, and of history; and those of law, merchandise and mechanical trades, so far as they can be supposed useful in the occurrences of common life.

But there ought, however, to be some distinction made between the different classes of words, and therefore it will be proper to print those which are incorporated into the language in the usual character, and those which are still considered to be foreign, in the Italick letter.

Another question may arise, with regard to appellatives, or the names of species. It seems of no great use to set down the words, *horse*, *dog*, *cat*, *willow*, *alder*, *dasy*, *rose*, and a thousand others, of which it will be hard to give an explanation not more obscure than the word itself. Yet it is to be considered, that, if the names of animals be inserted, we must admit those which are more known, as well as those with which we are, by accident, less acquainted; and if they are all rejected how will the reader be relieved of the difficulties produced by allusions to the crocodile, the camæleon, the ichneumon, and the hyæna? If no plants are to be mentioned, the most pleasing part of nature will be excluded, and many beautiful epithets be unexplained. If only those which are less well known are to be mentioned, who shall fix the limits of the reader's learning? The importance of such explications appears from the mistakes which the want of them has occasioned. Had Shakspear had a dictionary of this kind he had not made the *woodbine* entwine the *honeysuckle*; nor would Milton, with such assistance, have disposed so improperly of his *ellops* and his *scorpion*.

Besides, as such words, like others, require that their accents should be settled, their sounds ascertained, and their etymologies deduced, they cannot properly be omitted in the dictionary. And though the explanations of some may be censured as trivial, because they are almost universally understood, and those of others as unnecessary, because they will seldom occur, yet it seems not proper to omit them, since it is rather to be wished that many readers should find more than they expect, than that one should miss what he expect to find.

When all the words are selected and arranged, the first part of the work to be considered is the ORThOGRAPHY, which was long vague and uncertain, which at last, when its fluctuations ceased, was in many cases settled by accident, and in which, according to your Lordship's observation, there is still great uncertainty amongst the best critics; nor is it easy to state a rule by which we may decide between custom and reason, or between the equiponderant authorities of writers alike eminent for judgment and accuracy.

The great orthographical contest has long subsisted between etymology and pronunciation. It has been demanded, on one hand, that men should write as they speak; but as it has been shown that this conformity never was attained in any language, and that it is not more easy to perswade men to agree exactly in speaking than in writing, it may be asked with equal propriety, why men do not rather speak as they write. In France, where this controversy was at its greatest height, neither party, however ardent, durst adhere readily to their own rule; the etymologist was often forced to spell with the people; and the advocate for the authority of pronunciation, found it sometimes deviating so capriciously from the received use of writing, that he was constrained to comply with the use of his adversaries, lest he should loose the end by the means, and be left alone by following the croud.

When a question of orthography is dubious, that practice has, in my opinion, a claim to preference, which preserves the greatest number of radical letters, or seems most to comply with the general custom of our language. But the chief rule which I propose to follow, is to make no innovation, without a reason sufficient to balance the inconvenience of change; and such reasons I do not expect often to find. All change is of itself an evil, which ought not to be hazarded but for evident advantage; and as inconstancy is in every case a mark of weakness, it will add nothing to the reputation of our tongue. There are, indeed, some who will despise the inconveniencies of confusion, who seem to take pleasure in departing from custom, and to think alteration desirable for its own sake, and the reformation of our orthography, which these writers have attempted, should not pass without its due honours, but that I suppose they hold singularity its own reward, or may dread the fascination of lavish praise.

The present usage of spelling, where the present usage can be distinguished, will therefore in this work be generally followed, yet there will be often occasion to observe, that it is in itself inaccurate, and tolerated rather than chosen; particularly, when by a change of one letter, or more, the meaning of a word is obscured, as in *farrier*, for *ferrier*, as it was formerly written, from *ferrum*, or *fer*; in *gibberish* for *gebrish*, the jargon of Geber and his chymical followers, understood by none but their own tribe. It will be likewise sometimes proper to trace back the orthography of different ages, and shew by what gradations the word departed from its original.

Closely connected with orthography is PRONUNCIATION, the stability of which is of great importance to the duration of a language, because the first change will naturally begin by corruptions in the living speech. The want of certain rules for the pronunciation of former ages, had made us wholly ignorant of the metrical art of our ancient poets; and since those who study their sentiments regret the loss of their numbers, it is surely time to provide that the harmony of the moderns may be more permanent.

A new pronunciation will make almost a new speech, and therefore since one great end of this undertaking is to fix the English language, care will be taken to determine the accentuation of all polysyllables by proper authorities, as it is one of those capricious phaenomena which cannot easily be reduced to rules. Thus there is no antecedent reason for difference of accent in the two words *dolorous* and *sonorous*, yet of the one Milton gives the sound in this line,

He pass'd oe'r many a region *dolorous*,

and that of the other in this,

Sonorous metal blowing martial sounds.

It may be likewise proper to remark metrical licences, such as contractions, *generous*, *gen'rous*, *reverend*, *rev'rend*; and coalitions, as *region*, *question*.

But it is still more necessary to fix the pronunciation of monosyllables, by placing them with words of correspondent sound, that one may guard the other against the danger of that variation, which to some of the most common, has already happened, so that the words *wound*, and *wind*, as they are now frequently pronounced, as *flow*, and *brow*, which may be thus registered *flow*, *woe*, *brow*, *now*, or of which the exemplification may be generally given by a distich. Thus the words *tear* or lacerate, and *tear* the water of the eye, have the same letters, but may be distinguished thus, *tear*, *dare*; *tear*, *peer*.

Some words have two sounds, which may be equally admitted, as being equally defensible by authority. Thus *great* is differently used.

For Swift and him despis'd the farce of state,
The sober follies of the wise and *great*.

(Pope)

As if misfortune made the throne her seat,
And none could be unhappy but the *great*.

(Rowe)

The care of such minute particulars may be censured as trifling, but these particulars have not been thought unworthy of attention in more polished languages.

The accuracy of the French, in stating the sound so of their letters, is well known; and, among the Italians, Crescembeni has not thought it unnecessary to inform his countrymen of the words, which, in compliance with different rhymes, are allowed to be differently spelt, and of which the number is now so fix'd, that no modern poet is suffered to encrease it.

When the orthography and pronunciation are adjusted, the ETY-MOLOGY or DERIVATION is next to be considered, and the words are to be distinguished according to their different classes, whether simple, as *day*, *light*, or compound as *day-light*; whether primitive, as, to *act*, or derivative, as *action*, *actionable*, *active*, *activity*. This will much facilitate the attainment of our language, which now stands in our dictionaries a confused heap of words without dependence, and without relation.

When this part of the work is performed, it will be necessary to inquire how our primitives are to be deduced from foreign languages, which may often be very successfully performed by the assistance of our own etymologists. This search will give occasion to many curious disquisitions, and sometimes perhaps to conjectures, which, to readers unacquainted with this kind of study, cannot but appear improbable and capricious. But it may be reasonably imagined, that what is so much in the power of men as language, will very often be capriciously conducted. Nor are these disquisitions and conjectures to be considered altogether as wanton sports of wit, or vain shows of learning; our language is well known not to be primitive or self-originated, but to have adopted words of every generation, and either for the supply of its necessities, or the encrease of its copiousness, to have received additions from very different regions; so that in search for the progenitors of our speech, we may wander from the tropic to the frozen zone, and find some in the valleys of Palestine, and some upon the rocks of Norway.

Beyond the derivation of particular words, there is likewise an etymology of phrases. Expressions are often taken from other languages, some apparently, as to *run a risque, courir un risque*; and some even when we do not seem to borrow their words; thus, to *bring about* or accomplish, appears an English phrase, but in reality our native word *about* has no such import, and is only a French expression, of which we have an example in the common phrase, *venir à bout d'une affaire.*

In exhibiting the descent of our language, our etymologists seem to have been too lavish of their learning, having traced almost every word through various tongues, only to shew what was sufficiently shewn by the first derivation. This practice is of great use in synoptical lexicons, where mutilated and doubtful languages are explained by their affinity to others more certain and more extensive, but is generally superfluous in English etymologies. When the word is easily deduced from a Saxon original, I shall not often enquire further, since we know not the parent of the Saxon dialect, but when it is borrowed from the French, I shall shew whence the French is apparently derived. Where a Saxon root cannot be found, the defect may be supplied from kindred languages, which will be generally furnished with much liberality by the writers of our glossaries; writers who deserve often the highest praise, both of judgment and industry, and may expect to be mentioned at least with honour by me, whom they have freed from the greatest part of a very laborious work, and on whom they have imposed, at worst, only the easy task of rejecting superfluities.

By tracing in this manner every word to its original, and not admitting, but with great caution, any of which no original can be found, we shall secure our language from being over-run with *cant*, from being crouded with low terms, the spawn of folly or affectation, which arise from no just principles of speech, and of which therefore no legitimate derivation can be shown.

When the etymology is thus adjusted, the ANALOGY of our language is next to be considered; when we have discovered whence our words are derived, we are to examine by what rules they are governed, and how they are inflected through their various terminations. The terminations of the English are few, but those few have hitherto remained unregarded by the writers of our dictionaries. Our substantives are declined only by the plural termination, our adjectives admit no variation but in the degrees of comparison, and our verbs are conjugated by auxiliary words, and are only changed in the preter tense.

To our language may be with great justness applied the observation of *Quintilian*, that speech was not formed by an analogy sent from heaven. It did not descend to us in a state of uniformity and perfection, but was produced by necessity and enlarged by accident, and is therefore composed of dissimilar parts, thrown together by negligence, by affectation, by learning, or by ignorance.

Our inflections therefore are by no means constant, but admit of numberless irregularities, which in this dictionary will be diligently noted. Thus *fox* makes in the plural *foxes*, but *ox* makes *oxen*. *Sheep* is the same in both numbers. Adjectives are sometimes compared by changing the last syllable, as *proud, prouder, proudest*; and sometimes by particles prefixed, as *ambitious, more* ambitious, *most* ambitious. The forms of our verbs are subject to great variety; some end their preter tense in *ed*, as I *love*, I *loved*, I have *loved*, which may be called the regular form, and is followed by most of our verbs of southern original. But many depart from this rule, without agreeing in any other, as I *shake*, I *shook*, I have *shaken*, or *shook* as it is sometimes written in poetry; I *make*, I *made*, I have *made*; I *bring*, I *brought*; I *wring*, I *wrung*, and many others, which, as they cannot be reduced to rules, must be learned from the dictionary rather than the grammar.

The verbs are likewise to be distinguished according to their qualities, as actives from neuters; the neglect of which has already introduced some barbarities into our conversation, which, if not obviated by just animadversions, may in time creep into our writings.

Thus, my Lord, will our language be laid down, distinct in its minutest subdivisions, and resolved into its elemental principles. And who upon this occasion can forbear to wish, that these fundamental atoms of our speech might obtain the firmness and immutability of the primogenial and constituent particles of matter, that they might retain their substance while they alter their appearance, and be varied and compounded, yet not destroyed.

But this is a privilege which words are scarcely to expect; for, like their author, when they are not gaining strength, they are generally losing it. Though art may sometimes prolong their duration, it will rarely give them perpetuity, and their changes will be almost always informing us, that language is the work of man, of a being from whom permanence and stability cannot be derived.

Words having been hitherto considered as separate and unconnected, are now to be likewise examined as they are ranged in their various relations to others by the rules of SYNTAX or construction, to which I do not know that any regard has yet been shewn in English dictionaries, and in which the grammarians can give little assistance. The syntax of this language is too inconstant to be reduced to rules, and can only be learned by the distinct consideration of particular words as they are used by the best authors. Thus, we say, according to the present modes of speech, the soldier died *of* his wounds, and the sailor perished *with* hunger; and every man acquainted with our language would be offended by a change of these particles, which yet seem originally assigned by chance, there being no reason to be drawn from grammar why a man may not, with equal propriety, be said to die *with* a wound, or perish *of* hunger.

Our syntax therefore is not to be taught by general rules, but by special precedents; and in examining whether Addison has been with justice accused of a solecism in this passage,

> The poor inhabitant . . .
> Starves in the midst of nature's bounty curst,
> And in the loaden vineyard *dies for thirst*,

it is not in our power to have recourse to any established laws of speech, but we must remark how the writers of former ages have used the same word, and consider whether he can be acquitted of impropriety, upon the testimony of Davies, given in his favour in a similar passage.

> She loaths the watry glass wherein she gaz'd,
> And shuns it still, although *for thirst she dye*.

When the construction of a word is explained, it is necessary to pursue it through its train of PHRASEOLOGY, through those forms where it is used in a manner peculiar to our language, or in senses not to be comprised in the general explanations; as from the verb *make*, arise these phrases, to *make love*, to *make an end*, to *make way*, as he *made way* for his followers, the ship *made way* before the wind; to *make a bed*, to *make merry*, to *make a mock*, to *make presents*, to *make a doubt*, to *make out an assertion*, to *make good* a breach, to *make good* a cause, to *make nothing* of an attempt, to *make lamentation*, to *make* a merit, and many others which will occur in reading with that view, and which only their frequency hinders from being generally remarked.

The great labour is yet to come, the labour of interpreting these words and phrases with brevity, fulness and perspicuity; a task of which the extent and intricacy is sufficiently shown by the miscarriage of those who have generally attempted it. This difficulty is encreased by the necessity of explaining the words in the same language, for there is often only one word for one idea; and though it be easy to translate the words *bright, sweet, salt, bitter,* into another language, it is not so easy to explain them.

With regard to the INTERPRETATION many other questions have required consideration. It was some time doubted whether it be necessary to explain the things implied by particular words. As under the term *baronet,* whether instead of this explanation, *a title of honour next in degree to that of baron,* it would be better to mention more particularly the creation, privileges and rank of baronets; and whether under the word *barometer,* instead of being satisfied with observing that it is *an instrument to discover the weight of the air,* it would be fit to spend a few lines upon its invention, construction and principles. It is not to be expected that with the explanation of the one the herald should be satisfied, or the philosopher with that of the other; but since it will be required by common readers, that the explications should be sufficient for common use, and since without some attention to such demands the dictionary cannot become generally valuable, I have determined to consult the best writers for explanations real as well as verbal, and perhaps I may at last have reason to say, after one of the augmenters of Furetier, that my book is more learned than its author.

In explaining the general and popular language, it seems necessary to sort the several senses of each word, and to exhibit first its natural and primitive signification, as

To *arrive,* to reach the shore in a voyage. He *arrived* at a safe harbour.

Then to give its consequential meaning, *to arrive,* to reach any place, whether by land or sea; as, he *arrived* at his country seat.

Then its metaphorical sense, to obtain anything desired; as, he *arrived* at a peerage.

Then to mention any observation that arises from the comparison of one meaning with another; as, it may be remarked of the word *arrive,* that in consequence of its original and etymological sense, it cannot properly be applied but to words signifying something desirable; thus, we say a man *arrived* at happiness, but cannot say without a mixture of irony, he *arrived* at misery.

Ground, the earth, generally as opposed to the air or water. He swam till he reached *ground.* The bird fell to the *ground.*

Then follows the accidental or consequential signification, in which *ground* implies anything that lies under another; as, he laid colours upon a rough *ground.* The silk had blue flowers on a red *ground.*

Then the remoter or metaphorical signification; as, the *ground* of his opinion was a false computation. The *ground* of his work was his father's manuscript.

After having gone through the natural and figurative senses, it will be proper to subjoin the poetical sense of each word, where it differs from that which is in common use; as, *wanton* applied to any thing of which the motion is irregular without terror, as

In wanton ringlets curl'd her hair.

To the poetical sense may succeed the familiar; as of *toast*, used to imply the person whose health is drunk.

The wise man's passion, and the vain man's toast.

(Pope)

The familiar may be followed by the burlesque; as of *mellow*, applied to good fellowship.

In all thy humours whether grave, or mellow.

(Addison)

Or of *bite* used for *cheat*.

. . . More a dupe than wit,
Sappho can tell you, how this man was bit.

(Pope)

And lastly, may be produced the peculiar sense, in which a word is found in any great author. As *faculties* in Shakspeare signifies the powers of authority.

. . . This Duncan
Has born his faculties so meek, has been
So clear in his great office, that &c.

The signification of adjectives, may be often ascertained by uniting them to substantives, as *simple swain*, *simple sheep*; sometimes the sense of a substantive may be elucidated by the epithets annexed to it in good authors, as the *boundless ocean*, the *open lawns*, and where such advantage can be gained by a short quotation it is not to be omitted.

The difference of signification in words generally accounted synonimous, ought to be carefully observed; as in *pride*, *haughtiness*, *arrogance*; and the strict and critical meaning ought to be distinguished from that which is loose and proper; as in the word *perfection*, which though in its philosophical and exact sense, it can be of little use among human beings, is often so much degraded from its original signification, that the academicians have inserted in their work *the perfection of a language*, and with a little more licentiousness might have prevailed on themselves to have added the *perfection of a dictionary*.

There are many other characters of words which it will be of use to mention. Some have both an active and passive signification, as *fearful*, that which gives or which feels terror, *a fearful prodigy, a fearful hare*. Some have a personal, some a real meaning, as in opposition to *old* we use the adjective *young* of animated beings, and *new* of other things. Some are restrained to the sense of praise, and others to that of disapprobation, so commonly, though not always, we *exhort* to good actions, we *instigate* to ill; we *animate*, *incite*, and *encourage* indifferently to good or bad. So we usually *ascribe* good, but *impute* evil; yet neither the use of these words, nor perhaps of any other in our licentious language, is so established as not to be often reversed by the correctest writers. I shall therefore, since the rules of stile, like those of law, arise from precedents often repeated, collect the testimonies on both sides, and endeavour to discover and promulgate the decrees of custom, who has so long possessed, whether by right or by usurpation, the sovereignty of words.

It is necessary likewise to explain many words by their opposition to others; for contraries are best seen when they stand together. Thus the verb *stand* has one sense as opposed to *fall*, and another as opposed to *fly*; for want of attending to which distinction, obvious as it is, Dr. Bentley has squandered his criticism to no purpose, on these lines of Paradise Lost.

> . . . In heaps
> Chariot and charioteer lay overturn'd,
> And fiery foaming steeds. What *stood, recoil'd*,
> O'erwearied, through the faint Satanic host,
> Defensive scarce, or with pale fear surpris'd
> *Fled* ignominious . . .

'Here,' says the critic, 'as the sentence is now read, we find that what *stood*, *fled*,' and therefore he proposes an alteration, which he might have spared if he had consulted a dictionary, and found nothing more was affirmed than that those *fled* who did *not fall*.

In explaining such meanings as seem accidental and adventitious, I shall endeavour to give an account of the means by which they were introduced. Thus to *eke out* anything, signifies to lengthen it beyond its just dimensions by some low artifice, because the word *eke* was the usual refuge of our old writers when they wanted a syllable. And *buxom*, which means only *obedient*, is now made, in familiar phrases, to stand for *wanton*, because of an antient form of marriage, before the reformation, the bride promised complaisance and obedience in these terms: 'I will be bonair and *buxom* in bed and at board.'

I know well, my Lord, how trifling many of these remarks will appear separately considered, and how easily they may give occasion to the contemptuous merriment of sportive idleness, and the gloomy censures of arrogant stupidity; but dulness it is easy to despise, and laughter it is easy to repay. I shall not be solicitous what is thought of my work by such as know not the importance of philological studies, nor shall think those that have done nothing qualified to condemn me for doing little. It may not, however, be improper to remind them, that no terrestial greatness is more than an aggregate of little things, and to inculcate after the Arabian proverb, that drops added to drops constitute the ocean.

There remains yet to be considered the DISTRIBUTION of words into their proper classes, or that part of lexicography which is strictly critical.

The popular part of the language, which includes all words not appropriated to particular sciences, admits of many distinctions and subdivisions; as, into words of general use; words employed chiefly in poetry; words obsolete; words which are admitted only by particular writers, yet not in themselves improper; words used only in burlesque writing; and words impure and barbarous.

Words of general use will be known by having no sign of particularity, and their various senses will be supported by authorities of all ages.

The words appropriated to poetry will be distinguished by some mark prefixed, or will be known by having no authorities but those of poets.

Of antiquated or obsolete words, none will be inserted but such as are to be found in authors who wrote since the accession of Elizabeth, from which we date the golden age of our language; and of these many might be omitted, but that the reader may require, with an appearance of reason, that no difficulty should be left unresolved in books which he finds himself invited to read, as confessed and established models of stile. These will be likewise pointed out by some note of exclusion, but not of disgrace.

The words which are found only in particular books, will be known by the single name of him that has used them; but such will be omitted, unless either their propriety, elegance, or force, or the reputation of their authors affords some extraordinary reason for their reception.

Words used in burlesque and familiar compositions, will be likewise mentioned with their proper authorities, such as *dudgeon* from Butler, and *leasing* from Prior, and will be diligently characterised by marks of distinction.

Barbarous or impure words and expressions may be branded with some note of infamy, as they are carefully to be eradicated wherever they are found; and they occur too frequently even in the best writers. As in Pope,

> . . . *in* endless error *hurl'd*
> '*Tis these* that early taint the female soul.

In Addison,

> Attend to what a *lesser* muse indites.

And in Dryden,

> A dreadful quiet felt, and *worser* far
> Than arms . . .

If this part of the work can be well performed, it will be equivalent to the proposal made by Boileau to the academicans, that they should review all their polite writers, and correct such impurities as might be found in them, that their authority might not contribute, at any distant time, to the depravation of the language.

With regard to questions of purity, or propriety, I was once in doubt whether I should not attribute too much to myself in attempting to decide them, and whether my province was to extend beyond the proposition of the question, and the display of the suffrages on each side; but I have been since determined by your Lordship's opinion, to interpose my own judgement, and shall therefore endeavour to support what appears to me most consonant to grammar and reason. Ausonius thought that modesty forbad him to plead inability for a task to which Caesar had judged him equal.

> Cur me posse negem posse quod ille putat?

And I may hope, my Lord, that since you, whose authority in our language is so generally acknowledged, have commissioned me to declare my own opinion, I shall be considered as exercising a kind of vicarious jurisdiction, and that the power which might have been denied to my own claim, will be readily allowed me as the delegate of your Lordship.

In citing authorities, on which the credit of every part of this work must depend, it will be proper to observe some obvious rules, such as of preferring writers of the first reputation to those of an inferior rank, of noting the quotations with accuracy, and of selecting, when it can be conveniently done, such sentences as, beside their immediate use, may give pleasure or instruction by conveying some elegance of language, or some precept of prudence, or piety.

It has been asked, on some occasions, who shall judge the judges? And since with regard to this design, a question may arise by what authority the judges are selected, it is necessary to obviate it, by declaring that many of the writers whose testimonies were alleged, were selected by Mr. Pope, of whom I may be justified in affirming, that were he still alive, solicitous as he was for the success of this work, he would not be displeased that I have undertaken it.

It will be proper that the quotations be ranged according to the ages of the authors, and it will afford an agreeable amusement, if to the words and phrases which are not of our own growth, the name of the writer who first introduced them can be affixed, and if, to words which are now antiquated, the authority be subjoined of him who last admitted them. Thus for *scathe* and *buxom*, now obsolete, Milton may be cited.

> . . . The mountain oak
> Stands *scath'd* to heaven . . .
> . . . He with broad sails
> Winnow'd the *buxom* air . . .

By this method every word will have its history, and the reader will be informed of the gradual changes of the language, and have before his eyes the rise of some words, and the fall of others. But observations so minute and accurate are to be desired rather than expected, and if use be carefully supplied, curiosity must sometimes bear its disappointments.

This, my Lord, is my idea of an English Dictionary, a dictionary by which the pronunciation of our language may be fixed; by which its purity may be preserved, its use ascertained, and its duration lengthened. And though, perhaps, to correct the language of nations by books of grammar, and amend their manners by discourses of morality, may be tasks equally difficult; yet as it is unavoidable to wish, it is natural likewise to hope, that your Lordship's patronage may not be wholly lost; that it may contribute to the preservation of antient, and the improvement of modern writers; that it may promote the reformation of those translators, who for want of understanding the characteristical differences of tongues, have formed a chaotic dialect of heterogeneous phrases; and awaken to the care of purer diction, some men of genius, whose attention to argument makes them negligent of stile, or whose rapid imagination, like the Peruvian torrents, when it brings down gold, mingles it with sand.

When I survey the Plan which I have laid before you, I cannot, my Lord, but confess, that I am frighted at its extent, and like the soldiers of Caesar, look on Britain as a new world, which it is almost madness to invade. But I hope, that though I should not complete the conquest, I shall at least discover the coast, civilize part of the inhabitants, and make it easy for some other adventurer to proceed farther, to reduce them wholly to subjection, and settle them under laws.

We are taught by the great Roman orator, that every man should propose to himself the highest degree of excellence, but that he may stop with honour at the second or third: though therfore my performance should fall below the excellence of other dictionaries, I may obtain, at least, the praise of having endeavoured well, nor shall I think it any reproach to my diligence, that I have retired without a triumph from a contest with united academies and long successions of learned compilers. I cannot hope in the warmest moments, to preserve so much caution through so long a work as not often to sink into negligence, or to obtain so much knowledge of all its parts, as not frequently to fail by ignorance. I expect that sometimes the desire of accuracy, will urge me to superfluities, and sometimes the fear of prolixity betray me to omissions; that in the extent of such variety I shall be often bewildred, and that in the mazes of such intricacy, be frequently entangled; that in one part refinement will be utilised beyond exactness, and evidence dilated in another beyond perspicuity. Yet I do not despair of approbation from those who knowing the uncertainty of conjecture, the scantiness of knowledge, the fallibility of memory, and the unsteadiness of attention, can compare the causes of error with the means of avoiding it, and the extent of art with capacity of man.

TEXT AND SELECTED READING

The text is that of the 1747 edition which was addressed to the Earl of Chesterfield. The general importance of the *Plan* (along with that of the Preface to the *Dictionary* itself) is discussed in J. Barrell, 'The Language Properly So-Called' in *English Literature in History 1730-80* (London: Hutchinson, 1983), M. Cohen, *Sensible Words* (Baltimore: Johns Hopkins University Press, 1977) and A.P.R. Howatt, *A History of English Language Teaching* (Oxford: Oxford University Press, 1984). An account of the *Dictionary* is given in J. Sledd and G. Kolb, *Dr Johnson's Dictionary* (Chicago: Chicago University Press, 1955). And an interesting, though brief, interpretation of the cultural and political significance of Johnson's work is presented in Terry Eagleton's *The Function of Criticism* (London: Verso, 1984).

4

Thomas Sheridan

If Johnson had signalled the developing demarcation of different classes by the language they use, we can see in the texts of many of the late eighteenth-century elocution masters a sensitivity to language which is clearly related to the emerging stratification of social life which was so rapid in the period. Of course such sensitivity was not restricted to the elocutionists' texts and appears frequently in the literature of the period. In *Joseph Andrews* for example the character of Mrs Slipslop is positioned both socially and morally not just by her name but by her verbal infelicities. Railing against Joseph for his lack of attention to her she says: 'Do you intend to *result* my passion? Is it not enough, ungrateful as you are, to make no return to all the favours I have done you: but you must treat me with *ironing?*' And this technique is perfected later in Richard Sheridan's Mrs Malaprop in *The Rivals*. However, it is in the work of Thomas Sheridan, the playwright's father, that we find a theoretical account of the role of language, and pronunciation in particular, in the construction of social identity.

Sheridan's *Course* on elocution interestingly returns to Locke (as indeed do so many of the eighteenth-century language texts), taking up his theory of communication. He agrees with Locke's argument that we need to analyse our words, and the ideas they stand for, in order to ensure social intercourse; though he too fails to see the central paradox of Locke's theory. However, he criticises Locke for not probing into the practical reasons for the misunderstanding of words and offers his own remedy, which he specifies as the need to educate children in their own language. The aim of such an education in the English language, Sheridan claims, would be to attain perfect communication. That is, to reach a uniformity in the use of words which would bring about an easy transfer of ideas.

63

In one sense Sheridan's argument is an attempt to propose education as the means to resolve the problem pointed out by Locke. Yet its significant novelty lies in suggesting that an important part of the solution would be the teaching of pronunciation. For what, Sheridan asks, would be the point of being able to be sure of the meanings of words if their pronunciation by differing speakers resulted in our not being able to recognise those words? It is for this reason that pronunciation has an important role to play in the enhancement of communication. After the philosophers have clarified the words, the elocution masters then have the task of making sure that they are uniformly pronounced and thus mutually recognisable.

Variation in pronunciation had of course long been recognised along with variation in vocabulary and grammar. Caxton, for example, had noted in the Prologue to *Eneydos* (1490) 'that comyn englysshe that is spoken in one shyre varyeth from a nother'. The importance of Sheridan's project in the eighteenth century, however, was to delineate a particular form of pronunciation, elevate its status, downgrade other forms and take the elevated form as the model by means of which 'proper English' pronunciation could be taught. The form which is delineated and elevated is of course that of the court which is called the 'polite pronunciaton'. All other forms, ranging from the cockney to the Irish, are described as 'provincial dialects' which bear the stigma of 'a rustic, provincial, pedantic, or mechanic education', and are therefore to be avoided.

What is of most interest in this argument in fact is the shift from the criterion of intelligibility to that of social disgrace in the teaching of pronunciation. For what is really at stake here is not the problem of making oneself understood (though of course there may certainly have been difficulties with some differences), but that of making a claim for the right kind of social identity in the rapidly changing social formation of mid- to late eighteenth-century Britain. It is, as the reader will see below, not the last time that this problem appears.

A COURSE OF LECTURES ON ELOCUTION

Introductory Discourse

There has been no maxim more frequently inculcated, or more generally assented to, than that human nature, ought to be the chief study of human kind; and yet it is of all subjects, about which the busy mind of man has been employed, that which has been least attended to; or with regard to which, the fewest discoveries have been made, founded upon any certain knowledge.

Is it not amazing to reflect, that from the creation of the world, there was no part of the human mind clearly delineated, till within the last sixty years? When Mr. Locke arose, to give us a just view, of one part of our internal frame, 'the understanding', upon principles of philosophy founded upon reason and experience.

The chief cause of the very erroneous, or inaccurate views, given of that part of our nature, before his time, was, as he himself confesses, accidentally discovered by Mr. Locke, long after he had begun his work; and not 'till after he had found himself intangled in many perplexities, during the pursuit of his subject; when lighting accidentally upon this clue, he was happily guided thro' all the mazes of that labyrinth, in which so many had fruitlessly wandered, or been lost before.

His discovery was, that as we cannot think upon any abstract subject, without the use of abstract terms; and as in general we substitute the terms themselves, in thinking, as well as speaking, in the room of the complex ideas for which they stand; it is impossible we can think with precision, till we first examine whether we have precise ideas annexed to such terms: and it is equally impossible to communicate our thoughts to others with exactness, unless we are first agreed in the exact meaning of our words.

ACCORDINGLY, this acute philosopher, entered into a scrupulous examination of all the terms he used, for his own purpose, in private meditation; and afterwards gave clear definitions of those terms, for the benefit of others, in communicating to them his thoughts. His labours were attended with success. It must be evident to all who examine his works with care, that he has treated his subject with the utmost precision, and perspicuity; and that all who are properly qualified to read his essay, will, with due attention, agree in comprehending his meaning in exactly the same way.

BUT in this age of speculative philosophy, they who turn their thoughts to writings of that sort, seem to have no other object in view than that of merely acquiring knowledge; without once considering how that knowledge may be rendered useful to society. For the mastery of one speculative point, they run to another, with the same kind of avidity, that misers pursue the accumulation of wealth; and much to the same end: the one, rejoicing in his hoard of concealed knowledge; the other, in his heaps of hidden gold; tho' both are equally useless to themselves, and to the world.

EVEN Mr. Locke himself seems to have been so totally absorbed in pursuits of that sort, that he has not in any part of his works pointed out to us, how his discoveries might turn out to the benefit of mankind, by any practical plan to try their effects. And accordingly, little or no advantage has hitherto resulted from them, excepting the fascination they have given, to men of a speculative turn.

AFTER having shewn that most errors in thinking arose from an abuse of words; and that most controversies and disputes, which have been carried on without coming to any conclusion, were owing to the want of clear and precise ideas being affixed to the terms used by the disputants; the only remedy Mr. Locke suggests, is, that men should carefully examine the meaning of each word, and use it steadily in one sense. And that upon any difference of opinion, the parties should define such terms as are capable of ambiguity, or are of most importance in the argument.

BUT he might have judged from the great difficulty which he himself found in accomplishing this point, and from his own experience of the great care and pains it cost, to separate ideas from words to which they were early associated, and cemented by long use; that this was a task not likely to be performed by many. One would imagine that a philosopher, before he prescribed a cure, would have traced the disorder to its source. Nor had he far to seek for the source of our impropriety in the use of words, when he should reflect that the study of our own language, has never been made part of the education of our youth. Consequently the use of words is got wholly by chance, according to the company we keep, or the books that we read. And if neither the companions with whom we converse, nor the authors whom we consult, are exact in the use of their words, I cannot see how it is to be expected that we should arrive at any precision in that respect.

IF then, irregularity and disorder, in this case, as in all others, must necessarily follow from neglect, and leaving things to chance; regularity and order, as in all other cases, can proceed only from care and method. The way to have clear and precise ideas affixed to the use of words, would be to have mankind taught from their early days, by proper masters, the precise meaning of all the words they use.

THE rising generation, so instructed, would be uniform in the use of words, and would be able to communicate their ideas to each other, with ease and perspicuity. Nor would their understandings be clouded, in private meditation, by the mists of obscurity; nor their sentiments, when delivered in conversation, perplexed by the intanglements of verbal disputation. And this might easily be effected, if only a fourth part of that time were dedicated to the study of our own tongue, which is now wasted in acquiring a smattering in two dead languages, without proving either of use or ornament to one in a hundred so instructed.

IT is true, Mr. Locke, in his Essay on Education, grievously complains of our neglect of studying our mother tongue. But he lays the fault at the wrong door, when he imputes this neglect to the masters of grammar schools, and tutors at the universities. This is not part of their province. They neither profess to teach it, nor do they know how. Nothing effectual can be done, without making that a distinct branch of education, and encouraging proper masters to follow it as their sole employment, in the same way as the several masters in the other branches do. And certainly whether we consider the difficulty of the thing, or the great ends which might be answered by it, the masters in that branch, ought to meet with as great encouragement, as those in any other.

Lecture II

Pronunciation

THE next article which I propose to treat of is pronunciation. This word which had such a comprehensive meaning amongst the antients, as to take in the whole compass of delivery, with its concomitants of look and gesture; is confined with us to very narrow bounds, and refers only to the manner of sounding our words. This indeed is the only article relative to elocution, which claims any part of our attention. The reason of which seems to be this. In all other points of elocution, all ranks and orders of men, wherever born, or in whatever situation of life, are equally liable to the same defects, and to fall into the same errors. Amongst those bred at the university, or at court, as well as amongst mechanics, or rustics; amongst those who speak in the senate-house, pulpit, or at the bar, as well as amongst men in private life; we find stammerers, lispers, a mumbling indistinct utterance; ill-management of the voice, by pitching it in too high, or too low a key; speaking too loud, or so softly as not to be heard; and using discordant tones, and false cadences. These being, I say, common to all ranks and classes of men, have not any marks of disgrace upon them, but on the contrary meet with general indulgence, from a general corruption.

BUT it is not so with regard to pronunciation; in which tho' there be as great difference between men, as in any other article, yet this difference, is not so much between individuals, as whole bodies of men; inhabitants of different countries, and speaking one common language, without agreeing in the manner of pronouncing it. Thus not only the Scotch, Irish and Welsh, have each their own idioms, which uniformly prevail in those countries, but almost every county in England, has its peculiar dialect. Nay in the very metropolis two different modes of pronunciation prevail, by which the inhabitants of one part of the town, are distinguished from those of the other. One is current in the city, and is called the cockney; the other at the court end, and is called the polite pronunciation. As amongst these various dialects, one must have the preference, and become fashionable, it will of course fall to the lot of that which prevails at court, the source of fashions of all kinds. All other dialects, are sure marks, either of a provincial, rustic, pedantic, or mechanic education; and therefore have some degree of disgrace annexed to them. And as the court pronunciation is no where methodically taught, and can be acquired only by conversing with people in polite life, it is a sort of proof that a person has kept good company, and on that account is sought after by all, who wish to be considered as fashionable people, or members of the beau monde. This is the true reason that the article of pronunciation has been the chief, or rather only object of attention, in the whole affair of delivery. Yet tho' this is a point, the attainment of which is ardently desired by an infinite number of individuals, there are few who succeed in the attempt, thro' want of method, rules, and assistance of masters; without which old habits can not easily be removed.

THE difficulties of those who endeavour to cure themselves of a provincial or vicious pronunciation are chiefly three. 1st, The want of knowing exactly where the fault lies. 2dly, Want of method in removing it, and of due application. 3dly, Want of consciousness of their defects in this point. The way of getting over these difficulties I shall endeavour to point out.

AS to the first article, the want of knowing exactly where the fault lies; most persons who have a provincial dialect, finding that in every sentence they utter, there are many things to be reprehended, are apt to imagine that their whole speech is infected; and therefore look upon a total cure, against the strong power of early habit, as impracticable: whereas were they to examine into the source of this irregularity, they would find it to arise perhaps, only from a different manner of sounding some of the vowels, which occurring generally in every sentence, seems to infect their whole discourse.

THUS the gentlemen of Ireland for instance, differ from those of England, chiefly in two of the sounds belonging to the vowels ä and ë, sounded by them ā and ē, and even with regard to those also, not always, but only in certain words. In many of which they give the sound ā to the first vowel where it is pronounced ă, and the sound ĕ to the second, where it is pronounced ĕ. Thus the words patron, matron, are pronounced by them patron, matron, the *a* being sounded as it is in father; fever sea please are pronounced like savour say plays. They soon become conscious of this diversity of sound, and not knowing exactly in what words it is used, in order to imitate the English pronunciation, they adopt the sound ee in all words without distinction; instead of great they say greet, for occasion occeesion, days dees, &c.

NOW this mistake is evidently owing to want of method; for were there a vocabulary made, containing all the words in alphabetical order, in which the English pronunciation differs from the Irish with regard to these two sounds, their number would not be very considerable, and all might by moderate practice, in a short time, make themselves completely masters of polite pronunciation; for they scarcely differ in any other points, or at least the exceptions are so few, that they may be brought into a very narrow compass.

THIS brings me to the consideration of the second impediment in the way of such as would be desirous of getting rid of a provincial dialect, the want of method; often the source of want of due application.

AS there is no method ready to his hands, each individual must form one to himself. Let him in the first place employ his attention in discovering the particular vowels in the sounding of which the provincial manner differs from the polite pronunciation. Let him by the help of dictionaries and vocabularies, make out a list of the words, in which those vowels are to be found; and get some friend to attend him whilst he reads those words over, and mark their particular sounds, distinguishing those which differ from the general rule. When by these means he is able to sound them all right, let him practice them daily over by himself, and let him select such words as he finds most difficult of pronunciation, and form them into sentences, verses, or anagrams; which he may get by heart and frequently repeat. Tho' this may seem laborious at first, the task in the progress will be found easier than is imagined, and he who makes use of this method will be encouraged to proceed, from the certainty of success which will attend every step of his progress. Whereas they who attempt to alter their pronunciation without method, only plunge from one errour into another, and soon grow weary of fruitless pains.

BESIDE such as have a provincial pronunciation of certain letters perceptible in all words wherein those letters are sounded, there are few gentlemen of England who have received their education at country schools, that are not infected by a false pronunciation of certain words, peculiar to each county. It will not be difficult for them to collect all such words, as they seldom are numerous; and after having collected them, if they will daily repeat them, till the tongue gets the habit of pronouncing the new sounds with ease, they will soon take place of the others in their common speech. And surely every gentleman will think it worth while, to take some pains, to get rid of such evident marks of rusticity.

HOW easy it would be to change the cockney pronunciation, by making use of a proper method! The chief difference lies in the manner of pronouncing the ve, or u consonant as it is commonly called, and the w; which they frequently interchangeably use for each other. Thus they call veal weal, vinegar winegar. On the other hand they call winter vinter, well vell. Tho' the converting the *w* into a *v* is not so common as the changing the *v* into a *w*.

WHOEVER will allot a certain portion of time every day, to read aloud in the hearing of a friend, all words in the dictionary beginning with those two letters, will find in a short time the true pronunciation become familiar to him. In children this errour might in a great measure be prevented, if when they are taught to spell, the letter were called by the name which marks its power, ve instead of u consonant; for in that case the very sound of the letter would guide them to the true pronunciation; whereas in the other the sound itself confirms them in the vulgar one. A child might be soon made sensible of the absurdity of sounding v e a l weal, tho' it is impossible that he should perceive any impropriety in pronouncing u e a l in that manner.

ANOTHER vice in the cockney pronunciation is, the changing the sound of the last syllables of words ending in ow, wherever it is not sounded like a dipthong, but like a simple o, (which is always the case when the last syllable is unaccented) into er – as feller for fellow – beller, holler, foller, winder, – for bellow, hollow, follow, window. As also adding the letter r to all proper names ending in *a* unaccented, as Belindar, Dorindar, for Belinda, Dorinda. But the words in our language which come under either of the above cases are so few, that a list of them might be soon made, and the vicious habit give place to a just one by the method of practice before recommended.

70

WITH respect to the rustic pronunciation, prevailing in the several counties, I mean amongst the gentry, there does not seem to be any general errour of this sort; their deviations being for the most part, only in certain words, sounded in a peculiar manner by each county; and which probably owe their present pronunciation, to the continuation of the old custom; which like other antiquated modes, changes more slowly in their distance from, or want of communication with the court. And these deviations not being very numerous, as was before observed, may easily be set right. But there is one defect which more generally prevails in the counties than any other, and indeed is daily gaining ground amongst the politer part of the world, I mean the omission of the aspirate in many words by some, and in most by others. Were this custom to become general, it would deprive our tongue of one great fund of force and expression. For not only certain words have a peculiar energy, but several emotions of the mind are strongly marked, by this method of shooting out the words (if I may be allowed the expression) with the full force of the breath. As in exclamations what! when? where? why? how! hark! hist! — In the words hard, harsh, heave, hurt, whirl, whisper, whistle. If anyone were to pronounce the following sentence, Hail ye high ministers of Heav'n! how happy are we in hearing these your heavenly tydings! without an aspirate thus – Ail ye igh ministers of eaven! ow appy are we in earing these your eavenly tydings! who does not see that the whole expression of triumph and exultation would be lost? And the same may be observed with regard to the opposite expression of abhorrence and detestation, if the following sentence, How I hate, how I abhor such hell-hounds! were pronounced in the same manner, ow I ate, ow I abor such ell-ounds. But let no one imagine, that because he would not pronounce so many successive words, or a whole sentence in such manner, he is therefore entirely free from defect in this point; for I have met with but few instances in the course of my experience, and those only in the most correct speakers, of persons who have not been guilty of omitting the aspirate from some words, or of giving it too faintly to others. The best method of curing this will be to read over frequently all words beginning with the letter *H* and those beginning with *Wh* in the dictionary, and push them out with the full force of the breath, 'til an habit is obtained of aspirating strongly: nor need any one so circumstanced be apprehensive of falling into an extreme on that side, as the old habit will pull as strongly on the opposite side, and in this, as in all other points, reduce it to a medium.

71

THERE is another article which has produced frequent disputes with regard to pronunciation, as whether the word should be pronounced concordance or concordance — refractory or refractory — but points of this kind come more properly under the next head which I shall treat of, that of Accent.

THERE are some other words also of dubious sound, such as goold or gold, wind or wind; pronunciations of this kind have their several advocates, and there is no impropriety in using either. In cases of this nature all who have the opportunity of being informed of that pronunciation, most used by men of education at court, will have the best authority on their side; as that is indeed the only standard we can refer to, in critical cases, as well as others.

TEXT AND SELECTED READING

The text is taken from Sheridan's *A Course of Lectures on Elocution*, published in 1762 and addressed to the Earl of Northumberland. Sheridan's work is discussed in J. Barrell, 'The Language Properly So-Called' in *English Literature in History 1730-80* (London: Hutchinson, 1983) and M. Cohen, *Sensible Words* (Baltimore: Johns Hopkins University Press, 1977), and the general context is outlined in L. Formigari's 'Language and Society in the Late Eighteenth Century', *Journal of the History of Ideas*, 35 (1974). A detailed evaluation of his work can be found in W. Benzie, *The Dublin Orator* (Leeds: Leeds University Press, 1972).

5

James Buchanan

Sheridan was Irish, Buchanan was a Scot; it is no small irony that it is from the edges of the dominant culture that these two prominent elocution masters arrive with their prescriptions for 'proper English'. No small irony but perhaps too not really a surprise since it was precisely those who were the marginalised but aspirant who were most sensitive to the indices of linguistic and social identity in a turbulent culture. However, if Sheridan's prescriptions were couched in terms of the desirability of laying down the foundations for successful communication, then Buchanan's know no such pretensions. The intentions of his work announce themselves in his title: the task is to establish a mode of pronunciation, uniform of course, but elegant too, throughout the different countries which constitute Britain. And naturally it is to be the pronunciation practised by the learned and polite. Again then what we find in this text is the imposition of a certain form of pronunciation as the model and once more this has a long-standing precedent. As early as Puttenham's *Arte of English Poesie* (1589) for example, there is a clear social and geographical delimitation of the acceptable form of the language: 'that which is spoken in the King's court, or in the good townes and cities within the land, than in the marches and frontiers, or in port townes, where strangers haunt for traffic's sake.' In Buchanan's case, however, the imposition of the standard of pronunciation is not justified in terms of the ease of communication, but by the political prestige it would bring to the nation, the clear demarcation of the form of speech to be used in public speaking, and the social unity it would engender amongst the nation's subjects.

Buchanan's task, as he describes it, is to forge a standard, based on the pronunciation of 'the best speakers', in order to allow both foreigners and natives to acquire a proper access to the language and

73

thus 'to avoid a provincial dialect, so unbecoming gentlemen'. It is clear then that his aim at one level is similar to that of Sheridan in that both wish to provide the means by which those who do not have it already can attain the prescribed English pronunciation. In this respect they both share the aim of providing one of the key elements in the education of gentlemen and those who aspire to such status. That is, to lay down the guidelines for speaking in the public sphere for those who are to exercise power. It would be a great advantage, he notes, to

> British youth, especially of our young nobility and gentry, whose fortune it will be to speak in public whether in the senate, in the pulpit, on the bench or at the bar, were a Standard of Pronunciation to be taught in all our public schools.

Since the ear is the door to the heart as he says, or hegemony is the key to political victory as a later thinker might have put it, those who are to be in a position to influence others in the exercise of power have to be able to use correct pronunciation in order to do so successfully.

His aim, however, is not solely to prescribe the proper language of the powerful. For what he also seeks to do is to suggest that a standard of pronunciation can engender the social unity in a kingdom which although formally united by the 1707 Act of Union, is still culturally divided. The inhabitants of North Britain (Scotland), or at least the 'gentlemen at the bar', 'ministers' and 'schoolmasters' amongst them, are asked to take up the pronunciation of the 'best speakers' in order to reduce the national differences between the two kingdoms. For as Buchanan says, it is the 'different forms of speech' which have long fostered the 'national prejudice' which divides them and it is to language that he turns in order to heal the rift. The problem of course is that the first and second of his objectives, that is the attempt to lay down guidelines for gentlemen and the attempt to forge national unity, are contradictory. For the pronunciation of the powerful, as Sheridan had made clear, was to be based on the English court and therefore becomes more of a marker of political and national difference than a means to overcome it. Differing forms of social and cultural identity, centred upon differing forms of the language itself, are clearly in conflict here and the attempt to impose linguistic uniformity only forces the questions and problems to reappear at another level.

JAMES BUCHANAN

AN ESSAY TOWARDS ESTABLISHING A STANDARD FOR AN ELEGANT AND UNIFORM PRONUNCIATION OF THE ENGLISH LANGUAGE, THROUGHOUT THE BRITISH DOMINIONS AS PRACTISED BY THE MOST LEARNED AND POLITE SPEAKERS

The Preface

Whoever has been conversant with gentlemen of polite learning, must have heard them expressing their surprise, that, for the honour of our country, no attempt had been made towards a Standard for the proper and uniform Pronunciation of the English Language, now so elegant and learned, as justly to attract the attention of all Europe.

Some years since, I published an English Dictionary, with a view to obviate a vicious provincial dialect, and to remove the complaints of foreign gentlemen, desirous of learning English; several of whom, of a liberal education, then under my tuition, expostulated, that notwithstanding the acquisition of a proper English Pronunciation, yet there was no method exhibited to one just and regular. This charge being too well grounded, and reflecting what pains the French had taken to refine their language, and to make the study and pronunciation of it easy and familiar to other nations; I determined to rescue my country from any such imputation for the future, as far, at least, as my experience had at that time suggested. Accordingly, in the above-mentioned Dictionary, I marked the long and short sounds of the vowels throughout the alphabetical words, distinguished every quiescent letter, pointed out the number of syllables each word consisted of where doubtful, and ascertained the various sounds of the vowels and dipthongs, and of the single and double consonants, &c.

Thus was I the first who endeavoured to make the proper Pronunciation of our language of easy acquisition to foreigners, and to introduce an uniform one for the sake of natives; amongst whom it is still so notoriously vague and unstable.

After a long interval, there appeared last year a book entitled, 'A Spelling and pronouncing Dictionary', formed much upon the same plan. The author, Mr. Johnstone, has certainly shown himself a good judge of proper Pronunciation. He says, 'Having carried this book so far as to transcribe the substance of this book for the press, Mr. Buchanan's new English Dictionary first came into my hands; in which he has made a laudable effort of the same nature with this of mine, and which, on this account, and especially on account of the concise and accurate explications he has given of English words, is well worth consulting.'

However, further experience and reflection informed me, that all I had done was only a large advance towards making a proper Pronunciation general and uniform; and that it was impossible to represent a just one, and retain the true orthography, as from verbal expression the vocal sounds are constantly running into one another. I found it expedient, therefore, to denote every word as it actually came from the mouths of the best speakers, who, for ease or elegance, have receded from the written orthography, and expelled all harsh and troublesome contacts, according to the polite and learned of every language.

Though a dissertation upon articulate sounds may be both entertaining and useful to those who have made some progress in the study of the English language, yet it is but trifling with the bulk of people to say anything, even in a practical manner, about the various sounds of our letters, otherwise than by the *viva vox*.

For example, if I signify in writing, that [a] has five different sounds; and that 1. it sounds long in same, fair, compare, profane, &c. 2. broad, like German [a] in call, war, walk, bald, ward, water, &c. whoever has not been taught these sounds *viva voce*, or considered them abstractedly, has received no instruction. But let these sounds be properly represented in combination, and a child that can read a little will readily pronounce them thus, saim, fair, compair, profain, kaul, waur, wauk, bauld, waurd, wautir, &c. So if I signify that the dipthong [ea] has different sounds, and that, 1. in sounds like double [e] in arrear, appear, sear, dear, &c. 2. like short [e] in breast, head, deaf, sweat, ready, &c. and, 3. like long [a] in swear, bear, pear, great, &c. I have conveyed little or no instruction to the generality of people: But when these different sounds are represented in combination, as in the pronouncing columns of this work, an indifferent reader will easily express them thus, arreer, appeer, seer, deer, brest, hed, swet, redy, swair, bair, pair, grait, &c. We might here proceed to more examples; but for a view of the whole see the Introduction, where both the utility and plainness of this Essay as being adapted to the lowest capacity, will sufficiently appear.

When we consider the great anomaly of words in our language wherein the Pronunciation differs from the orthography, can we wonder that strangers should complain of the difficulty of acquiring a proper English Pronunciation, when, for want of a general guide, numbers of our own natives cannot pronounce with propriety?

In the following work the columns with the initial letters over them shew the true orthography, and the opposite columns the true pronunciation, in the most simple and easy manner, according to the best verbal expression. The orthographical columns will serve the purpose of a spelling dictionary far superior to anything of that kind ever offered to the public; as few of them contain above a third of the words of the English language. The spelling and pronouncing columns being face to face, will prevent those who have made but small progress in orthography from spelling as they used to pronounce. And as the difference betwixt the orthography and the proper Pronunciation is ascertained, it will also for the future prevent all unnecessary and pedantic deviations from our present orthography. To avoid crowding or confusing the pronouncing words, I have placed the common accent, denoting the elevation or emphasis of the voice, over its proper syllable in the orthographical words. And as in the pronouncing columns all redundant or silent letters are left out, and all the various sounds and changes of vowels, dipthongs, and consonants, are there properly denoted, every person that can read, by a proper attention to accent, must of necessity pronounce justly. It is true that foreigners must be taught the sounds of our vowels and dipthongs *viva voce*; for it is not to be supposed that they can utter sounds they never heard. But as it is only the general sounds they want, in order to become their own teachers, they may learn them in five minutes.

It must give great pleasure to every lover of his country, that our language is so highly esteemed abroad, as to become a part of polite education, and even necessary to finish a learned one: The following letter, dated in August last, is a proof. 'A gentleman writes from Hamburg to his friend, that he meets with great encouragement in Germany for teaching the English language; that several princes did him the honour of an invitation to teach at their courts, so great an esteem at present, says he, is put upon the English language, as well as the nation, by a great many of the Germanic body, who seem not to be inclined to be so much frenchified as of late.' Shall we ourselves then, unmindful of the richness and elegance of our own language, justly incur contempt by a shameful neglect in training up our youth in a masterly knowledge of it? Forbid it, Britain's genius! Let it rather be published in all the cities on the continent, that after the British nation had carried their victorious arms all over the four quarters of the globe, and compelled their enemies to sue for peace, they had the good policy to set about the further improvement of their language, and made it more acceptable and familiar to other nations, by rendering its Pronunciation regular, and of easy attainment. Formerly their young nobility and gentry set out on their travels with very little knowledge of their own country, and more deeply skilled in the French, than in their mother tongue: But, to the honour of that brave and free people be it spoken, the case is quite altered: the British youth are now taught in all their schools a grammatical and scientific knowledge of their own tongue; and to avoid a provincial dialect, so unbecoming gentlemen, they are early instructed, while the organs of speech are flexible, to pronounce properly, to read aloud gracefully; an accomplishment that many men who do not want good ears cannot perform, because they have been ill taught. In short, every Briton, now sensible of the importance of his own language, thinks it his interest to study it correctly, as being that which he is to use every day of his life, be his station ever so high, or ever so insignificant.

The establishing an uniform pronunciation at home is doing an honour to our country: and by making it of easy acquisition to foreigners, is, to my knowledge, removing more than half the trouble they have in acquiring a competent skill in our language, otherwise so easy and simple in its formation.

It was long ago supposed that a Standard for English pronunciation would be set under the sanction of government; but it remains a question whether any such thing ever was in agitation. Whether a work of this nature merits the attention of the present government, I shall not say; but certainly it would turn greatly to the advantage of British youth, especially of our young nobility and gentry, whose fortune it will be to speak in public, whether in the senate, in the pulpit, on the bench or at the bar, were a Standard Pronunciation to be taught in all our public schools. This would soon exclude all local dialects, with which the speech of some, who are otherwise accounted polite, is too much tinctured. The clergy are not ignorant how much the utterance of several amongst them is exceptionable; and a young gentleman, when he enters into holy orders, must be deaf to all sense of his duty, as well as to a laudable ambition, who does not study to secure the attention of his audience, by a proper delivery, a just and well-regulated Pronunciation. The ear is the door of the entrance to the heart, and whoever holds captive the former, will be sure to impress the latter.

With respect to the inhabitants of North Britain, as every word in the following work is presented to their view as it is actually pronounced by the best speakers, so that every one may become his own private teacher, it would be needless to say anything to so sensible a people, farther than just to put persons of distinction there in mind, that it is highly consistent with their duty in their several districts, even for the sake of their own offspring, cheerfully to lead the van towards a just and polished utterance. Let gentlemen at the bar, and those that minister in holy things, be especially exemplary, nor be diverted from such a gentlemen-like accomplishment by any foolish names that low-breeding can suggest. And let both clergy and laity enjoin the schoolmasters over that part of the united kingdom, to acquire and teach a proper Pronunciation to the rising generation. To carry this truly momentous design into proper execution, cries aloud for the helping hand of every man of sense; particularly when he considers, that he will be promoting one of the grandest moral ends that can possibly employ the human mind with relation to so great a community; even nothing less than removing national prejudice, which has too long subsisted, and been chiefly fostered between the two kingdoms from their different forms of speech! In fine, it will be joining them into one social family, and connecting them by much more benevolent and generous ties than that of political union.

May the Supreme Disposer of events prosper the glorious intention! and as, in the course of his admirable providence, he reduced a heptarchy into one great family, so may he unite for ever the hearts of a mighty and formidable people, under one sovereign, in the strictest and most lasting bonds of brotherly love and affection! which, to human eyes, nothing is likely to effect and thoroughly rivet, as their being of one language and of one speech.

TEXT AND SELECTED READING

The text is taken from Buchanan's *Essay* which was originally published in 1764 and addressed to 'the two august houses of the British parliament'. The general context of Buchanan's work is set out in M. Cohen, *Sensible Words* (Baltimore: Johns Hopkins University Press, 1977), A.P.R. Howatt, *A History of English Language Teaching* (Oxford: Oxford University Press, 1984) and Olivia Smith, *The Politics of Language 1791-1819* (Oxford: Oxford University Press, 1984). The political and cultural significance of his work is evaluated in J. Barrell, 'The Language Properly So-Called' in *English Literature in*

History 1730-80 (London: Hutchinson, 1983) and B. Emsley, 'James Buchanan and the Eighteenth-Century Regulation of English Usage', *PMLA*, 48 (1933).

6

Noah Webster

If Buchanan had attempted to forge unity between two nations by means of language then Webster's aim is to create division between two nations by precisely the same means. In a stark reversal of Buchanan's effort to conjure up cultural unity by the imposition of a standard pronunciation, Webster strives to highlight the cultural and political differences between Britain and America by focusing on the variation in pronunciation and language in the two nations.

Webster's position on spelling reform is interesting in that it progresses through a number of shifts. Initially his argument in the *Grammatical Institute* (1783) was that the dropping, for example, of 'superfluous letters' by particular writers amounted to nothing more than 'absurdities' induced by a 'rage for singularity'. In the extract set out below, however, he shifts his position radically. He did so partly under the influence of Benjamin Franklin's scheme of 'modern innovations in the English language and printing' (1789), and partly for political reasons. The extent of his conversion to the reformation of spelling can be seen in the Preface to his *Collection of Essays and Fugitive Writings*, where he argues that,

> Every possible reezon that could ever be offered for altering the spelling of wurds, stil exists in full force; and if a gradual reform should not be made in our language, it will proov that we are less under the influence of reezon than our ancestors.

His final position, however, was one of modification rather than radical change and the *American Dictionary* (1828) is not remarkable for great orthographical shifts.

Webster is most famous for those small amendments in spelling, such as the spelling *honor* rather than *honour*, or *theater* rather than *theatre*, which were to cause so much irritation to later British

81

commentators. Yet it is important to recall the political significance of his work since if the *Declaration of Independence* had asserted the severance of political and economic ties with Britain, then Webster's work is an attempt to extend that break into the linguistic and cultural realms. There are two aspects of his work which are particularly important from the perspective of examining the role of language in the formation of cultural identity. These are the tasks assigned to language of marking and indeed maintaining cultural difference between Britain and America, and the function which language was to play in the construction of national unity within the newly independent states.

Webster's assertion of the need for linguistic as well as political independence is made most explicit in his *Dissertations on the English Language* (1789). In it he argues that 'as an independent nation, our honor requires us to have a system of our own in language as well as government'. Later in the same text he declares,

> Customs, habits, and *language*, as well as government should be national. America should have her *own* distinct from all the world. Such is the policy of other nations, and such must be *our* policy, before the states can be either independent or respectable.

This was a position to which he remained faithful throughout his life and it reappears in the Preface to his final and most important work the *American Dictionary of the English Language*. In that text he proposes that,

> it is not only important, but, in a degree necessary that the people of this country should have an *American Dictionary* of the English language; for although the body of the language is the same as in England, and it is desirable to perpetuate that sameness, yet some differences must exist.

The examples of the differences in language and ideas which are selected by Webster are significant for no American, he claims, could possibly be satisfied with the English use and definition of terms such as 'congress', 'senate', 'assembly', 'court' and so on.

The declaration of linguistic and cultural independence being one part of his work, the other was the assertion of unity. For in 1789 the American nation was still to be forged and Webster saw a clear role for language in that process. Thus the *Dissertations* are an attempt to set out 'the general custom of speaking' and to separate and reject the local or particular. Within the text there is evidence of that rejection of the usage of particular groups within the nation which always follows from the call to social unity over and above actually existing differences. For it is clear that what is invoked is national unity rather than social equality: 'every engine should be employed to make the people of this country national; to call their attachments home to their own country; and to inspire them with the pride of national character.' It was a rallying call for the federation which does much to illustrate the role of language in the creation of forms of social identity:

> Let us then seize the present moment, and establish a *national language* as well as a national government. Let us remember that there is a certain respect due to the opinions of other nations. As an independent people, our reputation abroad demands that, in all things, we should be federal; be *national*; for if we do not respect *ourselves*, we may be assured that other nations will not respect us.

DISSERTATIONS ON THE ENGLISH LANGUAGE

Appendix
An Essay on the Necessity, Advantages and Practicability Of Reforming the Mode of Spelling, And of Rendering the Orthography of Words Correspondent to the Pronunciation

It has been observed by all writers on the English language, that the orthography or spelling of words is very irregular; the same letters often representing different sounds, and the same sounds often expressed by different letters. For this irregularity, two principal causes may be assigned:

1. The changes to which the pronunciation of a language is liable, from the progress of science and civilisation.

2. The mixture of different languages, occasioned by revolutions in England, or by a predilection of the learned, for words of foreign growth and ancient origin.

To the first cause may be ascribed the difference between the spelling and pronunciation of Saxon words. The northern nations of Europe originally spoke much in gutturals. This is evident from the number of aspirates and guttural letters, which still remain in the orthography of words derived from those nations; and from the modern pronunciation of the collateral branches of the Teutonic, the Dutch, Scotch and German. Thus *k* before *n* was once pronounced; as in *knave*, the *gh* in *might, though, daughter*, and other similar words; the *g* in *reign, feign*, &c.

But as savages proceed in forming languages, they lose the guttural sounds, in some measure, and adopt the use of labials, and the more open vowels. The ease of speaking facilitates this progress, and the pronunciation of words is softened, in proportion to a national refinement of manners. This will account for the difference between the ancient and modern languages of France, Spain, and Italy; and for the difference between the soft pronunciation of the present languages of those countries, and the more harsh and guttural pronunciation of the northern inhabitants of Europe.

In this progress the English have lost the sounds of most of the guttural letters. The *k* before *n* in *know*, the *g* in *reign*, and in many other words, are become mute in practice; and the *gh* is softened into the sound of *f*, as in *laugh*, or is silent, as in *brought*.

To this practice of softening the sounds of letters, or wholly suppressing those which are harsh and disagreeable, may be added a popular tendency to abbreviate words of common use. Thus *Southwark*, by a habit of quick pronunciation, is become *Suthark*; *Worcester* and *Leicester*, are become *Wooster* and *Lester*; *business, bizness*; *colonel, curnel; cannot, will not, cant, wont*. In this manner the final *e* is not heard in many modern words, in which it formerly made a syllable. The words *clothes, cares*, and most others of the same kind, were formerly pronounced in two syllables.

Of the other cause of irregularity in the spelling of our language, I have treated sufficiently in the first Dissertation. It is here necessary only to remark, that when words have been introduced from a foreign language into the English, they have generally retained the orthography of the original, however ill adapted to express the English pronunciation. Thus *fatigue, marine, chaise*, retain their French dress, while, to represent the true pronunciation in English, they should be spelt *fateeg, mareen, shaze*. Thus thro an ambition to exhibit the etymology of words, the English in *Philip, physic, character, chorus*, and other Greek derivatives, preserve the representatives of the original ϕ and χ; yet these words are pronounced, and ought ever to have been spelt, *Fillip, fyzzic* or *fizzic, karacter, korus*.

But such is the state of our language. The pronunciation of the words which are strictly *English*, has gradually been changing for ages, and since the revival of science in Europe, the language has received a vast accession of words from other languages, many of which retain an orthography very ill-suited to exhibit the true pronunciation.

The question now occurs; ought the Americans to retain these faults which produce innumerable inconveniencies in the acquisition and use of the language, or ought they at once to reform these abuses, and introduce order and regularity into the orthography of the AMERICAN TONGUE?

Let us consider this subject with some attention.

Several attempts were formerly made in England to rectify the orthography of the language. But I apprehend their schemes failed of success, rather on account of their intrinsic difficulties, than on account of any necessary impracticability of a reform. It was proposed in most of these schemes, not merely to throw out superfluous and silent letters, but to introduce a number of new characters. Any attempt on such a plan must undoubtedly prove unsuccessful. It is not to be expected that an orthography, perfectly regular and simple, such as would be formed by a 'Synod of Grammarians on principles of science', will ever be substituted for that confused mode of spelling which is now established. But it is apprehended that great improvements may be made, and an orthography almost regular, or such as shall obviate most of the present difficulties which occur in learning our language, may be introduced and established with little trouble and opposition.

The principal alterations, necessary to render our orthography sufficiently regular and easy, are these:

1. The omission of all superfluous or silent letters; as *a* in *bread*. Thus *bread, head, give, breast, built, meant, realm, friend*, would be spelt, *bred, hed, giv, brest, bilt, ment, relm, frend*. Would this alteration produce any inconvenience, any embarrassment or expense? By no means. On the other hand, it would lessen the trouble of writing, and much more, of learning the language; it would reduce the true pronunciation to a certainty; and while it would assist foreigners and our own children in acquiring the language, it would render the pronunciation uniform, in different parts of the country, and almost prevent the possibility of changes.

2. A substitution of a character that has a certain definite sound for one that is more vague and indeterminate. Thus by putting *ee* instead of *ea* or *ie*, the words *mean, near, speak, grieve, zeal*, would become *meen, neer, speek, greev, zeel*. This alteration could not occasion a moment's trouble; at the same time it would prevent a doubt respecting the pronunciation; whereas the *ea* and *ie* having different sounds, may

give a learner much difficulty. Thus *greef* should be substituted for *grief*; *kee* for *key*; *beleev* for *believe*; *laf* for *laugh*; *dawter* for *daughter*; *plow* for *plough*; *tuf* for *tough*; *proov* for *prove*; *blud* for *blood*; and *draft* for *draught*. In this manner *ch* in Greek derivatives, should be changed into *k*; for the English *ch* has a soft sound, as in *cherish*; but *k* always a hard sound. Therefore *character, chorus, cholic, architecture,* should be written *karacter, korus, kolic, arkitecture*; and were they thus written, no person could mistake their true pronunciation.

Thus *ch* in French derivatives should be changed into *sh*; *machine, chaise, chevalier,* should be written *masheen, shaze, shevaleer*; and *pique, tour, oblique,* should be written *peek, toor, obleek.*

3. A trifling alteration in a character, or the addition of a point would distinguish different sounds, without the substitution of a new character. Thus a very small stroke across *th* would distinguish its two sounds. A point over a vowel, in this manner à, or o̊, or ī, might answer all the purposes of different letters. And for the dipthong *ow*, let the two letters be united by a small stroke, or both engraven on the same piece of metal, with the left hand line of the *w* united to the *o*.

These, with a few other inconsiderable alterations, would answer every purpose, and render the orthography sufficiently correct and regular.

The advantages to be derived from these alterations are numerous, great and permanent.

1. The simplicity of the orthography would facilitate the learning of the language. It is now the work of years for children to learn to spell; and after all, the business is rarely accomplished. A few men, who are bred to some business that requires constant exercise in writing, finally learn to spell most words without hesitation; but most people remain, all their lives, imperfect masters of spelling, and liable to make mistakes, whenever they take up a pen to write a short note. Nay, many people, even of education and fashion, never attempt to write a letter, without frequently consulting a dictionary.

But with the proposed orthography, a child would learn to spell, without trouble, in a very short time, and the orthography being very regular, he would ever afterwards find it difficult to make a mistake. It would, in that case, be as difficult to spell *wrong*, as it is now to spell *right*.

Besides this advantage, foreigners would be able to acquire the pronunciation of English, which is now so difficult and embarrassing, that they are either wholly discouraged on the first attempt, or obliged, after many years labor, to rest contented with an imperfect knowledge of the subject.

A correct orthography would render the pronunciation of the language, as uniform as in the spelling books. A general uniformity thro the United States, would be the event of such a reformation as I am here recommending. All persons, of every rank, would speak with some degree of precision and uniformity. Such a uniformity in these states is very desirable; it would remove prejudice, and conciliate mutual affection and respect.

3. Such a reform would diminish the number of letters about one sixteenth or eighteenth; this would save a page in eighteen; and a saving of an eighteenth in the expense of books, is an advantage that should not be overlooked.

4. But a capital advantage of this reform in these states would be, that it would make a difference between the English orthography and the American. This will startle those who have not attended to the subject; but I am confident that such an event is an object of vast political consequence. For,

The alteration, however small, would encourage the publication of books in our own country. It would render it, in some measure, necessary that all books should be printed in America. The English would never copy our orthography for their own use; and consequently the same impressions of books would not answer for both countries. The inhabitants of the present generation would read the English impressions; but posterity, being taught a different spelling, would prefer the American orthography.

Besides this, a *national language* is a band of *national union*. Every engine should be employed to make the people of this country *national*; to call their attachments home to their own country; and to inspire them with the pride of national character. However they may boast of Independence, and the freedom of their government, yet their *opinions* are not sufficiently independent; an astonishing respect for the arts and literature of their parent country, and a blind imitation of its manners, are still prevalent among the Americans. Thus an habitual respect for another country, deserved indeed and once laudable, turns their attention from their own interests, and prevents their respecting themselves.

Objections

1. 'This reform of the Alphabet would oblige people to relearn the language, or it could not be introduced.'

But the alterations proposed are so few and so simple, that an hour's attention would enable any person to read the new orthography with facility; and a week's practice would render it so familiar, that a person would write it without hesitation or mistake. Would this small inconvenience prevent its adoption? Would not the numerous national and literary advantages, resulting from the change, induce Americans to make so inconsiderable a sacrifice of time and attention? I am persuaded they would.

But it would not be necessary that men advanced beyond the middle stage of life, should be at the pains to learn the proposed orthography. They would, without inconvenience, continue to use the present. They would read the *new* orthography, without difficulty; but they would write in the *old*. To men thus advanced, and even to the present generation in general, if they should not wish to trouble themselves with a change, the reformation would be almost a matter of indifference. It would be sufficient that children should be taught the new orthography, and that as fast as they come upon the stage, they should be furnished with books in the American spelling. The progress of printing would be proportioned to the demand for books among the rising generation.

This progressive introduction of the scheme would be extremely easy; children would learn the proposed orthography more easily than they would the old; and the present generation would not be troubled with the change; so that none but the obstinate and capricious could raise objections or make any opposition. The change would be so inconsiderable, and made on such simple principles, that a column in each newspaper, printed in the new spelling, would in six months, familiarize most people to the change, show the advantages of it, and imperceptibly remove their objections. The only steps necessary to ensure success in the attempt to introduce this reform, would be, a resolution of Congress, ordering all their acts to be engrossed in the new orthography, and recommending the plan to several universities in America; and also a resolution of the universities to encourage and support it. The printers would begin the reformation by publishing short paragraphs and small tracts in the new orthography; school books would first be published in the same; curiosity would excite attention to it, and men would gradually be reconciled to the plan.

2. 'This change would render our present books useless.'

This objection is, in some measure, answered under the foregoing head. The truth is, it would not have this effect. The difference in orthography would not render books printed in one, illegible to persons acquainted only with the other. The difference would not be so great as between the orthography of Chaucer, and of the present age; yet Chaucer's works are still read with ease.

3. 'This reformation would injure the language by obscuring etymology.'

This objection is unfounded. In general, it is not true that the change would obscure etymology; in a few instances, it might; but it would rather restore the etymology of many words; and if it were true that the change would obscure it, this would be no objection to the reformation.

It will perhaps surprize my readers to be told that, in many particular words, the modern spelling is less correct than the ancient. Yet this is a truth that reflects dishonour on our modern refiners of the language. Chaucer, four hundred years ago, wrote *bilder* for *builder*; *dedly* for *deadly*; *ernest* for *earnest*; *erly* for *early*; *brest* for *breast*; *hed* for *head*; and certainly his spelling was the most agreeable to the pronunciation. Sidney wrote *bin, examin, sutable*, with perfect propriety. Dr. Middleton wrote *explane, genuin, revele*, which is the most easy and correct orthography of such words; and also *luster, theater*, for *lustre, theatre*. In these and many other instances, the modern spelling is a corruption; so that allowing many improvements to have been made in orthography, within a century or two, we must acknowledge also that many corruptions have been introduced.

In answer to the objection, that a change of orthography would obscure etymology, I would remark, that the etymology of most words is already lost, even to the learned; and to the unlearned, etymology is never known. Where is the man that can trace back our English words to the elementary radicals? In a few instances, the student has been able to reach the primitive roots of words; but I presume the radicals of one tenth of the words in our language, have never yet been discovered, even by Junius, Skinner, or any other etymologist. Any man may look into Johnson or Ash, and find that *flesh* is derived from the Saxon *floce*; *child* from *cild*; *flood* from *flod*; *lad* from *leode*; and *loaf* from *laf* or *hlaf*. But this discovery will answer no other purpose, than to show, that within a few hundred years, the spelling of some words has been a little changed. We should still be at a vast difference from the primitive roots.

In many instances indeed etymology will assist the learned in understanding the composition and true sense of a word; and it throws much light upon the progress of language. But the true sense of a complex term is not always, nor generally, to be learnt from the sense of the primitives or elementary words. The current meaning of a word depends on its use in a nation. This true sense is to be obtained by attending to good authors, to dictionaries and to practice rather than derivation. The former *must* be *right*; the latter *may* lead us into *error*.

But to prove of how little consequence a knowledge of etymology is to most people, let me mention a few words. The word *sincere* is derived from the Latin, *sine cera*, without wax; and thus it came to denote *purity of mind*. I am confident that not a man in a thousand ever suspected this to be the origin of the word; yet all men, that have any knowledge of our language, use the word in its true sense, and understand its customary meaning, as well as Junius did, or any other etymologist.

Yea or *yes* is derived from the imperative of a verb, *avoir* to have, as the word is now spelt. It signifies therefore *have*, or *possess*, or *take* what you ask. But does this explication assist us in using the word? And does not every countryman who labours in the field, understand and use the word with as much precision as the profoundest philosophers?

The word *temper* is derived from an old root, *tem*, which signified *water*. It was borrowed from the act of *cooling*, or moderating heat. Hence the meaning of *temperate*, *temperance*, and all the ramifications of the original stock. But does this help us to the modern current sense of these words? By no means. It leads us to understand the formation of languages, and in what manner an idea of a visible action gives rise to a correspondent abstract idea; or rather, how a word, from a literal and direct sense, may be applied to express a variety of figurative and collateral ideas. Yet the customary sense of the word is known by practice, and as well understood by an illiterate man of tolerable capacity, as by men of science.

The word *always* is compounded of *all* and *ways*; it had originally no reference to time; and the etymology or composition of the word would only lead us into error. The true meaning of words is that which a nation in general annex to them. Etymology therefore is of no use but to the learned; and for them it will still be preserved, so far as it is now understood, in dictionaries and other books that treat of this particular subject.

4. 'The distinction between words of different meanings and similar sounds would be destroyed.'

'That distinction,' to answer in the words of the great Franklin, 'is already destroyed in pronunciation.' Does not every man pronounce *all* and *awl* precisely alike? And does the sameness of sound ever lead a hearer into a mistake? Does not the construction render the distinction easy and intelligible, the moments the words of the sentence are heard? Is the word *knew* ever mistaken for *new*, even in the rapidity of pronouncing an animated oration? Was *peace* ever mistaken for *piece*; *flour* for *flower*? Never, I presume, is this similarity of sound the occasion of mistakes.

If therefore an identity of *sound*, even in rapid speaking, produces no inconvenience, how much less would an identity of *spelling*, when the eye would have leisure to survey the construction? But experience, the criterion of truth, which has removed the objection in the first case, will also assist us in forming our opinion in the last.

There are many words in our language which, with the *same orthography*, have *two* or more *distinct meanings*. The word *wind*, whether it signifies *to move round*, or *air in motion*, has the *same spelling*; it exhibits no distinction to the *eye* of the silent reader; and yet its meaning is never mistaken. The construction shows at sight in which sense the word is to be understood. *Hail* is used as an expression of joy, or to signify frozen drops of water, falling from the clouds. *Rear* is to raise up, or it signifies the hinder part of an army. *Lot* signifies fortune or destiny; a plot of ground; or a certain proportion or share; and yet does this diversity, this contrariety of meanings ever occasion the least difficulty in the ordinary language of books? It cannot be maintained. This diversity is found in all languages; and altho it may be considered as a defect, and occasion some trouble for foreign learners, yet to natives it produces no sensible inconvenience.

5. 'It is idle to conform the orthography of words to the pronunciation, because the latter is continually changing.'

This is one of Dr. Johnson's objections, and it is very unworthy of his judgement. So far is this circumstance from being a real objection, that it is alone a sufficient reason for the change of spelling. On his principle of *fixing the orthography*, while the *pronunciation is changing*, any *spoken language* must, in time, lose all relation to the *written language*; that is, the sounds of words would have no affinity with the letters that compose them. In some instances, this is now the case; and no mortal would suspect from the spelling, that *neighbour, wrought*, are pronounced *nabur, rawt*. On this principle, Dr. Johnson ought to have gone back some centuries, and given us, in his dictionary, the primitive Saxon orthography, *wol* for *will*; *ydilnesse* for *idleness*; *eyen* for *eyes*; *eche* for *each*, &c. Nay, he should have gone as far as possible into antiquity, and, regardless of the changes in pronunciation, given us the primitive radical language in its purity. Happily for the language, that doctrine did not prevail till his time; the spelling of words changed with the pronunciation; to these changes we are indebted for numberless improvements; and it is hoped that the progress of them, in conformity with the national practice of speaking, will not be obstructed with the erroneous opinion, even of Dr. Johnson. How much more rational is the opinion of Dr. Franklin, who says, 'the orthography of our language began to be fixed too soon.' If the pronunciation must vary, from age to age, (and some trifling changes in language will always be taking place) common sense would dictate a correspondent change of spelling. Admit Johnson's principles; take his pedantic orthography for the standard; let it be closely adhered to in future; and the slow changes in the pronunciation of our national tongue, will in time make as great a difference between our *written* and our *spoken* language, as there is between the pronunciation of the present English and German. The *spelling* will be no more a guide to the pronunciation, than the orthography of the German or Greek. The event is actually taking place, in consequence of the stupid opinion, advanced by Johnson and other writers, and generally embraced by the nation.

All these objections appear to me of very inconsiderable weight, when opposed to the great, substantial and permanent advantages to be derived from a regular national orthography.

Sensible I am how much easier it is to propose improvements, than to *introduce* them. Every thing *new* starts the idea of difficulty; and yet it is often mere novelty that excites the appearance; for on a slight examination of the proposal, the difficulty vanishes. When we firmly *believe* a scheme to be practicable, the work is *half* accomplished. We are more frequently deterred by fear from making an attack, than repulsed in the encounter.

Habit also is opposed to changes; for it renders even our errors dear to us. Having surmounted all difficulties in childhood, we forget the labor, the fatigue, and the perplexity we suffered in the attempt and imagine the progress of our studies to have been smooth and easy. What seems intrinsically right, is so merely thro habit.

Indolence is another obstacle to improvements. The most arduous task a reformer has to execute, is to make people *think*; to rouse them from that lethargy, which, like the mantle of sleep, covers them in repose and contentment.

But America is in a situation most favourable for great reformations; and the present time is, in a singular degree, auspicious. The minds of men in this country have been awakened. New scenes have been, for many years, presenting new occasions for exertion; unexpected distresses have called forth the powers of invention; and the application of new expedients has demanded every possible exercise of wisdom and talents. Attention is roused; the mind expanded; and the intellectual faculties invigorated. Here men are prepared to receive improvements, which would be rejected by nations, whose habits have not been shaken by similar events.

Now is the time, and *this* is the country, in which we may expect success, in attempting changes favourable to language, science and government. Delay, in the plan here proposed, may be fatal; under the tranquil general government, the minds of men may again sink into indolence; a national acquiescence in error will follow; and posterity will be doomed to struggle with difficulties, which time and accident will perpetually multiply.

Let us then seize the present moment, and establish a *national language* as well as a national government. Let us remember that there is a certain respect due to the opinions of other nations. As an independent people, our reputation abroad demands that, in all things, we should be federal; be *national*; for if we do not respect *ourselves*, we may be assured that other nations will not respect us. In short, let it be impressed upon the mind of every American, that to neglect the means of commanding respect abroad, is treason against the character and dignity of a brave independent people.

TEXT AND SELECTED READING

The text is taken from the Appendix to Webster's *Dissertations on the English Language* first published in 1789. The best studies of the significance of Webster's work in its general context are provided by D. Baron, *Grammar and Good Taste* (London: Yale University Press, 1982) and D. Simpson, *The Politics of American English, 1776–1850* (Oxford: Oxford University Press, 1986), along with Julie Andresen, *Linguistics in America 1769–1924* (London: Routledge, 1990). Other interesting evaluations are V.P. Bynack's 'Noah Webster's Linguistic Thought and the Idea of an American National Culture', *Journal of the History of Ideas*, 45 (1984), along with R. Rollins' 'Words as Social Control: Noah Webster and the Creation of the American Dictionary', *American Quarterly*, 28 (1976). A contemporary essay by the poet Tom Paulin uses Webster's argument for a separate language in relation to Ireland and the use of English therein; 'A New Look at the Language Question' appears in T. Paulin, *Ireland and the English Crisis* (Newcastle: Bloodaxe, 1984).

7

John Walker

John Walker's *A Critical Pronouncing Dictionary* (1791) is in many ways the culmination of the elocution movement in the eighteenth century and played a role in regard to pronunciation similar to that performed by Johnson's *Dictionary* in regard to lexicography and to Lowth's *Short Introduction* to grammar. His methodology is to set out the English vocabulary in the style of a dictionary,

> in which not only the meaning of every word is clearly explained, and the sound of every syllable distinctly shown, but where words are subject to different pronunciations, the reasons for each are at large displayed, and the preferable pronunciation pointed out.

It is on the question of 'preferable pronunciation' that Walker makes his mark for in contradistinction to the rather vague formulations of the earlier elocutionists with regard to their model of pronunciation, he introduces a clearer and more interesting definition.

After having posited his own work as the final development in the study of eighteenth-century elocution, Walker turns his attention to the problem of settling upon a model of pronunciation. He tackles directly the question of the source from which the authority for his work is to be derived. Taking the common definition that authority in language resides with usage, after Horace's dictum that 'usus est jus at norma loquendi', Walker asserts that this is correct but then points out that the problem is that usage or custom has not yet declared itself. Therefore it remains for the elocutionist to specify what custom is, to draw it out from its recalcitrant silence and to capture its pronouncement in the *Dictionary*. It is clear, however, that Walker does not think that custom is simply what most people do in practice.

For as Quintilian had argued in an important modification of this principle in the *Institutio Oratoria*:

> if it be defined merely as the practice of the majority, we shall have a very dangerous rule affecting not merely style but life as well, a far more serious matter. For where is so much good to be found that what is right should please the majority?

> (Book I, V)

The search for custom then is not to be based solely on the practice of the majority but on quite different grounds.

Walker's specification of custom is a sort of amalgam of the language of the court, the language of the learned, and that of 'a certain number of the general mass of speakers'. And in essence 'good usage' in pronunciation consists of those modes of articulation used by the 'learned and polite' which have been taken up by a certain section of the nation. The precise delineation of that section of the nation will appear at the end of Walker's text and we shall return to it. First, however, it is important to see who does not partake of this definition of custom. Evidently no Irish speaker is in a position to be able to pronounce in accordance with custom since Walker indicates that even 'well-bred natives of Ireland' need to observe the rules he sets out for them in order 'to pronounce their words exactly in the same way as the more polished inhabitants of England do'. Likewise, the natives of Scotland have to be given instruction in order to conform to the regularities of custom. Even Cornwall, Lancashire, Yorkshire 'and every distant county in England' have their own dialects peculiar to them which mean that their speakers have to take the necessary lessons. Of course the whole drift of this argument is towards the metropolitan centre as the basis of custom and usage and yet even this is not quite the argument which is made. For Walker also specifies that 'cockneys' have their own peculiarities and also need the pre- and pro- scription which he offers. However, he does claim that 'though the pronunciation of London is certainly erroneous in many words, yet, upon being compared with that of any other place, it is undoubtedly the best.'

If it is not to be London speech in general then where is the authority of custom and usage to be found? The answer of course lies in the stipulation of that certain section of the nation mentioned earlier, of which Walker uses Campbell's definition: 'the language properly so called is found current, especially in the upper and middle ranks, over the whole British empire.' Which is to argue that custom, usage, 'the language properly so called', is not the practice of the majority, nor the practice of a certain region, but the practice of a class – the middle and upper ranks. This is a definition which will be taken up often in the texts below and one which had profound implications in British society.

A CRITICAL PRONOUNCING DICTIONARY AND EXPOSITOR OF THE ENGLISH LANGUAGE

Few subjects have of late years more employed the pens of every class of critics, than the improvement of the English language. The greatest abilities in the nation have been exerted in cultivating and reforming it; nor have a thousand minor critics been wanting to add their mite of amendment to their native tongue. Johnson, whose large mind and just taste made him capable of enriching and adorning the language with original composition, has condescended to the drudgery of disentangling, explaining, and arranging it, and left a lasting monument of his ability, labour, and patience: and Dr. Lowth, the politest scholar of the age, has veiled his superiority in his short Introduction to English Grammar. The ponderous folio has gravely vindicated the rights of analogy; and the light ephemeral sheet of news has corrected errors in Grammar, as well as Politics, by slyly marking them in italics.

Nor has the improvement stopped there. While Johnson and Lowth have been insensibly operating the orthography and construction of our language, its pronunciation has not been neglected. The importance of a consistent and regular pronunciation was too obvious to be overlooked; and the want of this consistency and regularity induced several ingenious men to endeavour at a reformation; who, by exhibiting the anomalies of pronunciation, and pointing out its analogies, have reclaimed some words that were not irrevocably fixed in a wrong sound, and prevented others from being perverted by ignorance and caprice.

Among those writers who deserve the first praise on this subject, is Mr. Elphinstone; who, in his Principles of the English Language, has reduced the chaos to a system, and laid the foundation of a just and regular pronunciation. But this gentleman, by treating his subject with an affected obscurity, and by absurdly endeavouring to alter the whole orthography of the language, has unfortunately lost his credit with the publick for that part of his labours which entitles him to the highest applause.

After him, Dr. Kendrick contributed a portion of improvement by his Rhetorical Dictionary; in which the words are divided into syllables as they are pronounced, and figures placed over the vowels to indicate their different sounds. But though this gentleman, in his Rhetorical Grammar prefixed to his Dictionary, has given several rational strictures on language in general, and the English language in particular, he has rendered his Dictionary extremely imperfect, by entirely omitting a great number of words of doubtful and difficult pronunciation — those very words for which a Dictionary of this kind would naturally be consulted.

To him succeeded Mr. Sheridan; who not only divided the words into syllables, and placed figures over the vowels as Dr. Kendrick had done, but by spelling those syllables as they are pronounced, seemed to complete the idea of a Pronouncing Dictionary, and to leave but little expectation of future improvement. It must, indeed, be confessed, that Mr. Sheridan's Dictionary is greatly superior to everything that preceded it; and his method of conveying the sound of words, by spelling them as they are pronounced, is highly rational and useful — But sincerity here obliges me to stop. The numerous instances I have given of impropriety, inconsistency, and want of acquaintance with the analogies of the language, sufficiently show how imperfect I think his Dictionary is on the whole, and what ample room was left for attempting another that might better answer the purpose of a guide to pronunciation.

The last writer on this subject is Mr. Nares; who, in his Elements of Orthoepy, has shewn a clearness of method and an extent of observation which deserve the highest encomiums. His preface alone proves him an elegant writer, as well as a philosophical observer of language; and his alphabetical index adding five thousand words to the rules of pronouncing them, is a new and useful method of treating the subject; but he seems, on many occasions, to have mistaken the best usage, and to have paid too little attention to the first principles of pronunciation.

Thus I have ventured to give my opinion of my rivals and competitors, and I hope without envy or self-conceit. Perhaps it would have been policy for me to have been silent upon this head, for fear of putting the publick in mind that others have written on the subject as well as myself: but this is a narrow policy which, under the colour of tenderness to others, is calculated to raise ourselves at their expense. A writer, who is conscious he deserves the attention of the public, (and unless he is thus conscious he ought not to write) must not only wish to be compared with those who have gone before him, but will promote the comparison by informing his readers what others have done, and on what he founds his pretension to a preference; and if this be done with fairness and impartiality, it can be no more offensive to modesty, than it is to honesty and plain dealing.

The work I have to offer on the subject has, I hope, added something to the public stock. It not only exhibits the principles of pronunciation, as others have done, divides the words into syllables, and marks the sounds of the vowels like Dr. Kendrick, spells the words as they are pronounced like Mr. Sheridan, and directs the inspector to the word by the rule like Mr. Nares; but where words are subject to different pronunciations, it shows the reasons from analogy for each; produces for authorities for one side and the other, and points out the pronunciation which is preferable. In short, I have endeavoured to unite the science of Mr. Elphinstone, the method of Mr. Nares, and the general utility of Mr. Sheridan; and to add to these advantages, have given critical observations on such words as are subject to a diversity of pronunciation. How I have succeeded must be left to the decision of the publick.

But to all works of this kind there lies a formidable objection; which is, that the pronunciation of a language is necessarily indefinite and fugitive, and that all endeavours to delineate or settle it are in vain. Dr. Johnson, in his Grammar prefixed to his Dictionary, says:

Most of the writers of English grammar have given long tables of words pronounced otherwise than they are written; and seem not sufficiently to have considered, that, of English, as of all living tongues, there is a double pronunciation; one, cursory and colloquial; the other, regular and solemn. The cursory pronunciation is always vague and uncertain, being made different, in different mouths, by negligence, unskilfulness, or affectation. The solemn pronunciation, though by no means immutable and permanent, is yet always less remote from the orthography, and less liable to capricious innovation. They have, however, generally formed their tables according to the cursory speech of those with whom they happened to converse; and concluding, that the whole language combines to vitiate language in one manner, have often established the jargon of the lowest of the people as the model of speech. For pronunciation, the best general rule is, to consider those as the most elegant speakers who deviate least from the written words.

Without any derogation from the character of Dr. Johnson, it may be asserted, that in these observations we do not perceive that justness and accuracy of thinking for which he is so remarkable. It would be doing great injustice to him to suppose, that he meant to exclude all possibility of conveying the actual pronunciation of many words that depart manifestly from their orthography, or of those that are written alike, and pronounced differently and inversely. He has marked these differences with great propriety himself in many places of his Dictionary; and it is to be regretted that he did not extend these remarks farther. It is impossible, therefore, that he could suppose, that, because the almost imperceptible glances of colloquial pronunciation were not to be caught and described by the pen, that the very perceptible difference between the initial accented syllables of *money* and *monitor*, or the final unaccented syllables of *finite* and *infinite*, could not be sufficiently marked upon paper. Cannot we show that *cellar*, a vault; and *seller*, one who sells, have exactly the same sound; or that the monosyllable *full*, and the first syllable of *fulminate*, are sounded differently, because there are some words in which solemnity will authorise different pronunciation from familiarity? Besides, that colloquial pronunciation which is perfect, is so much the language of solemn speaking, that, perhaps, there is no more difference than between the same picture painted to be viewed near and at a distance. The symmetry in both is exactly the same; and the distinction lies only in the colouring. The English language, in this respect, seems to have a great superiority over the French; which pronounces many letters in the poetic and solemn style that are wholly silent in the prosaic and familiar. But if a solemn and familiar pronunciation really exists in our language, is it not the business of a grammarian to mark both? And if he cannot point out the precise sound of *unaccented* syllables, (for these only are liable to obscurity) he may, at least, give those sounds which approach the nearest; and by this means approximate to the desired point, though he can never fully arrive at it.

The truth is, Dr. Johnson seems to have had a confused idea of the distinctness and indistinctness with which, on solemn or familiar occasions, we sometimes pronounce the *unaccented* vowels; and with respect to these, it must be owned, that his remarks are not entirely without foundation. The English language, with respect to its pronunciation, is evidently divisible into accented and unaccented sounds. The accented syllables, by being pronounced with greater force than the unaccented, have their vowels as clearly and distinctly sounded as any given note in music; while the unaccented vowels, for want of the stress, are apt to slide into an obscurity of sound, which, though sufficiently distinguishable to the ear, cannot be so definitely marked out to the eye by other sounds as those vowels that are under the accent. Thus some of the vowels, when neither under the accent, nor closed by a consonant, have a longer or a shorter, an opener or a closer sound, according to the solemnity or familiarity, the deliberation or rapidity of delivery. This will be perceived in the sound of the *e* in *emotion*, of the *o* in *obedience*, and of the *u* in *singular*. In the fast pronunciation of common speaking, the *e* in *emotion* is often shortened, as if divided into *em-o-tion*; the *o* in *obedience* is shortened and obscured, as if written *ub-be-dience*; and the *u* in *singular*, changed into short *i*, as if written *sing-il-ar*; while the deliberate and elegant sound of these vowels is the long open sound they have, when the accent is on them in *equal*, *over*, and *unit*; but *a*, when unaccented, seems to have no such diversity; it has generally a short obscure sound, whether ending a syllable, or closed by a consonant. Thus the *a* in *able* has its definite and distinct sound; but the same letter in *tolerable* goes into an obscure indefinite sound approaching to short *u*; nor can any solemnity or deliberation give it the long open sound it has in the first word. Thus, by distinguishing vowels into their accented and unaccented sounds, we are able to see clearly what Dr. Johnson saw but obscurely; and by this distinction entirely to obviate the objection.

Equally indefinite and uncertain is his general rule, that those are to be considered as the most elegant speakers who deviate least from the written words. It is certain, where custom is equal, this ought to take place; and if the whole body of respectable English speakers were equally divided in their pronunciation of the word *busy*, one half pronouncing it *bew-ze*, and the other half *biz-ze*, that the former ought to be accounted the most elegant speakers; but till this is the case, the latter pronunciation, though a gross deviation from orthography, will still be esteemed the most elegant. Dr. Johnson's general rule, therefore, can only take place where custom has not plainly decided; but unfortunately for the English language, its orthography and pronunciation are so widely different, that Dr. Watts and Dr. Jones lay it down as a maxim in their treatise on spelling, that all words, which can be sounded different ways, must be written according to that sound which is most distant from the true pronunciation; and consequently, in such language, a Pronouncing Dictionary must be of essential use.

But it still may be objected to such an undertaking, that the fluctuation of pronunciation is so great as to render all attempts to settle it useless. What will it avail us, it may be said, to know the pronunciation of the present day, if, in a few years, it will be altered? and how are we to know what even the present pronunciation is, when the same words are often differently pronounced by different speakers, and those, perhaps, of equal numbers and reputation? To which, it may be answered, that the fluctuation of our language, with respect to its pronunciation, seems to have been greatly exaggerated. Except a very few single words, which are generally noted in the following Dictionary, and the words where *e* comes before *r*, followed by another consonant, as *merchant*, *service*, &c. the pronunciation of the language is probably in the same state it was in a century ago; and had the same attention been then paid to it as now, it is not likely even that change would have happened. The same may be observed of those words which are differently pronounced by different speakers: if the analogies of the language were better understood, it is scarcely conceivable that so many words in polite usage would have a diversity of pronunciation, which is at once so ridiculous and embarrassing; nay, perhaps it may be with confidence asserted, that if the analogies of the language were sufficiently known, and so near at hand as to be applicable on inspection to every word, that not only many words which are wavering between contrary usages would be settled in their true sound, but that many words, which are fixed by custom to an improper pronunciation, would by degrees grow regular and analogical; and those which are so already would be secured in their purity, by a knowledge of their regularity and analogy.

But the utility of a work of this kind is not confined to those parts of language where the impropriety is gross and palpable; besides those imperfections in pronunciation, which disgust every ear not accustomed to them, there are a thousand insensible deviations, in the more minute parts of language, as the unaccented syllables may be called, which do not strike the ear so forcibly as to mark any direct impropriety in particular words, but occasion only such a general imperfection as gives a bad impression upon the whole. Speakers with these imperfections pass very well in common conversation; but when they are required to pronounce with emphasis, and for that purpose to be more distinct and definite in their utterance, here their ear fails them; they have been accustomed only to loose cursory speaking, and for want of firmness of pronunciation are like those painters who draw the muscular exertions of the human body without any knowledge of anatomy. This is one reason, perhaps, why we find the elocution of so few people agreeable when they read or speak to an assembly, while so few offend us by their utterance in common conversation. A thousand faults lie concealed in a miniature, which a microscope brings to view; and it is only by pronouncing on a larger scale, as public speaking may be called, that we prove the propriety of our elocution. As, therefore, there are deviations from analogy which are not at any rate tolerable, there are others which only, as it were, tarnish the pronunciation and make it less brilliant and agreeable. There are few who have turned their thoughts upon this subject without observing, that they sometimes pronounce the same word or syllable in a different manner; and as neither of these manners offends the ear, they are at a loss to which they shall give the preference; but as one must necessarily be more agreeable to the analogy of the language than the other, a display of these analogies, in a Dictionary of this kind, will immediately remove this uncertainty; and in this view of the variety we shall discover a fitness in one mode of speaking, which will give a firmness and security to our pronunciation, from a confidence that it is founded on reason, and the general tendency of the language.

But, alas! reasoning on language, however well founded, may all be overturned by a single quotation from Horace:

> . . . usus
> Quem penes arbitrium est, & jus & norma loquendi.

This, it must be owned, is a succinct way of ending the controversy; and by virtue of this argument we may become critics in language without the trouble of studying it. Not that I would be thought, in the most distant manner, to deny, that Custom is the sovereign arbiter of language. I acknowledge its authority, and know there is no appeal from it: I only wish to dispute whether this arbiter has not decided; for if once Custom speaks out, however absurdly, I sincerely acquiesce in its sentence.

But what is this custom to which we must so implicitly submit? Is it the usage of the greater part of the speakers, whether good or bad? This has never been asserted by the most sanguine abbettors of its authority. Is it the majority of the studious in schools and colleges, with those of the learned professions, or of those who, from their elevated birth or station, give laws to the refinements and elegancies of a court? To confine propriety to the latter, which is too often the case, seems an injury to the former; who, from their very profession, appear to have a natural right to a share, at least, in the legislation of language, if not to an absolute sovereignty. The polished attendants on a throne are as apt to depart from simplicity in language as in dress and manners; and novelty, instead of custom, is too often the *jus & norma loquendi* of a court.

Perhaps an attentive observation will lead us to conclude, that the usage, which ought to direct us, is neither of these we have been enumerating, taken singly, but a sort of compound ratio of all three. Neither a finical pronunciation of the court, nor a pedantic Graecism of the schools, will be denominated respectable usage, till a certain number of the general mass of speakers have acknowledged them; nor will a multitude of common speakers authorise any pronunciation which is reprobated by the learned and polite.

As those sounds, therefore, which are most generally received among the learned and polite, as well as the bulk of speakers, are the most legitimate, we may conclude that a majority of two of these states ought always to occur, in order to constitute what is called good usage.

But though custom, when general, is commonly well understood, there are several states and degrees of it which are exceedingly obscure and equivocal; and the only method of knowing the extent of custom in these cases, seems to be an inspection of those Dictionaries which professedly treat of pronunciation. We have now so many works of this kind, that the general current of custom, with respect to the sound of words, may be collected from them with almost as much certainty as the general sense of words from Johnson. An exhibition of the opinions of Orthoepists about the sound of words always appeared to me a very rational method of determining what is called custom. This method I have adopted in the following work; and if I have sometimes dissented from the majority, it has been, either from a persuasion of being better informed of what was actually the custom of speaking, or from a partiality to the evident analogies of the language. . . .

Rules to be Observed by the Natives of IRELAND in order to obtain a just Pronunciation of English

As Mr. Sheridan was a native of Ireland, and had the best opportunities of understanding those peculiarities of pronunciation which prevail there, I shall extract his observations on that subject as the best general direction, and add a few of my own by way of supplement, which I hope will render this article of instruction still more compleat.

The reader will be pleased to take notice, that as I have made a different arrangement of the vowels, and have adopted a notation different from Mr. Sheridan, I am obliged to make use of different figures to mark the vowels, but still such as perfectly correspond to his.

The chief mistakes made by the Irish in pronouncing English, lie for the most part in the sound of the two first vowels, *a* and *e*; the former being generally sounded a̅ by the Irish, as in the word ba̅r, in most words where it is pronounced a̍, as in *day*, by the English. Thus the Irish say pa̅tron, ma̅tron, the vowel a̅ having the same sound as in the word fa̅ther; whilst the English pronounce them as if written *paytron*, *maytron*. The following rule, strictly attended to, will rectify this mistake through the whole language.

When the vowel a finishes a syllable, and has an accent on it, it is invariably pronounced a̍ [day] by the English. To this rule there are but three exceptions in the whole language to be found in the words fa̅ther, papa̅, mama̅. The Irish may think also the word *rather* an exception, as well as *father*, and so it would appear to be in their manner of pronouncing it ra̅-ther, laying the accent on the vowel *a*; but in the English pronunciation *th* is taken into the first syllable, as thus *rath' er*, which makes the difference.

Whenever a consonant follows the vowel *a* in the same syllable, and the accent is on the consonant, the vowel *a* always has its fourth sound, as ha̍t, ma̍n; as also the same sound lengthened when it precedes the letter *r*, as fa̅r, ba̅r, though the accent be on the vowel; as likewise when it precedes *lm*, as ba̅lm, pa̅lm. The Irish, ignorant of this latter exception, pronounce all words of that structure as if they were written *bawn*, *psawm*, *quawm*, *cawm*, &c. In the third sound of *a*, marked by different combinations of vowels, or consonants, such as *au* in Paul; *aw* in law; *all*, in call; *ald*, in bald; *alk* in talk, &c. the Irish make no mistake, except in that of *lm*, as before mentioned.

The second vowel *e*, is for the most part sounded *ee* by the English, when the accent is upon it; whilst the Irish in most words give it the sound of slender a̍, as in *hate*. This sound of e̍ [ee] is marked by different combinations of vowels, such as *ea*, *ei*, *e* final mute, *ee*, and *ie*. In the last two combinations of *ee* and *ie*, the Irish never mistake; such as in *meet*, *seem*, *field*, *believe*, &c.; but in all the others, they almost universally change the sound of

104

é into à. Thus in the combination *ea*, they pronounce the words *tea, sea, please*, as if they were spelt *tay, say, plays*; instead of *tee, see, pleese*. The English constantly give this sound to *ea* whenever the accent is on the vowel *e*, except in the following words, *great*, a *pear*, a *bear*, to *bear*, to *forbear*, to *swear*, to *wear*, in all of which the *e* has the sound of à in hàte. For want of knowing these exceptions, the gentlemen of Ireland, after some time of residence in London, are apt to fall into the general rule, and pronounce these words as if spelt, *greet, beer, sweer*, &c.

Ei is also sounded *ee* by the English, and as à by the Irish; thus the words *deceit, receive*, are pronounced by them as if written *desate, resave. Ei* is always sounded *ee*, except when a *g* follows it, as in the words *reign, feign, deign*, &c. as also in the words *rein* (of a bridle), *rein-deer, vein, drein, veil, heir*, which are pronounced like *rain, vain, drain, vail, air*.

The final mute *e* makes the preceding *e* in the same syllable, when accented, have the sound of *ee*, as in the words supréme, sincere, repléte. This rule is almost universally broken through by the Irish, who pronounce all such words as if written supràme, sinsàre, replàte, &c. There are but two exceptions to this rule in the English pronunciation, which are the words *there, where*.

In the way of marking this sound, by a double *e*, as thus *ee*, as the Irish never make any mistakes, the best method for all who want to acquire the right pronunciation of these several combinations is, to suppose that *ea, ei*, and *e* attended by a final mute *e*, are all spelt with a double *e*, or *ee*.

Ey is always sounded like à by the English, when the accent is upon it; as in the words *prey, convey*, pronounced *pray, convay*. To this there are but two exceptions, in the words kéy and léy, sounded *kee, lee*. The Irish, in attempting to pronounce like the English, often give the same sound to *ey*, as usually belongs to *ei*; thus for *prey, convey*, they say *pree, convee*.

A strict observation of these few rules, with a due attention to the very few exceptions enumerated above, will enable the well-educated natives of Ireland to pronounce their words exactly in the same way as the more polished part of the inhabitants of England do, so far as the vowels are concerned. The dipthongs they commit no fault in, except in the sound of 1, which has already been taken notice of in the Grammar: where, likewise, the only difference in pronouncing any of the consonants has

105

been pointed out; which is, the thickening the sounds of *d* and *t*, in certain situations; and an easy method proposed of correcting this habit. . . .

There are dialects peculiar to Cornwall, Lancashire, Yorkshire, and every distant county in England; but as a consideration of these would lead to a detail too minute for the present occasion, I shall conclude these remarks with a few observations on the peculiarities of my countrymen, the Cockneys; who, as they are the models of pronunciation to the distant provinces, ought to be the more scrupulously correct.

FIRST FAULT OF THE LONDONERS – *Pronouncing s indistinctly after st*

The letter *s* after *st*, from the very difficulty of its pronunciation, is often sounded inarticulately. The inhabitants of London, of the lower order, cut the knot, and pronounce it in a distinct syllable, as if *e* were before it; but this is to be avoided as the greatest blemish in speaking: the last three letters in *posts, fists, mists,* &c. must all be distinctly heard in one syllable, and without permitting the letters to coalesce. For the acquiring of this sound, it will be proper to select nouns that end in *st* or *ste*; to form them into plurals, and pronounce them forcibly and distinctly every day. The same may be observed of the third person of verbs ending in *sts* or *stes*, as *persists, wastes, hastes,* &c.

For this purpose the *Rhyming Dictionary*, where all words are arranged according to their terminations, will be found peculiarly useful.

SECOND FAULT – *Pronouncing w for v, and inversely*

The pronunciation of *v* for *w*, and more frequently of *w* for *v*, among the inhabitants of London, and those not always of the lower order, is a blemish of the first magnitude. The difficulty of remedying this defect is the greater, as a cure of one of these mistakes has a tendency to promote the other.

Thus, if you are very careful to make a pupil pronounce *veal* and *vinegar*, not as if written *weal* and *winegar*, you will find him very apt to pronounce *wine* and *wind*, as if written *vine* and *vind*. The only method of rectifying this habit seems to be this: let the pupil select from a dictionary, not only all the words that begin with *v*, but as many as he can of those that have this letter in any other part. Let him be told to bite his under lip while he is sounding the *v* in those words, and to practise this every day till he pronounces the *v* properly at first sight: then, and not till then, let him pursue the same method with the *w*; which he must be directed to pronounce by a pouting out of the lips without suffering them to touch the teeth. Thus, by giving all the attention to only one of these letters at a time, and fixing by habit the true sound of that, we shall at last find both of them reduced to their proper pronunciation in a shorter time than by endeavouring to rectify them both at once.

THIRD FAULT – *Not sounding h after w*

The aspirate *h* is often sunk, particularly in the capital, where we do not find the least distinction of sound between *white* and *wile*, *whet* and *wet*, *where* and *were*, &c. The best method to rectify this is, to collect all the words of this description from a dictionary, and to write them down, and instead of the *wh* to begin them with *hoo* in a distinct syllable, and so pronounce them. Thus let *while* be pronounced *hoo-ile*; *whet*, *hoo-et*; *where*, *hoo-are*; *whip*, *hoo-ip*, &c. This is no more, as Dr. Lowth observes, than placing the aspirate in its true position before the *w*, as it is in the Saxon, which the words come from; where we may observe, that though we have altered the orthography of our ancestors, we have still preserved their pronunciation.

FOURTH FAULT – *Not sounding h where it ought to be sounded, and inversely*

A still worse habit than the last prevails, chiefly among the people of London, that of sinking the *h* at the beginning of words where it ought to be sounded, and of sounding it, either where it is not seen, or where it ought to be sunk. Thus we not unfrequently hear, especially among children, *heart* pronounced *art*, and *arm*, *harm*. This is a vice perfectly similar to that of pronouncing the *v* for the *w*, and the *w* for the *v*, and requires a similar method to correct it.

As there are so very few words in the language where the initial *h* is sunk, we may select these from the rest, and, without setting the pupil right when he mispronounces these, or when he prefixes the *h* improperly to other words, we may make him pronounce all the words where *h* is sounded, till he has almost forgot there are any words pronounced otherwise. Then he may go over those words to which he improperly prefixes the *h*, and those where *h* is seen but not sounded, without any danger of an interchange. As these latter words are but few, I shall subjoin a catalogue of them for the use of the learner. *Heir, heiress, herb, herbage, honest, honesty, honestly, honour, honorable, honorably, hospital, hostler, hour, hourly, humble, humbly, humbles, humour, humourist, humourous, humourously, humoursome.* Where we may observe, that *humour* and its compounds not only sink the *h*, but sound the *u* like the pronoun *you*, or the noun *yew*, as if written *yewmore, yewmorous*, &c.

Thus I have endeavoured to correct some of the more glaring errors of my countrymen; who, with all their faults, are still upon the whole the best pronouncers of the English language. For though the pronunciation of London is certainly erroneous in many words, yet, upon being compared with that of any other place, it is undoubtedly the best; that is, not only the best by courtesy, and because it happens to be the pronunciation of the capital, but best by a better title; that of being more generally received: or, in other words, though the people of London are erroneous in the pronunciation of many words, the inhabitants of every other place are erroneous in many more. Nay, harsh as the sentence may seem, those at considerable distance from the capital do not only mispronounce many words taken separately, but they scarcely pronounce with purity a single word, syllable, or letter. Thus, if the short sound of the letter *u* in *trunk, sunk*, &c. differ from the sound of that letter in the northern parts of England, where they sound it like the *u* in *bull*, and nearly as if the words were written *troonk, soonk*, &c. it necessarily follows that every word where the letter occurs must by those provincials be mispronounced.

Perhaps I cannot conclude these observations better than by quoting a passage from Dr. Campbell's Philosophy of Rhetorick, where what is called *national*, or general use in language, is treated with the greatest depth, clearness, and vivacity. To which I would premise, that what he observes with respect to England as distinct from the provinces, may, with very few exceptions, be applied to London − the centre of them all.

In every province there are peculiarities of dialect, which affect not only the pronunciation and the accent, but even the inflection and combination of words, whereby their idiom is distinguished from that of the nation, and from that of every other province. The narrowness of the circle to which the currency of the words and phrases of such dialects is confined, sufficiently discriminates them from that which is properly styled the language, and which commands a circulation incomparably wider. This is one reason, I imagine, why the term *use* on this subject is commonly accompanied with the epithet *general*. In the generality of provincial idioms there is, it must be acknowledged, a pretty considerable concurrence both of the middle and of the lower ranks. But still this use is bounded by the province, country, or district, which gives name to the dialect, and beyond which its peculiarities are sometimes unintelligible, and always ridiculous. But the language properly so called is found current, especially in the upper and middle ranks, over the whole British empire. Thus though in every province they ridicule the idiom of every other province, they all vail to the English idiom, and scruple not to acknowledge its superiority over their own.

For example; in some parts of Wales (if we may credit Shakespeare in his character of Fluellin in Henry V.) the common people say *goot* for *good*; in the South of Scotland they say *gude*; and in the North *gueed*. Wherever one of these pronunciations prevails, you will never hear from a native either of the two; but the word *good* is to be heard everywhere from natives, as well as strangers; nor do the people ever dream that there is anything laughable in it, however much they are disposed to laugh at the country accents and idioms they discern in one another. Nay more; though the people of distant provinces do not understand one another, they mostly all understand one who speaks properly. It is a just and curious observation of Dr. Kendrick, in his Rhetorical Grammar, that the case of language, or rather speech, being quite contrary to that of science; in the former, the ignorant understand the learned, better than the learned do the ignorant; in the latter it is otherwise.

But though the inhabitants of London have this manifest advantage over all the other inhabitants of the island, they have the disadvantage of being more disgraced by their peculiarities than any other people. The grand difference between the metropolis and the provinces is, that people of education in London are free from all the vices of the vulgar; but the best educated people in the provinces, if constantly resident there, are sure to be strongly tinctured with the dialect of the country in which they live. Hence it is that the vulgar pronunciation of London, though not half so erroneous as that of Scotland, Ireland, or any of the provinces, is, to a person of correct taste, a thousand times more offensive and disgusting.

TEXT AND SELECTED READING

The text is taken from Walker's *A Critical Pronouncing Dictionary* (1791) whose full title stipulates: 'in which not only the meaning of every word is clearly explained, and the sound of every syllable distinctly shown, but where words are subject to different pronunciations, the reasons for each are at large displayed, and the preferable pronunciation is pointed out'. It also offers 'rules to be observed by the natives of Scotland, Ireland, and London, for avoiding their respective peculiarities; and directions to foreigners for acquiring a knowledge of the use of this dictionary'. The general context and significance of this and related works is explored in M. Cohen, *Sensible Words* (Baltimore: Johns Hopkins University Press, 1977), A.P.R. Howatt, *A History of English Language Teaching* (Oxford: Oxford University Press, 1984), D. Simpson, *The Politics of American English 1776–1850* (Oxford: Oxford University Press, 1986) and O. Smith, *The Politics of Language 1791– 1819* (Oxford: Oxford University Press, 1984).

8

John Pickering

Webster had argued for linguistic as well as political independence from Britain but his call was not unopposed. Pickering's *Vocabulary*, for example, can be seen as an attack on Webster, as may be noted from his Preface:

> In this country, as is the case in England, we have thirsty reformers and presumptuous sciolists, who would unsettle the whole of our language for the purpose of making it conform to their whimsical notions of propriety. Some of our corruptions have originated with them.

In fact the *Vocabulary* is testimony to the weight of feeling against Webster's work, and that of the reform movement in general, not just in America but in Britain too. As the reader will see from the extracts from British reviewers, the tradition of haughty, arrogant and insulting comments on American usage has a long history in Britain.

Pickering's argument is based on the premise that American usage may eventually destroy the possibility of inter-national communication between British and American writers by dint of the variation in their respective use of 'the language'. In a sense this anxiety is related to Swift's argument about linguistic change which takes place in time; that is, that it will prevent communication between present and future. In fact Pickering uses this argument too but the most important point about such linguistic change, in his eyes, is that it will mean the loss of a common inheritance. 'Our religion and our laws are studied in the language of the nation, from which we are descended', he says, and thus the loss of the common language will result in differences arising in the social and political habits of America as compared with Britain. It was precisely this of course that Webster desired.

The tone of the British reviews which were, it should be remembered, written in or around a time of war between the two nations, is revealing in its intensity. Thus the *British Critic* argues in effect that it would be better if America had a language of its own (Hebrew, Greek and French had been proposed by American revolutionaries in the recent past), rather than introducing 'confusion' into English by its distinctive usage. This was taken up by the *Annual Review* which attacked that 'torrent of barbarous phraseology, with which the American writers threaten to destroy the purity of the English language'. And it was extended in the *Edinburgh Review* which criticised writers 'in that other England, which they are building in the West', on the grounds that they were corrupting the language and thus tarnishing 'the only badge, that is still worn, of our consanguinity'. Pickering's account was at one with such views and he too finds three main faults with American usage. These are the introduction of neologisms, the rendering of new significance to old words and the retention of obsolete words. Such developments were evidently taken as markers of wholescale cultural and political change.

Pickering's authority for such strictures is interesting in that it replicates that which we have seen emerging in earlier pieces. He too talks of the metropolitan model as the source for evaluation and judgement. Indeed he says that just as the usage of the 'polite and educated' of the British metropolis can be used to condemn Scotticisms (Witherspoon's origin for his coinage 'Americanism' in the eighteenth century), 'peculiarities of the Irish' and 'provincial corruptions', likewise it can be used to reject American 'corruptions'. 'Well educated Englishmen' are Pickering's standard, or perhaps 'intelligent Americans, who shall have an opportunity of residing in England'; and they are to be the source of authority which can dictate rejection or permission. They, not American authors, and particularly not 'presumptuous sciolists' like Webster.

After the turmoils of the revolution and independence it is perhaps surprising to find an American author turning to London as the cultural centre. Particularly one who repeats the doctrines of earlier English commentators such as Johnson or Swift. Surprising perhaps, but it is no doubt indicative of the cultural and social conflicts in the new nation. Of course Pickering's work was itself challenged, not least in an important way by Webster. For in his *Letter to Pickering* (1817) Webster made explicit the connection between language, politics and war which lay behind many of the arguments:

There is nothing which, in my opinion, so debases the genius and character of my countrymen, as the implicit confidence they place in English authors, and their unhesitating submission to their *opinions*, their *derision*, and their *frowns*. But I trust that the time will come when the English will be convinced that the intellectual faculties of their descendants have not degenerated in America; and that we can contend with them in *letters*, with as much success, as upon the ocean.

A VOCABULARY OR COLLECTION OF WORDS AND PHRASES WHICH HAVE BEEN SUPPOSED TO BE PECULIAR TO THE UNITED STATES OF AMERICA

Essay

The preservation of the *English language* in its purity throughout the United States is an object deserving the attention of every American, who is a friend to the literature and science of his country. It is in a particular manner entitled to the consideration of the Academy; for, though subjects, which are usually ranked under the head of *Physical Science*, were doubtlessly chiefly in view with the founders of the Academy, yet, our *language* also, which is to be the instrument of communicating to the public the speculations and discoveries of our countrymen, seems necessarily 'to fall within the design of the institution;' because, unless that language is well settled, and be read with ease by all to whom it is addressed, our authors will write and publish, certainly under many disadvantages, though perhaps not altogether in vain.

It is true, indeed, that our countrymen may speak and write in a *dialect* of English, which will be understood in the *United States*; but if they are ambitious of having their works read by Englishmen as well as by Americans, they must write in a language that Englishmen can read with pleasure. And if for some time to come it should not be the lot of many Americans to publish works, which will be read out of their own country, yet all, who have the least tincture of learning, will continue to feel an ardent desire to acquaint themselves with *English* authors. Let us then imagine for a moment the time to have arrived, when *Americans* shall no longer be able to understand the works of Milton, Pope, Swift, Addison, and other English authors, justly styled classic, without the aid of a *translation* into a language, that is to be called at some future day the *American* tongue. By such a change, it is true, our loss would not be so great in works purely scientific, as in those usually termed works of taste; for the obvious reason, that the design of the former is merely to communicate information, without regard to elegance of language or the force and beauty of the sentiments. But the excellencies of works of taste cannot be felt even in the best translations; – a truth, which, without resorting to the example of the matchless ancients, will be acknowledged by every man, who is acquainted with the admirable works extant in various living languages. Nor is this the only view in which a radical change of language would be an evil. To say nothing of the facilities afforded by a *common language* in the ordinary intercourse of business, it should not be forgotten, that our religion and our laws are studied in the language of the nation, from which we are descended; and, with the loss of the language, we should finally suffer the loss of those particular advantages, which we now derive from the investigations of the jurists and divines of that country.

But it is often asked among us, do not the people of this country speak and write the English language with purity? A brief consideration of the subject will furnish a satisfactory answer to this question; it will enable us to correct the erroneous opinions entertained by some Americans on this point, and at the same time defend our countrymen against the charge made by some English writers, of a *design* to effect an entire change in the language.

As the inquiry before us is a simple question of fact, it is to be determined, like every other question of this nature, by proper evidence. What evidence then have we, that the English language is not spoken and written in America, with the same degree of purity that is to be found in the writers and orators of England.

In the first place, although it is agreed, that there is greater uniformity of dialect throughout the United States (in consequence of the frequent removals of people from one part of our country to another) than is to be found throughout England; yet none of our countrymen, not even those, who are the most zealous in supporting what they imagine the honour of the *American* character will contend, that we have not in some instances departed from the standard of the language. We have formed some *new* words; and to some *old* ones, that are still used in England, we have fixed *new significations*: while others, which have long been *obsolete* in England, are still retained in *common use* with us. If then, in addition to these acknowledgements of our *own countrymen*, we allow any weight to the opinions of *Englishmen* (who must be competent judges in this case,) it cannot be denied, that we have in several instances deviated from the standard of the language, *as spoken and written in England at the present day*. By this, however, I do not mean, that so great a deviation has taken place, as to have rendered any considerable part of our language unintelligible to Englishmen; but merely, that so many corruptions have crept into *our English*, as to have become the subject of much animadversion and regret with the learned of Great Britain. And as we are hardly aware of the opinion entertained by them of the extent of these corruptions, it may be useful, if it should not be very flattering to our pride, to hear their remarks on this subject in their own words. We shall find that these corruptions are censured, not by mere pretenders to learning, but, (so far as the fact is to be ascertained from English publications,) by all the scholars of that country, who take an interest in American literature. In proof of this, I request the attention of the Academy to the following extracts from several of the British Reviews; some of which are the most distinguished of the present day, and all of which together may be considered as expressing the general opinion of the literary men of Great Britain, who have attended to this subject. That all the remarks are just, to the extent in which the will naturally be understood, few of our countrymen will be willing to admit.

The *British Critic* (for February 1810) in a review of the Rev. Mr. *Bancroft's* Life of Washington, says

> In the style we observe, with regret rather than with astonishment, the introduction of several *new* words, or *old* words in a new sense; a deviation from the rules of the English language, which, if it continues to be practised by good writers in America, will introduce confusion into the medium of intercourse, and render it a subject of regret that the people of that continent should not have an entirely separate language as well as government of their own. Instances occur at almost every page; without pains in selecting, the following may be taken as specimens, &c.

The Reviewers then mention several words, all of which are inserted in the following Vocabulary.

The same Reviewers (in April 1808) in their account of Chief Justice *Marshall's* Life of Washington, have the following remarks:

> In the writings of *Americans* we have *often* discovered deviations from the purity of the *English idiom*, which we have been

more disposed to censure than to wonder at. The *common speech* of the United States has departed very considerably from the standard adopted in England, and in this case it is not to be expected that *writers*, however cautious, will maintain a strict purity. Mr. Marshall deviates occasionally, but not grossly, &c.

The *Critical Review* (for September 1809) in remarks upon *Travels Through France, by Col. Pinckney*, says – 'He falls into occasional inaccuracies . . . but the instances are rare, and by no means so striking as we have *frequent* occasions of remarking in *most American* writers.'

The same Reviewers (in July 1807) in speaking of *Marshall's* Life of Washington, have the following among other remarks on the style of that work – that 'it abounds with many of those idioms which prevail on the other side of the Atlantic.'

The *Annual Review* (for 1808) in speaking of the same work, after pointing out several instances of false English (in respect to many of which, however, the Reviewers have been misled by the incorrectness of the *English edition* of that work, as will be seen in the following Vocabulary,) has the following observations; which, if they had been made in a manner somewhat different, would probably have been more favourably received by those for whose benefit they seem to be intended:

> We have been more particular in noticing these faults in Mr. Marshall's language, because we are not at all certain that the Americans do not consider them as beauties; and because we wish, if possible, to stem *that torrent of barbarous phraseology*, with which the *American* writers threaten to destroy the purity of the English language.

The *Monthly Reviewers* (in May 1808) in their account of a little work, entitled *A Political Sketch of America*, cite with approbation, the following passage

> The national *language* should be sedulously cultivated; and this is to be accomplished by means of schools. This circumstance demands particular attention, for the language of *conversation* is becoming incorrect; and even in America *authors* are to be found, who make use of *new* or *obsolete* words, which no good writer in this country would employ.

116

The *Eclectic Review* (for August 1813) in noticing *Sketches of Louisiana, by Major A. Stoddard*, makes the following observations on the style of that author and of our writers in general:

> For an American the composition is tolerable; but the Major has a good share of those words and phrases, which his literary countrymen must, however reluctantly, relinquish before they will rank with good writers. The standard is fixed, unless it were possible to consign to oblivion the assemblage of those great authors, on whose account the Americans themselves are to feel complacency in their language to the latest ages.

The *Edinburgh Review* (for October 1804) which is the last I shall cite, has the following general observations on this subject:

> If the men of birth and education in that other England, which they are building up in the West, will not *diligently study* the great authors, who purified and fixed the language of our common forefathers, we must soon lose the only badge, that is still worn, of our consanguinity.

The same Reviewers, in their remarks on *Marshall's* and *Ramsay's* Lives of Washington, say –

> In these volumes we have found *a great many words and phrases* which *English* criticism refuses to acknowledge. America has thrown off the yoke of the British nation, but she would do well for some time, to take the laws of composition from the Addisons, the Swifts and the Robertsons of her ancient sovereign. . . . These remarks, however, are not dictated by any paltry feelings of jealousy or pride. We glory in the diffusion of our language over a new world, where we hope it is yet destined to collect new triumphs; and in the brilliant perspective of American greatness, *we* see only pleasing images of associated prosperity and glory of the land in which we live.

Such is the strong language of British scholars on this subject. And shall we at once, without examination, ascribe it wholly to prejudice? Should we not by such a hasty decision expose ourselves to the like imputation. On the contrary, should not the opinions of such writers stimulate us to inquiry, that we may ascertain whether their animadversions are well founded or not? We see the same critics censure the Scotticisms of their *northern bretheren*, the peculiarities of the *Irish*, and the provincial corruptions of their own *English* writers. We cannot therefore be so wanting in liberality as to think, that, when deciding upon the literary claims of *Americans*, they are governed by prejudice or jealousy. A suspicion of this sort should be the less readily entertained, as we acknowledge that they sometimes do justice to our countrymen. The writings of Dr. Franklin, for example, have received the highest praise; and a few other American authors have been liberally commended by them. The opinions of these critics too are supported by those of some distinguished men in our own country. Dr. Franklin censures, without reserve, 'the popular errors several of our own states are *continually* falling into,' with respect to 'expressions and pronunciation.' Dr. Witherspoon, who, by having been educated in Great Britain, and by his subsequent long residence in the United States, was particularly well qualified to judge on this subject, remarks:

> I shall also admit, though with some hesitation, that gentlemen and scholars in Great Britain speak as much with the vulgar in common chit chat, as persons of the same class do in America; but there is a remarkable difference in their public and solemn discourses. I have heard in this country, in the senate, in the bar, and from the pulpit, and see daily in dissertations from the press, errors in grammar, improprieties and vulgarisms, which hardly any person of the same class in point of rank and literature would have fallen into in Great Britain.

With these opinions of such distinguished writers before us, shall we entertain the illiberal jealousy that justice is intentionally withheld from us by our English bretheren? Let us rather imitate the example of the learned and modest Campbell, who, though he had devoted a great part of a long life to the study of the *English* language, yet thought it no disgrace to make an apology for his *style*, in the following terms: 'Sensible,' says he,

> of the disadvantages in point of style, which my northern situation lays me under, I have availed myself of every opportunity of better information, in regard to all those terms and phrases in the version, [of the Gospels] of which I was doubtful. I feel myself under particular obligations on this account, to one gentleman, my valuable friend and colleague, Dr. Beattie, who, though similarly situated with myself, has with greater success studied the genius and idiom of our language; and of whom it is no more than justice to add, that the acknowledged purity of his

own diction, is the least of his qualifications as an author. But if, notwithstanding all the care I have taken, I shall be found, in many places, to need the indulgence of the *English* reader, it will not much surprise me.

Upon an impartial consideration of the subject, therefore, it seems impossible to resist the conclusion, that, although the language of the United States has perhaps, changed less than might have been expected, when we consider how many years have elapsed since our ancestors brought it from England; yet it has in so many instances departed from the English standard, that our scholars should lose no time in endeavouring to restore it to its purity, and to prevent future corruption.

This, it is obvious, is to be effected, in the first place, by carefully noting every unauthorised word and phrase; or (as Dr. Franklin many years ago recommended, in his letter to Mr. Webster on this subject) by '*setting a discountenancing mark*' upon such of them, as are not rendered indispensably necessary by the peculiar circumstances of our country; and, even if we should continue to have a partiality for some of those expressions, and should choose to retain them, it will always be useful *to know* them. By knowing exactly what peculiar words are in use with us, we should, among other advantages, have it in our power to expose the calumnies of some prejudiced and ignorant writers, who have frequently laid to the charge of our countrymen *in general* the affected words and phrases of a few conceited individuals; – words and phrases, which are justly the subject of as much ridicule in *America* as they are in *Great Britain*. As a general rule also, we should undoubtedly avoid all those words which are noticed by English authors of reputation, as expressions with which *they are unacquainted*; for although we might produce some English authority for such words, yet the very circumstance of their being thus noticed by well educated *Englishmen*, is a proof that they are not in use at this day in England, and, of course, ought not to be used elsewhere by those who would speak *correct English*.

With a view to this important object I have taken some pains to make a collection of words and phrases, which I offer to the Academy, not as a perfect list of our real or supposed peculiarities of language, but merely as the beginning of a work, which can be completed only by long and accurate observation, especially of intelligent Americans, who shall have an opportunity of residing in England, and of well educated Englishmen who may visit this country. It has long been the wish of our scholars to see a work of this kind; but, though several words have been noticed by Dr. Witherspoon, Dr. Franklin, and some others, yet no one seems to have been willing to undertake the laborious task of making a general collection of them. Seeing no prospect of such a work, and observing, with no small degree of solicitude, the corruptions which are gradually insinuating themselves into our language, I have taken the liberty to ask the attention of the Academy to this subject, by laying before them the following Vocabulary; a performance, which I am sensible is not so worthy of their notice, as it might have been made, had more time and ability been devoted to it.

In making this Vocabulary, I have resorted to all the sources of information in my power, and have, under each word, given some authorities for and against the use of it. I have also subjoined to some of the words, the criticisms of Dr. Franklin, Dr. Witherspoon, and other writers, at large, in order that the reader may avail himself of their instructive observations, without the trouble of searching for them through the numerous volumes of their works; and in all cases, where any word had been noticed by English or American writers, which I had also myself observed, (particularly during my residence in England, where my attention was first directed to this subject), I have chosen to give it upon their authority, rather than my own. Many words will be found in the collection, which are not in fact of *American origin*, or peculiar to Americans; but it appeared to me that it would be useful to insert all words, the legitimacy of which had been questioned, in order that their claim to a place in the language might be discussed and settled. Several of the words have been obtained from British Reviews of American publications; and I may here remark, how much it is to be regretted, that the reviewers have not pointed out *all* the instances, which have come under their notice, of our deviations from the *English* standard. This would have been doing an essential service to our literature, and have been the most effectual means of accomplishing what those scholars appear to have so much at heart – the preservation of the English language in its purity, wherever it is spoken.

It has been asserted, that we have discovered a much stronger propensity than the English, to add new words to the language; and the little animadversion, which, till within a few years, such new-coined words have met with among us, seems to support that opinion. The passion for these senseless novelties, however, has for some time past been declining. Our greatest danger now is, that we shall

120

continue to use antiquated words, which were brought to this country by our forefathers nearly two centuries ago; (some of which too were at that day *provincial* words in England); and, that we shall affix a *new signification* to words, which are still used in that country solely in their original sense. Words of these descriptions having long formed a part of the language, we are not led to examine critically the authority on which their different significations rest; but those which are *entirely new*, like strangers on their first appearance, immediately attract our attention, and induce us to inquire into their pretensions to the rank they claim. [The reader will not infer from these remarks, that *our right* to make new words is here meant to be denied. We, as members of that great community or family which speaks the English language, have undoubtedly, as well as the other members, a right to make words and propose them for adoption into our common language. But unless those, who are the final arbiters in the case, that is, the body of the learned and polite of this whole community, wherever they may be, shall sanction such new terms, it will be presumptuous in the authors of them to attempt to force them into general use. We should hardly be willing to adopt all the words and phrases which the people of Scotland, of Ireland, or of the British Settlements in various parts of the world, should propose to make a part of our common language. Our right however in this respect is not contested by the English themselves; See, for instance, the remark of the *British Critic* on this subject, under the word *Lengthy* in the following Vocabulary.]

But it is not enough for us to note single *words*; our *idiom*, it should seem, is in some degree changed, and is in danger of still greater corruptions. At the same time, therefore that we are 'setting a discountenancing mark' upon unauthorised words, we should assiduously study the language of the best authors, especially Dryden, Swift, and Addison; to the last of whom, Dr. Blair, in his Lectures on Rhetoric, justly applies Quintilian's well-known remark upon Cicero — that 'to be highly pleased with his manner of writing is the criterion of a good taste in English style — Ille se profecisse sciat cui Cicero vale placebit;' and of whom Dr. Johnson emphatically says — 'whoever would attain a good English style, familiar but not coarse, and elegant but not ostentatious, must give his days and nights to the volumes of Addison.' Dr. Franklin, who in his *Life* informs us that it was *one of the greatest objects of his ambition to write English well*, formed his style upon that of *Addison*; and Franklin is one of the very few American writers, whose style has satisfied the English critics. This is the discipline to which the most distinguished scholars of Great Britain have submitted, and without which neither they nor the scholars of our own country, can acquire and preserve a pure English style. It is related of Mr. Fox, that when speaking of his intended History, he said, he would *'admit no word into his book for which he had not the authority of Dryden'*. This determination may perhaps seem, at first view, to have been dictated by too fastidious a taste, or an undue partiality for a favourite author; but unquestionably, a rule of this sort, adopted in the course of our education, and extended to a few of the best authors, would be the most effective method of acquiring a good English style. And, surely, if Fox found no necessity for any other words than Dryden had used, those writers have little excuse, who take the liberty, not only of using all the words they can find in the whole body of English authors, ancient and modern, but also of making new terms of their own at pleasure. Who shall have a right to complain of scarcity, where that distinguished orator found abundance? Such standard authors, therefore, should be made the *foundation* of *our English*; but as our language, like all others, is constantly though slowly changing, we should also, in order to perfect our style, as we advance to mature age, study those authors of our own time, who have made the older writers their models. Every word in the writings of Addison, is not now in general use, in England; and many words have been adopted since his time, and are now sanctioned by the best writers of that country. These writers, therefore, as well as their illustrious masters, ought to be diligently read; for we should always remember, that in language, as in the fine arts, we can only attain to excellence by an incessant study of the best models.

TEXT AND SELECTED READING

The text is that of the 'Essay' which begins Pickering's *Vocabulary* first published in 1816. The best studies of the place of Pickering in the American language debates are D. Baron, *Grammar and Good Taste* (London: Yale University Press, 1982), D. Simpson, *The Politics of American English 1776–1850* (Oxford: Oxford University Press, 1986) and J.T. Andresen, *Linguistics in America 1769–1924* (London: Routledge, 1990). More general surveys of the type of work in which Pickering was involved are J. Friend, *The Development of American Lexicography* (The Hague: Mouton, 1967) and G.P. Krapp, *The English Language in America* (New York: Century, 1925). An interesting collection of early writings on American English is M.M. Mathews, *The Beginnings of American English* (London: University of Chicago Press, 1931).

9

T. Watts

Published in the year before the Great Exhibition, Watts' essay is marked by the confidence of the period. Ranging over both past and contemporary pretenders to the title of universal language, Watts expresses a sanguinity and pride in the English language which is typical of the new discipline of 'the history of the language' to which this piece is a contribution. Universal language schemes have a long history, from Wilkins' *Essay Towards a Real Character and a Philosophical Language* (1668) to Basic and Esperanto in this century. However, the concern in this essay is not with projects for artificial languages which are intended for universal use, but with natural languages which, by dint of the fact that they are used all over the globe, have become universal in that sense. Watts notes that the last language to achieve such status was Latin, which was of course the language of the Catholic church and therefore for an extensive period the language of the European intelligentsia. The rise of the vernacular languages in the wake of the Reformation, however, coupled with the development of print-capitalism, brought about the end of such dominance and universality. Thus although Hobbes was famous in Europe on account of his use of Latin in the seventeenth century, his successor in the English philosophical tradition John Locke not only wrote in English but composed a treatise on education in which he argued that it, rather than Latin, should be the medium of instruction for the young.

The fall of Latin was also the signal for the use of the vernacular languages in major literary works which was in itself an important moment in the cultural history of nations. However, it is perhaps not until the late eighteenth and early nineteenth centuries that a language was deemed to be an essential component of a nation's identity. It was in this period, for example, that Herder asserted: 'Denn *jedes* Volk ist Volk; es hat *seine* National Bildung wie seine Sprache' (For every nation is a nation, it has its own national culture as well as its own language). And this linkage between language and nation was taken up in a variety of distinct contexts. In a sense the competition between languages which Watts refers to in this piece is a result of this linkage since the status of universal language is in effect to be the preserve of the nation which gains geographical and territorial supremacy in the world order. This is tantamount to arguing that the universal language will be the language of whichever is the major imperialist nation.

It is in fact imperialism which transforms the status of the English language and takes it from its somewhat anxious position in the seventeenth and eighteenth centuries. Imperialism, or as Watts describes it here 'fashion', 'emigration' and 'conquest', is the means by which the language of an insular culture became written and spoken all over the world. For as Watts argues, 'the fact that the dominions of England now stretch from the Ganges to the Indus' means that 'the whole space of India is dotted with the regimental libraries of its European conquerors, and that Rasselas has been translated into Bengalee'. This was a common view, and one which was echoed in Edwin Guest's assertion in 1838 that English

> is rapidly becoming the great medium of civilisation, the language of law and literature to the Hindoo, of commerce to the African, of religion to the scattered islanders of the Pacific. The range of its influence, even at the present day, is greater than ever was that of the Greek, the Latin, or the Arabic; and the circle widens daily.

The process by which 'the world is circled by the accents of Milton and Shakespeare' is one which subjugated and destroyed the cultures, languages and economies of the colonised. However, the dominant language did not merely enter into hierarchical relations with the languages and cultures of the subject nations since imperialism was also a process of competition between the imperialist nations themselves. A competition for ever more territory, resources and power which issued in war. It is on this account that Watts views English, the language of the major imperial nation, as a dominating force which will subjugate not only the languages of the colonised, but the languages of the other imperial powers too. The logic of the struggle between the imperial powers is clear: if other nations 'do not extend their empire beyond this quarter of the globe' then their languages 'will be reduced to this same degree of insignificance in comparison with English, as the subordinate languages of modern Europe to those of the state they belong to, — the Welsh to the English, the Basque to the Spanish', and so on. This is an outcome which Watts heralds: 'It will be a singular and a novel experiment in modern society, if a single language becomes so predominant over all others as to reduce them in comparison to the proportion of provincial dialects.' This may strike the reader as a rather peripheral way of thinking about imperialism but it was by no means uncommon in the period. It is in fact simply an extension of the historical process whereby all forms of cultural identity were evaluated, subjugated or destroyed in favour of that of the metropolitan, imperial centre.

'ON THE PROBABLE FUTURE POSITION OF THE ENGLISH LANGUAGE'

Since the revival of letters there has been a general tendency to the establishment of what may be called a universal language, that is, of a language universally understood by those who make any at all an object of liberal study. At the present time there can be no doubt that this honour, so far as possessed by any language in Europe, is still in possession of the French, though its position is no longer so commanding as it was. In any country foreign to France in which two modern languages are made an object of cultivation, French is one of the two; in those countries where only one is cultivated, French is the one.

The position now occupied by French was, it is often said, formerly in the possession of the Latin language; but this is not exactly the case. The Latin language not only enjoyed the distinction which French possesses, but one of much superior value. The French is read by scholars of different countries; the Latin was not only read, but written. The effects are widely different. At the commencement of the sixteenth century Erasmus of Rotterdam was the most distinguished author of Holland and the most distinguished author of Europe. His productions issued from the presses of Rotterdam, London, and Basil; they were read with equal advantage in every civilised country. At the commencement of the nineteenth century Bilderlijk was the most distinguished author of Holland, and almost unknown even by name beyond its boundaries. Southey, in his epistle to Allan Cunningham, mentions his name, and thus proceeds:–

> 'And who is Bilderlijk?' methinks thou sayest;
> A ready question, yet which, trust me, Allan,

Would not be ask'd had not the curse that came
From Babel, clip't the wings of Poetry.
Napoleon ask'd him once, with cold, fix'd look,
'Art thou then in the world of letters known?'
And meeting his imperial look with eye
As little wont to turn away before
The face of man, the Hollander replied,
'At least I have done that whereby I have
There to be known deserved'

Perhaps Bilderlijk had a genius equal to that of Erasmus, but Erasmus wrote in Latin and Bilderlijk wrote in Dutch, and these were the consequences.

This difference in the universality of the Latin and French – that the one was generally read and written, the other only read – is evidently one of great importance. The effect of the diffusion of the Latin language was to enable every writer of whatever country to assume the station to which his talents entitled him; the effect of the diffusion of the French has been to concentrate the attention of Europe on the writers of a particular country, who might or might not be worthy of it. There have been periods, such as during the reign of Napoleon for instance, when the literature of France was, beyond comparison, inferior to those of England and Germany. It was a poor consolation for the Englishman who was unable to read in the original Goethe and Schiller, or for the German who could have wished to study Scott and Byron, to give his nights and days to the pages of Chateaubriand and Lebrun.

There are no insuperable difficulties indeed in the way of a foreigner's attaining a sufficient mastery over the French language to use it as an author, at least as far as prose is concerned, and at one time, it seemed not unlikely that a fashion of doing so might arise. 'Several foreigners,' says Gibbon, 'have seized the opportunity of speaking to Europe in this common dialect, and Germany may plead the authority of Leibniz and Frederick, of the first of her philosophers and the greatest of her kings.' England was once in danger of losing to a foreign language the immortal productions of Gibbon himself, who had indeed published his youthful 'Essay on Literature,' in French, and it is to the advice of Hume, though he had himself once conceived the notion of retiring to France and adopting its language, that we are indebted for the enrichment of English with the 'Decline and Fall'. Goethe, it is said, regretted even in later life, the abandonment of an early project to compose his writings in the best-known language in Europe.

For the last century, however, the torrent of example has set the other way. It is now just about a hundred years ago that Klopstock paved the way to the recultivation of German, and a language till that time neglected and despised has assumed a position amongst the first and richest in Europe, rich both in its native resources and in the productions of genius. This lesson has been fertile in results. The countries of Scandinavia, though their combined population is scarcely equal to that of the seventh of Germany, have brought two languages into the field. These, from their similarity to English and German, might be acquired without great effort by those already acquainted with both, but with the Slavonic languages the case is very different. The Russian and the Polish literature, one of them brought into existence during this period, the other revived after a long trance which threatened to be fatal, are in languages quite unconnected with any that had previously been considered worthy of the cultivation of the scholar. The extent of Europe which belongs to the Slavonic tribes is however so vast, that it might have been considered probable that at some period one of their dialects, at all events, would rise into literary importance. But the cultivation of the Slavonic languages was followed by that of the Hungarian. A language wholly remote from any other European speech, except the Finnish and the Laplandic, has been made the vehicle, not only of poetry and fiction, but of natural history and mathematics.

The Hungarian makes the sixth language which, during the last century, has risen to the dignity of a language of books and literature. Within the century before there was not one that had changed its footing in this respect in a striking degree. There are still in different corners of Europe a few languages which remain in the same position that they then occupied, or in very nearly the same; and of these there is a remarkable number in the British islands. The progress of each of these six languages has been greeted as a sign and harbinger of the progress of cultivation, but should we be prepared to hail with similar gratulation a similar advance on the part of the Gaelic, the Irish, or the Welsh?

The tendency of all these languages has been to lessen the predominance of the French language, and to alter the literary centre of Europe. The cause of this pre-eminence of French has been the subject of some interesting speculation, and in the year 1783 the Academy of Berlin proposed the question for a prize. The answer which obtained the award was the well-known dissertation of Rivarol, 'De l'Universalité de la langue Française,' which has been frequently reprinted, and has obtained a reputation somewhat out of proportion to its merits. In this essay Rivarol passes but lightly over the claims of the Italian, the Spanish, and the German languages, to that supremacy which French has obtained, but enters at some length into an examination of the comparative claims of the French and ourselves. The Italian language, he observes, was too early ripe; at a time when it had the advantage over all its rivals, Europe was not yet sufficiently sensible of the necessity for a general dialect of literature to make choice of any. That harmony of Italian is also too monotonous; the constant termination of its words in vowels has been found so wearisome in prose, that poetical license in Italian has the unusual tendency to make the words shorter and harsher. To Spanish he hardly considers any claim to have ever belonged, yet that noble and harmonious language is free from the fault with which he reproaches the Italian, and was at one time spoken by a nation which held the fairest portion of the old world, and spread its conquests far and wide in the new. There was a time when Spanish was frequently introduced for whole scenes in Italian plays, and even occasionally on the stage at Paris, – when it was commonly spoken in the courts of Italy and in that of Vienna. To the deficiencies of Spanish literature, and to the remoteness of the peninsula from the other civilised nations of Europe, must no doubt be ascribed the singular neglect which has placed it as low in the list of cultivated languages as it once stood high. Of German Rivarol maintains that it came too late — that the place was already taken, and that it has the disadvantage of being a language entirely new in literature. There was he asserts, a necessity that the predominant language of Europe should be connected with the venerated languages of ancient Rome, since to all that the cultivated tongues, with the exception of German, exhibited undoubted affinities.

There is a geographical reason, on which Rivarol lays no stress, to which the Marquis Du Roure, who subsequently touched on the same subject, was inclined to attribute the whole weight of the decision. France, says Du Roure, is situated precisely in the centre of the five principal nations of Europe. The Englishman who wishes to visit either Spain, or Italy, or Germany, without incurring the fatigue of a long sea voyage, must necessarily pass through France, and in the same way the inhabitant of each of these countries is compelled to take the same road. What can be more natural than for a nation to study the language of its nearest neighbour? And France is the only near neighbour of some of these countries, as near as any to all. To this motive the Marquis attaches so much importance, that he states his belief, that if, owing to some startling revolution, the Basque or Breton were to become the general language of France, Basque or Breton would immediately become the most fashionable foreign language in England, Germany, Italy and Spain.

If however we admit the correctness of Du Roure's hypothesis, with regard to the original cause of the predominance of the French, it will not necessarily follow that the same causes are now in operation. Undoubtedly at the time that French was elected, the number of voters who would be supposed to influence the decision was but five; the constituency has now been extended; the Russians, the Poles, the Hungarians, the Scandinavians have obtained the suffrage. The same reasons that formerly decided the predominance of the French, have now a tendency to promote the advancement of German. The country of each of the rising literatures touches on Germany, and, as has been before remarked, the literary centre of Europe has changed.

There has been a similar alteration with regard to the affinity of the literary nations with the Latin language, the point which has been dwelt upon by Rivarol. Among the new competitors in the field, not one has the slightest connection with Latin or the Romanic dialects; many are closely akin to German; the others are more likely to regard with more favour a language entirely dependent on its own resources and that can be studied by itself, than one which to be fully intelligible requires some study of its ancient stock. Thus two of the advantages which France formerly possessed are turned against itself and transferred to German. That language has in addition a vast and striking recommendation which neither Rivarol nor Du Roure has adverted to. Of the cultivated languages of Europe, none is so weak an instrument of translation as the French, and none is more powerful than the German. This consideration, which must always have been an important one in discussing the claims of a language to the place of a representative, has become doubly so by the circumstances of the modern literary world. In French, there is not even a tolerable translation of Tasso, or Ariosto, or Dante, or Calderon, much less of Shakespeare, or Burns, or Byron. If only one of the modern languages of Europe can descend to posterity, or which is much the same, if posterity can only find time to make itself master of one, it is the interest of the world that that one should rather be German than French.

129

The time seems fast approaching when the predominance in point of language will have to undergo a revolution, and these considerations seem weighty enough to bend the decision to the side of the German, were it not for the existence of another language whose claims are still more demanding. That language is our own. Two centuries ago the proud position that it now occupies was beyond the reach of anticipation. We all smile at the well-known boast of Waller in his lines on the death of Cromwell, but it was the loftiest at the time that the poet found it in his power to make:

> Under the tropic is our language spoke
> And part of Flanders hath received our yoke.

'I care not', said Milton, 'to be once named abroad, though perhaps I could attain to that, being content with these islands as my world.' A French Jesuit Garnier, laying down rules for the arrangement of a library, thought it superfluous to say anything of English books, because, as he observed, 'libri Anglica scripti lingua vix mare transmittunt.' Swift, in the earlier part of the eighteenth century, in his 'Proposal for Correcting, Improving and Ascertaining the English Language', observed, 'the fame of our writers is usually confined to these two islands'. Not quite a hundred years ago Dr. Johnson seems to have entertained far from a lofty idea of the legitimate aspirations of an English author. He quotes in a number of the Rambler (No. 118, May 4th 1751) from the address of Africanus as given by Cicero, in his Dream of Scipio:

> The territory which you inhabit is no more than a scanty island inclosed by a small body of water, to which you give the name of the great sea and the Atlantic ocean. And even in this known and frequented continent what hope can you entertain that your renown will pass the stream of the Ganges or the cliffs of Caucasus, or by whom will your name be uttered in the extremities of the north or south towards the rising or the setting sun? So narrow is the space to which your fame can be propagated, and even there how long will it remain?

'I am not inclined,' remarks Johnson

> to believe that they who among us pass their lives in the cultivation of knowledge or acquisition of power, have very anxiously inquired what opinions prevail on the further banks of the Ganges. . . . The hopes and fears of modern minds are

content to range in a narrower compass; a single nation, and a few years have generally sufficient amplitude to fill our imagination.

What a singular comment is supplied on this passage by the fact that the dominions of England now stretch from the Ganges to the Indus, that the whole space of India is dotted with the regimental libraries of its European conquerors, and that Rasselas has been translated into Bengalee! A few years later the great historian of England had a much clearer perception of what was then in the womb of Fate. When Gibbon, as has been already mentioned, submitted to Hume a specimen of his intended History of Switzerland, composed in French, he received a remarkable letter in reply: 'Why', said Hume,

> do you compose in French and carry faggots into the woods, as Horace says with regard to the Romans who wrote in Greek? I grant that you have a like motive to those Romans, and adopt a language much more generally diffused than your native tongue, but have you not remarked the fate of those two ancient languages in following ages? The Latin, though then less cele- brated and confined to more narrow limits, has in some measure outlived the Greek, and is now more generally understood by men of letters. Let the French therefore triumph in the present diffusion of their tongue. Our solid and increasing establish- ments in America, where we need less dread the inundation of barbarians, promise a superior stability and duration to the English language.

Every year that has since elapsed has added a superior degree of probability to the anticipation of Hume. At present the prospects of the English language are the most splendid that the world has ever seen. It is spreading in each of the quarters of the globe by fashion, by emigration, and by conquest. The increase of population alone in the two great states of Europe and America in which it is spoken, adds to the number of its speakers in every year that passes, a greater amount than the whole number of those who speak some of the literary languages of Europe, either Swedish, or Danish, or Dutch. It is calculated that before the lapse of the present century, a time that so many now alive will live to witness, it will be the native and vernacular language of about one hundred and fifty millions of human beings.

What will be the state of Christendom at the time that this vast preponderance of one language will be brought to bear on all its relations, – at the time when a leading nation in Europe and a gigantic nation in America use the same idiom, – when in Africa and Australasia the same language is in use by rising and influential communities, and the world is circled by the accents of Milton and Shakespeare? At that time such of the other languages of Europe as do not extend their empire beyond this quarter of the globe will be reduced to this same degree of insignificance in comparison with English, as the subordinate languages of modern Europe to those of the state they belong to, – the Welsh to the English, the Basque to the Spanish, the Finnish to the Russian. This predominance, we may flatter ourselves, will be a more signal blessing to literature than that of any other language possibly could be. The English is essentially a medium language; – in the Teutonic family it stands midway between the Germanic and Scandinavian branches – it unites, as no other language unites, the Romanic and the Teutonic stocks. This fitted it admirably in many cases for translation. A German writer, Prince Puckler Muskau, has given it as his opinion that English is even better adapted than German to be the general interpreter of the literature of Europe. Another German writer, Jensich, in his elaborate 'Comparison of Fourteen Ancient and Modern Languages of Europe', which obtained a prize from the Berlin Academy in 1796, assigns the general palm of excellence to the English. In literary treasures what other language can claim the superiority? If Rivarol more than sixty years back thought the collective wealth of its literature able to dispute the preeminence with the French, the victory has certainly not departed from us in the time that has since elapsed, – the time of Wordsworth and Southey, of Rogers and Campbell, of Scott, of Moore, of Byron.

The prospect is so glorious that it seems an ungrateful task to interrupt its enjoyment by a shade of doubt; but as the English language has attained to this eminent station from small beginnings, may it not be advisable to consider whether obstacles are not in existence, which, equally small in their beginnings, have a probability of growing larger? The first consideration that presents itself is that English is not the only language firmly planted on the soil of America, the only one to which a glorious future is, in the probable course of things, assured.

A sufficient importance has not always been attached to the fact, that in South America, and in a portion of the northern continent, the languages of the peninsula are spoken by large and increasing populations. The Spanish language is undoubtedly of easier acquisition for the purposes of conversation than our own, from the harmony and clearness of its pronunciation; and it has the recommendation to the inhabitants of Southern Europe of greater affinity to their own languages and the Latin. Perhaps the extraordinary neglect which has been the portion of this language for the last century and a half may soon give place to a juster measure of cultivation, and indeed the recent labours of Prescott and Ticknor seem to show that the dawn of that period has already broken. That the men of the North should acquire an easy and harmonious Southern language seems in itself much more probable than that the men of the South should study a Northern language not only rugged in its pronunciation, but capricious in its orthography. The dominion of Spanish in America is however interrupted and narrowed by that of Portuguese, and to a singular degree by that of the native languages, some of which are possibly destined to be used for literary purposes in ages to come.

At the time when Hume wrote his letter to Gibbon, the conquest of Canada had very recently been effected. The rivalry of the French and English in North America had been terminated by the most signal triumph of English arms. Had measures been taken at that time to discourage the use of French and to introduce that of English, there can be little doubt that English would now be as much the language of Quebec and Montreal as it is of New York and the Delaware. Those measures were not taken. At this moment, when we are approaching a century from the battle of the Heights of Abraham, there is still a distinction of races in Canada, nourished by a distinction of language, and both appear likely to continue.

Within the United States themselves, a very large body of the inhabitants have remained for generation after generation ignorant of the English language. The number is uncertain. According to Stricker, in his dissertation 'Die Verbreitung des deutschen Volkes über die Erde', published in 1845, the population of German origin in the United States in 1844 was 4,886,632, out of a total of 18,980,650. This statement, though made in the most positive terms, is founded on an estimate only, and has been shown to be much exaggerated. Wappaus (in his 'Deutsche Auswanderung und Colonisation'), after a careful examination, arrives at the conclusion that the total cannot amount to a million and a half. Many of these are of course acquainted with both languages – in several cases where amalgamation has taken place, the German language has died out and has been replaced by the English, – but the number of communities where it is still prevalent is much larger than is generally supposed. In Pennsylvania, Ohio, and Missouri, to say nothing of other states, there are masses of population of German origin or descent, who are only acquainted with German. This tendency has of late years increased instead of declining. It has been a favourite project with recent German emigrants to form in America a state, in which the language should be German, and from the vast numbers in which they have crossed the Atlantic, there is nothing improbable in the supposition, that, by obtaining a majority in some one state, this object will be attained. In 1835 the legislature of Pennsylvania placed the German language in its legal rights on the same footing with the English.

It may be asked if any damage will be done by this? The damage, it may be answered, will be twofold. The parties who are thus formulated into an isolated community, with a language distinct from that of those around them, will be placed under the same disadvantages as the Welsh of our own day, who find themselves always as it were some inches shorter than their neighbours, and have to make an exertion to be on their level. Those of them who are only masters of one language are in a sort of prison, those who are masters of two might, if English had been their original speech, have had their choice of the remaining languages of the world to exert the same degree of labour on, with a better prospect of advantage. In the case of Welsh, the language has many ties: even those who see most clearly the necessity of forsaking it, must lament the harsh necessity of abandoning to oblivion the ancient tongue of an ancient nation. But these associations and feelings could not be pleaded in favour of transferring the Welsh to Otaheite; and when these feelings are withdrawn, what valid reason will remain for the perpetuation of Welsh, or even, it may be said, of German?

The injury done to the community itself is perhaps the greatest; but there is also damage done to the world in general. It will be a single and a novel experiment in modern society, if a single language becomes so predominant over all others as to reduce them in comparison to the proportion of provincial dialects. To have this experiment fairly tried is a great object. Every atom that is subtracted from the amount of the majority has its influence − it goes into the opposite scale. If the Germans succeed in establishing their language in the United States, other nations may follow. The Hungarian emigrants who are now removing thither from the vengeance of Austria may perpetuate their native Magyar, and America may in time present a surface as checkered as Europe, or in some parts, as Hungary itself, where the traveller often in passing from one village to another finds himself in the domain of a different language. That this consummation may be averted must be the wish not only of every Englishman and of every Anglo-American, but of every sincere friend of the advancement of literature and civilisation. Perhaps a few more years of inattention to the subject will allow the evil to make such progress that exertion to oppose it may come too late.

TEXT AND SELECTED READING

The text is that of a paper read before the Philological Society on February 22nd 1850 and published in the *Proceedings of the Philological Society*, 4 (1848–50). The best study of the historical context of Watts' work is Hans Aarsleff, *The Study of Language in England 1780–1860* (Princeton: Princeton University Press, 1967). A study of the political significance of Watts' essay and pieces like it is given in T. Crowley, *The Politics of Discourse* (London: Macmillan, 1989). The responses of contemporary colonial writers to many of the questions addressed by Watts can be found in F. Fanon, *Black Skin, White Masks* (London: Grove Press, 1967) and Ngugi Wa Thiongo, *Decolonising the Mind* (London: James Currey, 1986). An overview of such responses is given in B. Ashcroft, G. Griffiths and H. Tiffin, *The Empire Writes Back* (London: Routledge, 1989).

10

Archbishop R.C. Trench

If Watts had tied the fate of the language in with the fate of the nation in its quest for imperial status, then Trench's account of the language and nation is more complex. Although he too binds them together, he does so in a way which both encapsulates and advances important theoretical claims. Taking as his object the 'use, origin and distinction of words', Trench moulds his study in order to fulfil his belief that 'language is an instrument of knowledge'. The types of knowledge, and their deployment for particular purposes, form the most interesting aspects of his work.

The assertion that language is 'fossil poetry' was made by Emerson; but it is Trench who extends this claim into other areas of discourse. For as Trench says, language is indeed 'fossil poetry', yet it is also, at least as plausibly, 'fossil ethics' or 'fossil history'. The belief that language is 'fossil history' is one inherited from the romantics and one to which we shall return. Also interesting, however, is the claim concerning the 'morality in words'. The proposition is that once examined etymologically, words reveal messages to us by dint of the fact that the divine 'seal of truth on language' ensures that language records the post-lapsarian history of humanity in the semantic shifts and developments which affect single words. As words change their meanings they record the vicissitudes of humanity and this embodied history can then be read back from words in order to teach us moral lessons. It is in this way that language becomes a 'moral barometer' by which we can evaluate the nation and its history. It also means that language itself becomes an agent within history, a claim echoing a passage in Herder's *Essay on the Origin of Language* (1772). For words are not merely the 'passive vehicles' of truth and falsehood; as Trench says, they 'do not hold themselves neutral in the great conflict between good and evil . . . but receive from us the impressions of our good and of our evil, which again they are active to propagate amongst us.' Of course given the agency of language, Trench sees it as important that words should not simply be allowed to record history and engage in its future construction without constraint. His task is to remind us of what words originally meant, what their present use tells us about morality, and what they should mean in the future. Taking the word 'religion' as an example, Trench does not believe in simply recording its multi-accentual uses, but in challenging them from a particular standpoint. Holding the origin of the word to be the sense of being bound (though in fact the etymology is obscure), Trench argues that this means that the word's signification is thus properly the sense of being bound to God or to our 'fellow-men'. Later uses of the term, he argues, are misuses since they corrupt its origin and come to mean 'monkery' which is an immoral understanding of the word. Thus not only does language record morality here, it also allows the Archbishop to prescribe both the proper use of words and morals.

By the same process as that described above, language also acts as the transcript of history. Even single words can record 'great social revolutions, revolutions in nations and in the feelings of nations' and so on. Language records history even more faithfully than the narrative accounts which we have of the past. Indeed when such narratives fail, we can turn to language; for as one linguist of the period put it, 'often where history is utterly dumb concerning the past, language speaks' (W. Mathews, *Words; Their Use And Abuse*, 1882). If language speaks history then what it articulates most clearly is the history of the nation which uses it. This is a concept which was to gain a central place in German linguistic thought in the romantic period, but it is one which is expressed most clearly in James Harris' *Hermes or a Philosophical Inquiry Concerning Universal Grammar* (1751). In it Harris asserts,

> We shall be led to observe, how Nations, like single men, have their peculiar Ideas; how these peculiar Ideas become the genius of their language, since the Symbol must of course correspond to its Archetype; how the wisest nations, having the most and best Ideas, will consequently have the best and most copious languages.

It is in the sense set out here then that we might describe Trench's work as an attempt to give a proper account of the 'genius' of the English language and thus of the English nation. It is an attempt to read proper English identity from the history of the nation which has transcribed itself in the English language.

ON THE STUDY OF WORDS

Introductory Lecture

There are few who would not readily acknowledge that mainly in worthy books are preserved and hoarded the treasures of wisdom and knowledge that the world has accumulated; and that chiefly by aid of these are they handed down from one generation to another. I shall urge on you in these lectures something different than this; namely, that not in books only, nor yet in connected oral discourse, but often also in words contemplated singly, there are boundless stores of moral and historic truth, and no less of passion and imagination, laid up, − that from these, lessons of infinite worth may be derived, if only our attention is roused to their existence. I shall urge on you, (though with teaching such as you enjoy, the subject will not be new,) how well it will repay you to study the words which you are in the habit of using or of meeting, be they such as relate to the highest spiritual things, or our common words of the shop and the market, and all the familiar intercourse of life. It will indeed repay you far better than you can easily believe. I am sure, at least, that for many a young man his first discovery of the fact that words are living powers, are the vesture, yea, even the body, which thoughts weave for themselves, has been like the dropping of scales from his eyes, like the acquiring of another sense, or the introduction into a new world; he is never able to cease wondering at the moral marvels that surround him on every side, and ever reveal themselves more and more to his gaze.

We indeed hear it not seldom said that ignorance is the mother of invention. A falser word was never spoken, and hardly a more mischevious one; for it seems to imply that this healthiest exercise of the mind rests, for the most part on a deceit and illusion, and that with better knowledge it would cease; while, in truth, for once that ignorance leads us to admire that which with fuller insight we would perceive to be a common thing, and one demanding therefore no such tribute from us, an hundred, nay, a thousand times, it prevents us from admiring that which is admirable indeed. And this is so, whether we are moving in the region of nature, which is the region of God's wonders, or even in the region of art, which is the region of man's wonders; and nowhere truer than in this sphere and region of language, which is about to claim us now. Oftentimes here we move up and down in the midst of intellectual and moral marvels with vacant eye and careless mind, even as some traveller passes unmoved over fields of fame, or through cities of ancient reknown — unmoved, because utterly unconscious of the lofty deeds which have there been wrought, of the great hearts which spent themselves there. We, like him, wanting the knowledge and insight which would have served to kindle admiration in us, are oftentimes deprived of this pure and elevating excitement of the mind, and miss no less that manifold teaching and instruction which lie ever about our path, and nowhere more largely than our daily words, if only we knew where to put forth our hands and make it our own. 'What riches,' one exclaims, 'lie hidden in the vulgar tongue of our poorest and most ignorant. What flowers of paradise lie hidden under our feet, with their beauties and their parts undistinguished and undiscerned, from having been daily trodden on.'

And this subject upon which we are entering ought not to be a dull or uninteresting one in the handling, or one to which only by an effort you will yield the attention which I shall claim. If it shall prove so, this I fear must be through the fault of my manner of treating it; for certainly in itself there is no study which *may* be made at once more instructive and entertaining than the study of the use, origin, and distinction of words, which is exactly that which I propose to myself and to you. I remember a very learned scholar to whom we owe one of our best Greek lexicons, a book which must have cost him years, speaking in the preface of his great work with a just disdain of some, who complained of the irksome drudgery of such toils as those which had engaged him so long, — thus irksome, forsooth, because they only had to do with words; who claimed pity on themselves, as though they had been so many galley-slaves chained to the oar, or martyrs who had offered themselves to the good of the rest of the literary world. He declares that, for his part, the task of classing, sorting, grouping, comparing, tracing the derivation and usage of words had been to him no drudgery, but a delight and labour of love.

And if this may be true in regard of a foreign tongue, how much truer ought it to be in regard to our own, of our 'mother tongue', as we fondly call it. A great writer not very long departed from us has here borne witness to the pleasantness and profit of this study. 'In a language,' he says, 'like ours, where so many words are derived from other languages, there are few modes of instruction more useful or more amusing than that of accustoming young people to seek for the etymology or primary meaning of the words they use. There are cases in which more knowledge of more value may be conveyed by the history of a word than by the history of a campaign.'

And, implying the same truth, a popular American author has somewhere characterised language as 'fossil poetry'. He evidently means that just as in some fossil, curious and beautiful shapes of vegetable or animal life, the graceful fern of the finely vertebrated lizard, such as now, it may be, have been extinct for thousands of years, are permanently bound up with the stone, and rescued from that perishing which would have otherwise been theirs, — so in words are beautiful thoughts and images, the imagination and the feeling of past ages, of men long since in their graves, of men whose very names have perished, preserved and made safe for ever. The phrase is a striking one; the only fault which one might be tempted to find with it is, that it is too narrow. Language may be, and indeed is, this 'fossil poetry'; but it may be affirmed of it with exactly the same truth that it is fossil ethics, or fossil history. Words quite as often and as effectually embody facts of history, or convictions of the moral common sense, as of the imagination or passion of men; even as, so far as that moral sense may be perverted, they will bear witness and keep a record of that perversion. On all these points I shall enter at full in after lectures; but I may give by anticipation a specimen or two of what I mean, to make from the first my purpose and my plan more fully intelligible to all.

Language then is fossil poetry; in other words, we are not to look for the poetry which a people may possess only in its poems, or its poetical customs, traditions and beliefs. Many a single word also is itself a concentrated poem, having stores of poetical thought and imagery laid up in it. Examine it, and it will be found to rest on some deep analogy of things natural and things spiritual; bringing those to illustrate and to give an abiding form and body to these. The image may have grown trite and ordinary now; perhaps through the help of this very word may have become so entirely the heritage of all, as to seem little better than a commonplace; yet not the less he who first discerned the relation, and devised the new word which should express it, or gave to an old, never before but literally used, this new and figurative sense, this man was in his degree a poet – a maker, that is, of things which were not before, which would not have existed, but for him, or for some other gifted with equal powers.

He who spoke first of a 'dilapidated' fortune, what an image must have risen up before his mind's eye of some falling house or palace, stone detaching itself from stone, till all had gradually sunk into desolation and ruin. Or he who to that Greek word which signifies 'that which will endure to be held up to and judged by the sunlight',

140

gave first its ethical signification of 'sincere', 'truthful', or as we sometimes say, 'transparent', can we deny to him the poet's feeling and eye? Many a man had gazed, we may be sure, at the jagged and indented mountain ranges of Spain, before one called them 'sierras' or 'saws', the name by which they are now known, as *Sierra* Morena, *Sierra* Nevada; but that man coined his imagination into a word, which will endure as long as the everlasting hills which he named.

'Iliads without a Homer', someone has called, with a little exaggeration, the beautiful but anonymous ballad poetry of Spain. One may be permitted, perhaps, to push the exaggeration a little further in the same direction, and to apply the same language not merely to a ballad but to a word. Let me illustrate that which I have been here saying somewhat more at length by the word 'tribulation'. We all know in a general way that this word, which occurs not seldom in Scripture and in the Liturgy, means affliction, sorrow, anguish; but it is quite worth our while to know *how* it means this, and to question the word a little closer. It is derived from the Latin word 'tribulum' — which was the threshing instrument or roller, whereby the Roman husbandmen separated the corn from the husks; and 'tribulatio' in its primary significance was the act of this separation. But some Latin writer of the Christian Church appropriated the word and image for the setting forth of an higher truth; and sorrow, distress, and adversity being the appointed means for the separating in men of whatever in them was light, trivial, and poor from the solid and the true, their chaff from their wheat, therefore he called these sorrows and griefs 'tribulations', threshings, that is, of the inner spiritual man, without which there could be no fitting him for the heavenly garner. Now in proof of my assertion that a single word is often a concentrated poem, a little grain of gold capable of being beaten out into a broad extent of gold-leaf, I will quote, in reference to this very word 'tribulation', a graceful composition by George Wither, an early English poet, which you will at once perceive is all wrapped up in this word, being from the first to last only the expanding of the image and thought which this word has implicitly given:

> Till from the straw, the flail, the corn doth beat,
> Until the chaff be purged from the wheat,
> Yea, till the mill the grains in pieces tear,
> The richness of the flour will scarce appear.
> So, till men's persons great afflictions touch,
> If worth be found, their worth is not so much,

Because like wheat in straw, they have not yet
That value which in threshing they may get.
For till the bruising flails of God's corrections
Have threshed out of us our vain affections;
Till those corruptions which do misbecome us
Are by Thy sacred Spirit winnowed from us;
Until from us the straw of worldly treasures,
Till all the dusty chaff of empty pleasures,
Yea, till His flail upon us He doth lay,
To thresh the husk of this our flesh away;
And leave the soul uncovered; nay, yet more,
Till God shall make our very spirit poor,
We shall not up to highest wealth aspire;
But then we shall; and that is my desire.

This deeper religious use of the word 'tribulation' was unknown to Classical, that is, to heathen, antiquity, and belongs exclusively to the Christian writers: and the fact that the same deepening and elevating of the use of words recurs in a multitude of other, and many of them more striking, instances, is one well deserving to be followed up. Nothing, I think, would more strongly bring before us what a new power Christianity was in the world than to compare the meaning which so many words possessed before its rise, and the deeper meaning which they obtained, so soon as they were assumed by it as vehicles of its life, the new thought and feeling enlarging, purifying, and ennobling the very words which they employed. This is a subject which I shall have occasion to touch upon more than once in these lectures, but is itself well worthy of, as it would afford ample material, a volume.

But it was said just now that words often contain a witness for great moral truths — God having impressed such a seal of truth on language, that men are constantly uttering deeper things than they know, asserting mighty principles, it may be asserting them against themselves, in words that to them may seem nothing more than the current coin of society. Thus to what grand moral purposes Bishop Butler turns the word 'pastime'; how solemn the testimony which he compels the world, out of its own use of this word, to render against itself — obliging it to own that its amusements and pleasures do not really satisfy the mind and fill it with the sense of an abiding and satisfying joy; they are only 'pastime'; they serve only, as this word confesses, to *pass* away the *time*, to prevent it from hanging, an intolerable burden, on men's hands; all which they can do at the best is to prevent men from discovering and attending to their own internal poverty and dissatisfaction and want. He might have added that there is the same acknowledgement in the word 'diversion', which means no more than that which *diverts* or turns us aside from ourselves, and in this way helps us to forget ourselves for a little. And thus it would appear that, even according to the world's own confession, all which it proposes is — not to make us happy, but a little to prevent us from remembering that we are unhappy, to *pass* away our *time*, to *divert* us from ourselves. While on the other hand we declare that the good which *will* really fill our souls and fill them to the uttermost, is not *in* us, but *without* us and *above* us, in the words which we use to set forth any transcending delight. Take three or four of these words – 'transport', 'rapture', 'ravishment', 'ecstasy', – 'transport', that which *carries* us, as 'rapture', or 'ravishment', that which *snatches* us, out of and above ourselves; and 'ecstasy' is very nearly the same, only drawn from Greek.

And not less, where a perversion of the moral sense has found place, words preserve oftentimes a record of this perversion. We have a signal evidence of this, even as it is a notable evidence of the manner in which moral contagion, spreading from heart and manners, invades the popular language in the use, or misuse, of the word 'religion', during all the ages of Papal domination in Europe. Probably many of you are aware that in those times a 'religious person' did not mean anyone who felt and allowed the bonds that bound him to God and his fellow-men, but one who had taken peculiar vows upon him, a member of one of the monkish orders; a 'religious' house did not mean, nor does it now mean in the Church of Rome, a Christian household, ordered in the fear of God, but a house in which those persons were gathered together according to the rule of some man, Benedict, or Dominic, or some other. A 'religion' meant not a service of God, but an order of monkery; and taking the monastic vows was termed going into a 'religion'. Now what an awful light does this one word so used throw on the entire state of mind and habits of thought in those ages! That then was 'religion', and nothing else was deserving of the name! And 'religious', was a title which might not be given to parents and children, husbands and wives, men and women fulfilling faithfully and holily in the world the several duties of their stations, but only to those who had devised self-chosen service for themselves.

In like manner that 'lewd', which meant at one time no more than

'lay', or unlearned, — the 'lewd' people, the lay people, — should come
to signify the sinful, the vicious, is not a little worthy of note. How
forcibly we are reminded here of that saying of the Pharisees of old:
'This people which knoweth not the law is cursed'; how much of their
spirit must have been at work before the word could have acquired
this secondary meaning.

But language is fossil history as well. What a record of great social
revolutions, revolutions in nations and in the feelings of nations, the
one word 'frank' contains; which is used, as we all know, to express
aught that is generous, straightforward, and free. The Franks, I need
not remind you, were a powerful German tribe, or association of
tribes, which at the breaking up of the Roman Empire possessed
themselves of Gaul, to which they gave their own name. They were
the ruling conquering people, honourably distinguished from the
Gauls and the degenerate Romans among whom they established
themselves by their independence, their love of freedom, their scorn of
a lie; they had, in short, the virtues which belong to a conquering and
dominant race in the midst of an inferior and conquered one. And
thus it came to pass that by degrees the name 'frank', which may have
originally indicated merely a national, came to involve a moral,
distinction as well; and a 'frank' man was synonymous not merely
with a man of the conquering German race, but was an epithet
applied to a person possessed of high moral qualities, which for the
most part appertained to, and were found only in, men of that stock;
and thus in men's daily discourse, when they speak of a person as
being 'frank', or when they use the words 'franchise', 'enfranchisement',
to express civil liberties and immunities, their language here is the
outgrowth, the record, and the result of great historic changes, bears
testimony to facts of history, whereof it may well happen that the
speakers have never heard. Let me suggest to you the word 'slave', as
one which has undergone a process entirely analogous, although in an
opposite direction. . . .

Lecture II
On the Morality in Words

Seeing then that language contains so faithful a record of the good and
of the evil which in times past have been working in the minds and
hearts of men, we shall not err, regarding it as a moral barometer,
which indicates and permanently marks the rise or fall of a nation's

life. To study a people's language will be to study *them*, and to study them at best advantage; there where they present themselves to us under fewest disguises, most nearly as they are. Too many have had a hand in it, and in causing it to arrive at its present shape, it is too entirely the collective work of the whole nation, the result of the united contributions of all, it obeys too immutable laws, to allow any successful tampering with it, any making of it to witness other than the actual facts of the case.

Thus the frivolity of an age or nation, its mockery of itself, its inability to comprehend the true dignity and meaning of life, the feebleness of its moral indignation against evil, all this will find an utterance in the use of solemn and earnest words in senses comparatively trivial or even ridiculous, in the squandering of such as ought to have been reserved for the highest mysteries of the spiritual life on slight and secular objects, in the employment almost in jest and play, it may be in honour of words implying the deepest moral guilt — as the French 'perfide', 'malice', 'malin'; while, on the contrary, the high sentiment, the scorn of everything mean or base of another people or time, will as certainly in one way or another stamp themselves on the words which they employ; and thus will it be with whatever good or evil they may own.

Often a people's use of some single word will offer us a deeper insight into their real condition, their habits of thought and feeling, than whole volumes written expressly with the intention of imparting this insight. Thus our word 'idiot' is abundantly characteristic, not indeed of English but of Greek life, from which we have derived it and our use of it. The ἰδιώτης, or 'idiot', was in its earliest sense the *private* man, as contradistinguished from him who was clothed with some office, and had a share in the management of public affairs. In this its primary use it is occasionally employed in English; as by Jeremy Taylor, when he says 'Humility is a duty in great ones as well as in *idiots*'. It came then to signify a rude, ignorant, unskilled, intellectualy unexercised person, a boor; this derived or secondary use bearing witness, as has been most truly said, to 'the Greek notion of the indispensableness of public life, even to the right development of the intellect', a conviction which was clearly inwoven in the Greek habit of thought, and lay at the foundation of all schemes of mental culture. Nor is it easy to see how it could have uttered itself with greater clearness than in this secondary use of the word 'idiot'. Our tertiary, according to which the 'idiot' is one deficient in intellect, not merely with its powers unexercised, is but this secondary pushed a little further. — Again, the innermost distinctions between the Greek mind and the Hebrew reveal themselves in the several salutations of each, in the 'Rejoice' of the first, as contrasted with the 'Peace' of the second. The clear, cheerful, world-enjoying temper of the Greek embodies itself in the first; he could desire nothing better or higher for himself, nor wish it for his friend, than to have *joy* in his life. But the Hebrew had a deeper longing within him, and one which finds utterance in his 'Peace'. It is not hard to find why this latter people should have been chosen of the first bearers of that truth which indeed enables truly to *rejoice*, but only through first bringing *peace*; nor why from them the word of life should first go forth. It may be urged, indeed, that these were only forms, and so in great measure they have at length become; as in our 'good-by' or 'adieu' we can hardly be said now to commit our friend to Divine protection; yet still they were not such at the first, nor would they have held their ground, if ever they had become such altogether.

So too the modifications of meaning which a word has undergone, as it has been transplanted from one soil to another, the way in which one nation receiving a word from another, has yet brought into it some new force which was foreign to it in the tongue from whence it was borrowed, has deepened, or extenuated, or otherwise altered its meaning, — all this may prove profoundly instructive, and may reveal to us, as perhaps nothing else would, the most fundamental diversities existing between them. Observe, for instance, how different is the word 'self-sufficient' as used by us, and by the heathen nations of antiquity. The Greek word exactly corresponding is a word of honour, and applied to men in their praise. And indeed it was the glory of the heathen philosophy to teach man to find his resources in his own bosom, to be thus sufficient for himself; and seeing that a true centre without him and above him, a centre in God, had not been revealed to him, it was no shame for him to seek it there; better this than no centre at all. But the Gospel has taught us another lesson, to find our sufficiency in God; and thus 'self-sufficient', which with the Greek was a word in honourable use, is not so with us. 'Self-sufficiency' is not a quality which any man desires now to be attributed to him. We have a feeling about the word, which causes it to carry its own condemnation with it; and its different uses, for honour once, for reproach now, do in fact ground themselves on the central differences of heathenism and Christianity.

Once more, we might safely conclude that a nation would not be likely tamely to submit to tyranny and wrong, which had made 'quarrel' out of 'querela'. The Latin word means properly 'complaint', and we have in 'querelous' this its proper meaning coming distinctly out. Not so, however, in 'quarrel'; for Englishmen being wont not merely to complain, but to set vigorously about righting and redressing themselves, their griefs being also grievances, out of this word, which might have given them only 'querelous' and 'querelousness', have gotten 'quarrel' as well.

On the other hand we cannot wonder that Italy should have filled our Great Exhibition with beautiful specimens of her skills in the arts, with statues and sculptures of rare loveliness, but should only rivet her chains more closely by the weak and ineffectual efforts which she makes to break them, when she can degrade the word 'virtuoso', or the 'virtuous', to signify one accomplished in painting, music, and sculpture, such things as are the ornamental fringe of a nation's life, but can never be made, without loss of all manliness of character, its main texture and woof − not to say that excellence in these fine arts has been in too many cases divorced from all true virtue and worth. And what shall we say concerning the uses to which she turns her 'bravo'? The opposite exaggeration of the ancient dwellers in Italy, who often made 'virtus' to signify warlike courage alone, as if for them all virtues were included in this one, was at all events more tolerable than this; for there is a sense in which a man's 'valour' is his value. − How little, again, the modern Italians live in the spirit of their ancient worthies, or reverence the greatest among them, we may argue from the fact that they have been content to take the name of one among their nobles, and degrade it so far that every glib and loquacious hireling who shows strangers around their picture galleries, palaces and ruins, is termed by them a 'Cicerone', or a 'Cicero'! So too the French use of the word 'honnêteté', as external civilty, marks a tendency to accept the shows and pleasant courtesies of social life in the room of deeper moral qualities.

How much too may be learned by noting the words which nations have been obliged to borrow from other nations, as not having them of home-growth − this in most cases, if not in all, testifying that the thing itself was not native, was only an exotic, transplanted, like the word which indicated it, from a foreign soil. Thus it is singularly characteristic of the social and political life of England, as distinguished from that of the other European nations, that to it alone the word 'club' belongs; the French and German languages having been alike unable to grow a word of their own as its equivalent, having both been obliged to borrow this from us. And no wonder; for these voluntary associations of men for the furthering of such social or political ends as are near to the hearts of the associates could have only had their rise under such favourable circumstances as ours. In no country where there was not extreme personal freedom could they have sprung up; and as little in any where men did not know how to use this freedom with moderation and self-restraint, could they long have been endured. It was comparatively easy to adopt the word; but the ill success of the 'club' itself everywhere save here where it is native, has shown that it was not so easy to transplant the thing. While we have lent this and other words mostly political to the French and German, it would not be less instructive, were this a suitable opportunity, to trace our corresponding obligations to them.

But it is time to bring this lecture to an end. These illustrations, to which it would not be hard to add many more, are amply enough to justify what I have asserted of the existence of a moral element in words; they are enough to make us feel about them, that they do not hold themselves neutral in the great conflict between good and evil, light and darkness, which is dividing the world; that they are not content to be the passive vehicle, now of the truth, now of falsehood. We see on the contrary that they continually take their side, are some of them children of light, others children of this world, or even of darkness; they beat with the pulses of our life; they stir with our passions; they receive from us the impressions of our good and of our evil, which again they are active to propagate amongst us. Must we not own then that there is a wondrous and mysterious world, of which we may hitherto have taken too little account, around us and about us? And may there not be a deeper meaning than hitherto we have attached to it, lying in that solemn declaration, 'By thy words thou shalt be justified, and by thy words thou shalt be condemned'?

TEXT AND SELECTED READING

The text is taken from a set of lectures delivered by Trench to 'the pupils at the diocesan training school, Winchester' and first published as *On the Study of Words* in 1851. Again, the best study of the historical context of the piece is Hans Aarsleff, *The Study of Language in England 1780–1860* (Princeton: Princeton University Press, 1967), while Tony Crowley, *The Politics of Discourse* (London: Macmillan, 1989) examines the political and cultural significance of Trench's work. A specific view of approaches to language at the time is given in L. Dowling, 'Victorian Oxford and the Science of Language', *PMLA*, 97 (1982), and the theological background to much of the contemporary debate is examined in J. Burrow, 'The Uses of Philology in Victorian Britain' in *Ideas and Institutions of Victorian Britain*, ed. R. Robson (New York: Barnes and Noble, 1967). The more general history of linguistic thought in the nineteenth century is presented by H. Pedersen, *The Discovery of Language: Linguistic Science in the Nineteenth Century* (1931; trans. J.W. Spargo, Bloomington: Indiana University Press, 1959).

11

Proposal

It was Trench who read two important papers to the Philological Society in 1857 which led to the *Proposal* set out below. This in turn resulted in the project which became the *New* (subsequently *Oxford*) *English Dictionary* published between 1888 and 1933. Trench's papers 'On Some Deficiencies in Our English Dictionaries' fulfilled the task of reviewing previous dictionaries and setting out a plan for a future work which would rectify their faults. Many of the points in the *Proposal* are in fact taken from Trench's papers, not the least his contention that the dictionary should be 'an historical monument, the history of a nation contemplated from one point of view'. The linkage of language and nation demonstrates once more how important this line of thought was in the linguistic study of the period. It is a relationship which was to have important implications for the study of literature, history and politics.

The methodological difficulties of the lexicographer, discussed by Johnson, were treated in full in the *Proposal* and are worth considering. There are five main points:

1 The dictionary should be exhaustive.
2 It should take as 'authorities all English books'.
3 When dealing with these authorities it should be aware of the historical limits of possible quotation, and thereby impose an historical limit upon the language.
4 It was to treat each word according to the 'historical principle' by tracing the development of the senses of the word and the history of its use in the language.
5 It should ascertain the word's etymology within the language, and demonstrate its cognate history in other languages.

It may be best to consider these principles in reverse order. The fifth point concerns 'internal' and 'external' etymology and aims to find both the English *etymon* (root word) and the non-English *etymon* of the English root. This is interesting in that it means that at least at one level the word is considered to be an essence which remains the same despite all the historical differences of form and meaning. If the essential unity were not present then searching for the etymology would be a fruitless task; but the concept of an essential unity which resists historical variability is one which extends into other areas of discourse (such as nationalism) with profound effect. Point four is related to the fifth point in that it too reiterates the question of a word's essential unity by aiming to trace the history of a single coherent unit over and against variation in both form and sense (this time within the language). As with an individual life, a word constantly differs but essentially remains the same; and it is on this principle that the 'biographies of words' (as one linguist put it) could be constructed. Point three is likewise related to the former point since if it is possible to publish the birth and death notices for individual words, then it is clear that this can only take place if the language itself is given historical limits. For if the historical limits of the language are not fixed then it would not be possible to say when an English word 'first' appears. If, for example, the language is taken to date from 1250, then English words must be born after that date. Of course their cognate relations might pre-exist in other languages, but English words could not exist until the language itself 'first' appears. The implications of this necessary imposition of historical limits are profound indeed when we recall the inter-linking of language and nation; for what is at stake is not just the historical dating of the beginning of the language, but of the nation and people too. Needless to say, such a vexed question was to cause endless difficulties for the lexicographers.

The first and second points can be taken together, though they are related to the other points in that they are based on the conception of a national literature which has evolved historically. However, they are interesting in another way since they posit not only the place where the lexicographers are to find their material, but also what sort of material it was precisely that they were to seek. The location of the lexicographers' source material was of course English literature itself, the written records of the language. Thus the dictionary was to contain 'every word occurring in the literature of the language it professes to illustrate'. The effect that this had on the development of English studies cannot be underestimated; for as a practical measure it meant that the lexicographers and their co-workers would have to systematise, classify, and even distribute English literature in order to gain access to the linguistic material. It is thus no coincidence that this is the period in which the foundations of the discipline of English studies are set down. However, the problem with this material source for the lexicographers was quite simply its diversity, for it was rapidly discovered that if 'all English books' were taken as authorities, then confusion and indeterminacy would vanquish the attempt to impose order and clarity. It is for this reason that the lexicographers came up with the brilliant methodological solution to the problem of historical and geographical variation in the language of the literary texts which they were to examine. That is, they imposed a delimitation on the form of the language with which they were primarily concerned and it occurs thus in the *Proposal*: 'As soon as a standard language has been formed, which in England was the case after the Reformation, the lexicographer is bound to deal with that alone.' In fact the supplement to the *Oxford English Dictionary* has this as the first use of the term 'standard English' and it is important to note that it refers here to the standard literary language which is held to have appeared after a certain date and to take a particular, recognisable form. This definition will be of crucial importance in later texts when we shall see the term change its significance. If it refers here to a form of writing which was used nationally (an important political definition in its own right), then later it is to signify the spoken form of the language belonging to a certain class.

PROPOSAL FOR THE PUBLICATION OF A NEW ENGLISH DICTIONARY BY THE PHILOLOGICAL SOCIETY

In the year 1857 the Philological Society determined to form a collection of words hitherto unregistered in the Dictionaries of Johnson and Richardson, with a view to publishing a supplementary volume, which might be used with either of those works. A committee was appointed, circulars were issued, and the public as well as members of the Society were invited to take part in the work. The success of the experiment was so encouraging, that some members of the Society, unwilling that the energies thus brought into play should be expended in the production of a work necessarily of a subordinate and imperfect character, strongly urged the propriety of extending the scheme to the compilation of a new and more Scientific Dictionary than any at present existing. This proposal was, after much deliberation, entertained and accepted, and the Philological Society, at its meeting of January 7, 1858, resolved that, instead of the Supplement to the standard English Dictionaries, then in course of preparation by the Society's Unregistered Words Committee, a new Dictionary of the English Language should be prepared under the authority of the Philological Society. The work has been placed by the Society in the hands of two Committees; the one Literary and Historical, consisting of the Very Rev. the Dean of Westminster, F.J. Furnivall, Esq., and H. Coleridge, Esq., Secretary; and the other Etymological, consisting of Hensleigh Wedgwood, Esq., and Professor Malden; and the former of these will edit the Dictionary and direct the general working of the scheme. Arrangements for the publication of the work in 5s. Parts have been made with Messrs. Trubner and Co., of Paternoster Row.

The object of the present Prospectus is twofold: first, to lay before the public, as concisely as possible, the main outlines of the plan upon which the New Dictionary will be constructed, and to ask from that public such further help in the reading and noting of books as will enable the plan to be carried out satisfactorily; and, secondly, to furnish our contributors with such a system of rules as will direct them to the principal points to be attended to in perusing and analysing the books they may undertake, and also ensure general uniformity in the results arrived at. It will of course be understood that we cannot, within the limits of a mere circular like the present, do more than state the conclusions at which we have arrived, without attempting to enter into any arguments in their behalf, or any refutations by anticipation of possible objections. The whole subject will be most naturally and conveniently discussed in the preface to the work itself, and we must reserve our defence, if any be thought necessary, until that appears. Those who may wish for further satisfaction as to our lexicographical creed, than what can be gathered from this Prospectus, are referred to the Dean of Westminster's Essay 'On Some Deficiencies in our English Dictionaries', which leaves no important portion of the subject unnoticed.

I. We may begin then by stating that, according to our view, the first requirement of every lexicon is, that it should contain *every word occurring in the literature of the language it professes to illustrate*. We entirely repudiate the theory, which converts the lexicographer into an arbiter of style, and leaves it in his discretion to accept or reject words according to his private notions of their comparative elegance or inelegance. In the case of the dead languages, such as Greek, no lexicon of any pretensions would omit the ἄπαξ λεγόμενα of Lycophron, or the experimental coinages of Aristophanes and the other comedians; and as we are unable to perceive any difference between a dead and living language, so far as lexicographical treatment is concerned, it follows that we cannot refuse to admit words into the Dictionary which may not be sanctioned by the usage of more than one writer, or be conformable in their structure to our ideas of taste. However worthless they may be in themselves, they testify to a tendency of language, and on this account only, if on no other, have a distinct and appreciable value.

II. We admit as authorities all English books, except such as are devoted to purely scientific subjects, as treatises on electricity, mathematics, &c., and works written subsequently to the Reformation for the purpose of illustrating provincial dialects. As soon as a standard language has been formed, which in England was the case after the Reformation, the lexicographer is bound to deal with that alone; before that epoch, however, the English language was in reality another name for the sum of a number of local languages, all exhibiting an English type distinct from the Saxon, and therefore all equally entitled to notice as authorities in the formation of a Dictionary. At the same time we may reserve to ourselves a discretion of deciding, in doubtful cases, what shall or shall not be deemed a Dictionary authority, – a discretion which from special cases may often be required and usefully exercised without at all infringing on the generality of the principles we have just laid down.

III. The limits of quotation in point of time are next to be fixed. We have decided to commence with the commencement of English, or, more strictly speaking, with that definite appearance of an English type of language, distinct from the preceding semi-Saxon, which took place around the end of the reign of Henry III. Of course this, like every other line of demarcation, is hard to draw, and occasions a few apparent incongruities, some of the books included in our thirteenth-century list retaining much more of their Saxon matrix than others; but on the whole it would be difficult, if not impossible, to fix the limit lower down without excluding books which it would be most undesirable to lose.

IV. In the treatment of individual words the historical principle will be uniformly adopted; – that is to say, we shall endeavour to show more clearly and fully than has hitherto been done, or even attempted, the development of the sense or various senses of each word from its etymology and from each other, so as to bring into clear light the common thread which unites all together. The greatest care will also be taken to fix as accurately as possible, by means of appropriate quotations, the epoch of the appearance of each word in the language, and, in the case of archaisms and obsolete words, of their disappearance also; and the limits of the various phases of meaning exhibited by each individual will be defined, as far as possible, in like manner and by the same means.

V. Lastly, in the Etymological department of our work, where, as is well known, there is the most pressing need for improvement, we shall in addition to the proximate origin of each word, exhibit several of its affinities with the related languages for the sake of comparison, always including that language which seems to present the radical element contained in the word in its oldest form. Examples illustrating our meaning will be found in the sequel [to the Proposal].

The same principle of volunteer co-operation will apply to this portion of our work as to the other, and the labours of any contributors who may be willing to send in suggestions as to difficult etymologies, or emendations of those already in the Dictionaries, or lists of words illustrating any philological laws, such as those of letter-change, will receive every consideration.

And such contributions as the Etymological Committee shall deem worthy of insertion, in cases where there is room for a fair difference of opinion, although they may not themselves adopt the views therein propounded, will in all cases be distinguished by the initials of the contributors. It may be added here, that the following gentlemen have kindly consented to aid the Etymological Committee by their advice and assistance in doubtful cases:– The Lord Bishop of St. David's, Sir F. Madden, Professor Key, Professor Goldstucker, Thos. Watts, Esq., Rev. J. Davies, Professor Siegfried, Dr. Halbertsman, M. de Haan Hettema, &c.

We must now recur to the Literary and Historical portion of our work, in order to state the points on which we ask for help. The periods into which our language may, for philological purposes, be most conveniently divided, are three: 1. From its rise, cir. 1250, to the Reformation − of which the appearance of the first printed English translation of the New Testament may be taken as the beginning. 2. From the Reformation to Milton (1526–1674, the date of Milton's death). 3. From Milton to our own day. As a general rule, we desire to give instances of the use of every word in each of these periods, or in as

many of them as it occurs in, besides noting all changes of sense, &c.,
– though, considering the unequal importance of different words, we
reserve to ourselves the discretion of diminishing or increasing the
number of quotations to be given under any word. In order, therefore,
to carry out our desire, and recollecting that we have to catch every
word on its first appearance in our literature, we have recently issued
an alphabetical list of all A.D. 1250–1300 words; and we ask our
contributors to read among them all the printed books of the remainder
of the first period, viz. 1300–1526, the fourteenth-century literature
being taken first, – each contributor giving us extracts containing
both the new and obsolete words occurring in the particular books
taken by him that fall within our rules hereafter given.

For the period 1526–1674, we shall ask each contributor for a
quotation for every word, phrase idiom, &c. in his book that does not
occur in the Concordances to the Bible and Shakespere, or that to the
Bible only, if the Shakespere Concordance be unprocurable. It is true
that this plan will fail to give the earliest use of those few words which,
though used in the Bible or Shakespere, yet were first used by some of
the earliest writers of the interval between 1526 and Shakespere; but
the universal accessibility of Cruden's Concordance, as one of the
bases of comparison, presents advantages too great, as our former
experience has taught us, to be lightly overlooked; and we must trust
to the vigilance of our contributors to supply this unavoidable defect
in our scheme.

For the period from 1674 to the present day, we shall after a time
issue a list of Burke's works, and ask for a quotation from the modern
writers for all words &c. not in the list.

In the mean time, however, contributors who may prefer to work at
the literature of this period will render us an invaluable service by a
careful analysis of the works of any of the principal writers, extracting
all remarkable words, and all passages which contain definitions or
explanations, or which, by reason of their intrinsic merit, are specially
eligible as illustrative quotations. We have not given a list of these
writers, as their names must be familiar to all; but Wordsworth, Scott,
Coleridge, Southey, Tennyson, Ruskin, Macaulay, and Froude may
be mentioned as pre-eminently important. Let us say here, that the
whole of the 18th-century literature has been handed over to our
American collaborators, a subcommittee for the purpose of assisting
in the work having been recently organised in that country. Of this
sub-committee the Hon. G.P. Marsh, of Burlington, Vermont, has
kindly consented to act as Secretary.

And in each period we shall ask our contributors to give us extracts for words now obsolete, in order that we may, by comparing such extracts, ascertain the last appearance in our literature of every such obsolete word.

And further we shall gladly receive, 1st, any well-considered definitions of words; and, 2nd, any well-considered distinctions of words from the synonyms with which they are likely to be confounded.

A few practical remarks may be added in conclusion. Two great obstacles have to be encountered during the early part of the work which nothing but the earnest cooperation of those who have knowledge, and of those also who have leisure, will suffice to overcome. In the first place, the difficulties of the language, in which the early romances, &c., are written, will, we fear, operate to deter many from rendering assistance, whose services would prove valuable if employed on an Elizabethan author; and secondly, the excessive rarity of most of the books themselves, which form our authorities for this period, will exclude nearly all who cannot read them in the British Museum or the Bodleian, or some other large library, where alone they are likely to be found. Many poems and other pieces, a collation of which would be invaluable for such a work as this, still lie in MS. Others have been brought out by printing clubs of exclusive constitution, such as the Roxburghe and Abbotsford, or for private circulation only, and might, for all that the public in general is the better for them, just as well have remained in MS., being of course utterly unprocurable, except in great libraries, and not always there. We cannot but express an earnest hope that those who are qualified to assist us in this portion of our task (and there are many) will not hesitate to come forward at once, and save us from the necessity of delegating that, which no efforts of our own will enable us to accomplish by ourselves, to persons less fitted for this peculiar work.

We have endeavoured to include in the foregoing remarks all such information regarding the plan and theory of our Dictionary as may enable the public to judge of its pretensions and claims to support. Mere typographical and editorial details respecting the size of the work, or the arrangement of the articles, must be made the subjects of a special communication: it would obviously be premature to speak decidedly on such points now, or to bond ourselves down to adopt a certain form, which subsequent experience might lead us to modify with advantage. All that is desired at present is to enlist the sympathies of the public on behalf of the work, and to bring, as far as possible, the scattered learning and energy which exists plentifully enough in this country, if it can be but effectually reached and addressed, to bear upon a common, and we may add national, project. At present it is abundantly clear, that England does not possess a Dictionary worthy of her language; nor, as long as lexicography is confined to the isolated efforts of a single man, is it possible that such a work should be written. We do but follow the example of the Grimms when we call upon Englishmen to come forward and write their own Dictionary for themselves, and we trust that our invitation may be responded to still more effectually than theirs has been.

TEXT AND SELECTED READING

The text of the *Proposal* is taken from the Appendix to the *Transactions of the Philological Society*, 1858. The historical evolution of the Dictionary project is detailed in Hans Aarsleff, 'The Early History of the Oxford English Dictionary', *Bulletin of the New York Public Library*, 66 (Sept. 1962) and Hans Aarsleff, *The Study of Language in England 1780–1860* (Princeton: Princeton University Press, 1967). An interesting account is also given in K.M.E. Murray, *Caught in the Web of Words* (Oxford: Clarendon, 1979). The political significance of the project is examined in Tony Crowley, *The Politics of Discourse* (London: Macmillan, 1989) and T. Davies, 'Education, Ideology and Literature', *Red Letters*, 7 (1978).

12

G.F. Graham

Languages are not 'pure' in the strict sense of that term, argues Graham at the start of his essay. That is, languages are not free-standing, self-sufficient, and untainted by historical contact with other languages. In fact they interweave so tightly that one nineteenth-century linguist thought it pertinent to ask:

> In some cases it might even be made a question when it was that the language properly began, at what point in the unbroken thread which undoubtedly connects every form of human speech with a succession of preceding forms out of which it has sprung, we are to say that an old language has died and a new one come into existence.
>
> (George L. Craik, *Outlines of The History of the English Language For The Use of Junior Classes in Schools*, 1851)

Linguistic boundaries are amongst the most difficult to fix, and, as Graham's essay notes, also the hardest to police.

Arguing that languages are subject to attack from without (in effect the processes described by Saussure as falling under 'external linguistics'), Graham's major concern, however, is with 'internal corruptions'. His first example betrays the confusion which marks an approach which sees the impossibility of linguistic (and thus cultural) purity, but longs for it as a resolution. The contraction of words is viewed by Graham as probably originating in 'a loose, careless way of speaking', or 'vicious and slovenly pronunciation' and is therefore attacked as an impurity. Yet he also notes that words have 'a natural tendency to contraction' and that 'it may be laid down as a rule that words, as they grow older, degenerate in meaning and contract in form'. The tension between these two views can be taken as evidence of the difficulties such a commentator faced: the desire to preserve

159

purity coupled with the impossibility of changing rules and 'natural tendencies'. The example of linguistic contraction also offers interesting testimony to Saussure's remark that language users are not aware of the diachronic past of any unit and are only concerned with its present significance in the synchronic system. Graham's account of contraction is interesting in this respect since one of his examples embodies precisely the claim made by Saussure. For when Graham claims that 'mite' is the syncopated form of 'minute', and that 'minute' was known before 'mite', he illustrates that such knowledge of a form's past is irrelevant to its present use. In fact, 'mite' and 'minute' have distinct (though confused) etymological roots and both appear in the language at about the same time. Ironically enough, if the warping or distorting of a word by 'a mistaken notion of its derivation' is a 'corruption', then Graham has convicted himself of the offence.

However, Graham is quite specific about the responsibility for the worst corruptions and is not slow to attribute blame. For in a repetition of eighteenth-century emphases, it is the 'common people' who are viewed as the corrupters. Again, however, his own examples betray the prejudices upon which his own account is based. By far the majority of his examples are taken from what he calls 'high life': fashion, the bourgeois kitchen, parliament, the universities, the private schools of Eton and Harrow, lawyers and merchants. These examples are not stigmatised in the way that those taken from other classes of society are derided. For if slang consists of those 'vulgar, unauthorised terms which have come into fashion during the last eighty or ninety years', then the language of specific non-fashionable groups does not even rise to the level of slang. Their usage is 'cant': 'the secret language of thieves, beggars and tramps, by which they endeavour to conceal their evil deeds from the public'. Whatever the distinctions drawn between the different forms of illicit vocabulary, it is clear that Graham sees a need to purify the language. Slang, he comments, is a 'pest to society', an 'epidemic', 'an infectious disease' and an 'evil' which 'every Englishman who has a proper feeling for his language' would condemn.

If slang is one danger then Americanisms are another, the result of the 'recklessness with which the Americans use the English language'. Again we see the contestation of cultural ascendancy between America and Britain which centres upon the language. For Graham of course there is no question but that Americanisms are 'interlopers', which again indicates the logic of the inside and the outside, of those who belong and those who are aliens, which tends to dominate these debates. Americans may set great store by liberty, he says, 'and of course we have no right whatever to interfere with their opinions concerning principles or forms of political government', but when Americans 'think proper to take liberties with our language' then it becomes a serious matter. England has to be the source of authority for English usage since it is the location of the purest form of the language. Departures from sanctioned English usage 'must be looked upon as abortions or deformations of our language', 'monstrosities' which cannot be countenanced.

Of course the introduction 'of all sorts of meanings, words and phrases' was not a new development in the history of English usage. Shakespeare for example was a writer of 'fire-new words' as were many of his contemporaries in the period of the 'golden age' of the language. In fact if we return to that period we find a lesson that might also apply to Graham's strictures. For Jonson's *The Poetaster: Or His Arraignment* (1602) is at least in part a satire on the introduction of new 'wild outlandish terms' into the language. In the play Crispinus, a would-be poet, is given a physic in order that he should vomit and thus clear his system of his 'peculiar dialect'. The cathartic works and he pukes up such terms as 'glibbery', 'lubrical', 'magnificate', 'snotteries', 'turgidous', 'ventosity', 'oblatrant', 'furibund', 'fatuate', 'prorumped' and 'obstupefact'. After having brought up all such terms Crispinus is then cured of his verbal sickness. However, the lesson of the play is not the success of the satire but its historical failure. For along with the words mentioned above as examples of words which need to be banished from the language we also find others. These are (with the dates given to their coinage by the *OED*), 'reciprocal' (1570), 'defunct' (1548), 'spurious' (1598), 'clumsie' (1597) and 'inflate' (1502). What we see from this is that attempts to police the purity of the language are doomed to failure. It is true of Jonson's efforts, as it is true of those of Graham; for he too attempted to banish words which have since found a place in the language. 'Americanisms' such as 'to raise', 'to fix', 'recuperate', 'rowdy', 'rile', 'stampede', 'slick', 'spry', 'boss', 'to progress', 'right away', are his examples of words to be banished. What can be concluded from this failure is the general point that what counts as 'proper English' at any particular time depends upon a set of flexible and open-ended criteria which change constantly.

A BOOK ABOUT WORDS

Chapter XIII
Slang Words and Americanisms

No language is, or ever has been, in the strict sense of the word *pure*. All languages are continually borrowing and lending – adopting words from foreign sources, and contributing from their own store to that of others. It is now well known that the ancient Greeks borrowed largely from the Oriental tongues, and lent words and forms to Latin. Latin, again borrowed from Greek, and contributed to form the modern Italian, Spanish and French. The modern German language is just now strongly affected by a French influence; and French itself, though for the most part Latin, contains many Celtic and not a few Germanic words. Spanish, which is in the main Latin, has a very considerable admixture of Arabic, brought in by the Moors in the eighth century; and English is well known to be made up of Anglo-Saxon, Norman French, and Latin.

But languages are not only subject to these attacks from without, a process of internal corruption is also set up, and appears in various forms. One of these may be recognised in the principle of contraction. It may be laid down as a rule that words, as they grow older, degenerate in meaning and contract in form. This contraction probably originated in a loose, careless way of speaking, which afterwards affected the written language. Sometimes a letter or syllable is cut off from the beginning of a word; sometimes one is taken from the middle or the end. '*Bus*' is now all we have left (at any rate, in ordinary conversation) of '*omnibus*'. '*Fantasy*' has lost its middle syllable, and appears as '*fancy*', and '*cab*' does duty for '*cabriolet*'. One conclusion this result enables us to draw is that the contracted forms are always the more modern. The form 'courtesy' existed before 'curtsy'; 'procurator' preceded 'proctor'; and 'minute' was known before 'mite'. Whether these contractions are to be regarded favourably or otherwise may be a question, but there is no doubt that they are all produced by the operation of a natural law of language which no human power will ever be able to prevent.

When a word is warped or distorted from its original form, either by a vicious or slovenly pronunciation, or from a mistaken notion of its derivation, it is said to be a corruption. One of these corruptions appears in our word 'surgeon'. The French 'chirurgien', from which it immediately comes, shows more clearly its Greek origin – χείρ (cheir), a hand; and ἔργω (ergo), I work — i.e. a hand-worker, or manual operator. But a careless pronunciation, probably aided by a natural tendency to contraction, has caused the word with us to dwindle down to 'surgeon'.

As an illustration of corruption arising from a false notion of its derivation, we may take the word 'island'. How did the *s* get into it? This *s* is not sounded, and yet it must be written. In the one word 'island', there is a mixture of Latin and German. The first syllable is of Romance, and the second of Teutonic origin. The Latin for 'island' is 'insula', from 'in' and 'salo', the salt (sea, understood). The Anglo-Saxon word for the same idea was 'ea-land'. Here '*ea*' means 'water'. This '*ea*', or '*ey*', is found in many names of islands, as 'Angls*ea*', 'Jers*ey*', 'Guerns*ey*', &c. '*Ea*-land', then meant 'water-land', or 'land surrounded by water'. In the earlier editions of 'Paradise Lost', the word always appeared written 'iland' (without the s), which points more clearly to its Saxon derivation, and is nearer in spelling to the modern German — 'Eiland'. The '*s*' was afterwards inserted from a mistaken notion that the word was of Latin, and not German, origin.

A false analogy will sometimes give rise to a corrupted form of spelling. The past tense of 'can' was originally 'coude', not 'cou*l*d'; and the *l* was afterwards introduced, from the apparent analogy of the word to 'wou*l*d', from 'will', and 'shou*l*d', from 'shall'. This, then, is a corruption. But, though at first incorrect, it must now be retained.

Proper names, both of places and persons, have suffered a good deal from this influence. Words of this class are most likely to be corrupted, because they are most frequently in the mouths of the common people. That 'Birmingham' should be called 'Brummagem', 'Cirencester', 'Siseter', and 'Wavertree', 'Wartree', is not surprising when we remember that these corruptions originated with those who had often to pronounce, but seldom, if ever, to write these names. But what is, perhaps, more strange, many of these corruptions are now adopted by the upper classes. Thus, in all ranks of society, the proper name 'Beauchamp' is now pronounced 'Beecham'; 'St. John' is called 'Sinjon'; 'Choldmondeley' is pronounced 'Chumley', and 'Marjoribanks' 'Marchbanks'.

Slang Words

Among the many signs of the corruption of the English language, one, which is not the least remarkable, is the prevalent use of slang words and phrases. That certain terms should be peculiar to certain callings, trades, or professions, may be naturally expected, but that these should be extended into general conversation, is a corroborative proof of the strong liking people now have for anything unusual or out-of-the-way. One very curious fact may here be observed. While the style of most of our periodical writers soars upwards, and affects the lofty and sublime, that of general conversation is the very reverse, and sinks to the low and vulgar.

A difference must be here made between 'cant' and 'slang'. The first signifies the secret language of thieves, beggars and tramps, by which they endeavour to conceal their evil deeds from the public. The knowledge and practice of this kind of language is confined to the above-named fraternities. But slang consists of those vulgar, un-authorised terms, which have come into fashion during the last eighty or ninety years, and which are not confined to one class, but may be now heard in almost every grade of society.

In all trades and professions there are certain terms peculiar to each, which are properly called 'technical'; these can hardly be denominated slang. For example, in the language of actors, a '*length*' signifies forty-two lines of the part each has to study for the stage. They say, a part consists of so many 'lengths'. This, and other such terms, are seldom, if ever, heard beyond the circle to which they properly belong. But slang is found in almost all classes of society. That of high life is drawn from various sources. One of its phases may be seen in the French words and forms which would-be fashionable people so delight in using. To call a breakfast a *déjeuner* is absurd, especially as we have a good word of our own to express that meal. Leaders of fashion never speak of the fashionable world; but of the 'beau monde'. This 'beau monde', they tell us, give 'recherchés' entertainments, attended by the 'élite' of society. Lady *So-*and-*So* gave a 'thé dansant', which, of course, 'went off with éclat', &c. &c. Many so-called fashionable ladies and gentlemen would, probably, be deeply offended to hear such language termed slang; but any words or forms which are not recognised English certainly deserve to be so stigmatised.

This form of slang is confined chiefly to the would-be fashionables, and to those writers of very questionable taste, who use what they think funny and startling expressions in a novel and flippant way. Cookery also has given us much slang of this sort. If we were to ask, in an ordinary English hotel, for 'côtelettes à la jardinière', or a 'vol-au-vent à la financière', the people of the house would probably stare at us; but these and such expressions form the staple of the style of many popular novelists.

Of parliamentary slang, too, there is no lack of examples. Lord Palmerston, and Mr. Disraeli are perhaps better known as *Pam* and *Dizzy*, than by their proper names. A single vote to one candidate at an election is called a 'plumper'; and those who have boiled a pot in a house, to qualify themselves to vote, are termed 'potwallopers'. Among military men, anyone unusually particular about his dress or personal appearance is called a 'dandy' or a 'swell'. They also call a 'title' a 'handle to your name', and a kind-hearted, good-natured fellow is, with them, a 'trump', or a 'brick'.

The Universities also have their slang terms. The graduates use 'crib' for a house; 'deadmen' for empty wine-bottles; 'governor', or 'relieving-officer', for a father; 'plucked', for defeated or rejected in an examination; and 'row' for a disturbance.

The Eton and Harrow boys make use among themselves of many slang terms, which are not often heard outside their bounds; but when they return home from their holidays, they frequently infect their sisters with some of their strange phraseology. A boy will sometimes puzzle his sisters at home by asking them if they do not find his 'toggery' absolutely 'stunning'; or what they think of his 'tile', or white 'choker'; adding that they are not yet paid for; but that he supposes the 'governor' will have to 'stump up', or 'fork out the blunt', &c.

Lawyers also have their slang; and this is not surprising when we remember the many opportunities they must have of hearing it, from their connection with the police courts, and with life in its worst phases. With them, taking the benefit of the Insolvent Debtors Act, is to be 'whitewashed'; and to draw up a fraudulent balance sheet is to 'cook' accounts, &c.

But of all the forms of slang, the one most abundant in variety of terms is the mercantile. It has been calculated that there are as many as thirty-six vulgar synonyms for the one simple word *money*. The following are a few of them: '*blunt*', '*tin*', '*coppers*', '*browns*', '*shiners*', '*yellow-boys*', '*flimsies*' (bank notes); '*fivers*' (five pound notes), &c. &c. In city phraseology, 100,000*l*. is called a *plum*, and one million sterling is a *marigold*. On the Stock Exchange buyers and sellers for the account are called 'bulls' and 'bears': a broker who is unable to pay his debts, is there called a 'lame-duck'; and if expelled from the house, is said to 'waddle'.

But though most of these terms will never form a legitimate part of the English language, some of them are certainly not considered so vulgar as others. It is said that the elegant Lord Chesterfield was the author of the word 'humbug', which, though it may have been considered slang in his day, can hardly be so called now. Another word, 'hoax', was condemned by Swift as low and vulgar, this, too, has made its way; and is not so revolting to good taste as it probably was when first used. Both these words, 'humbug' and 'hoax', are to be found in Dr. Latham's edition of Johnson's Dictionary.

Thackeray immortalised 'snob' in his celebrated 'papers'; and though the word is not to be recommended, it must be allowed that it is very expressive. Lord Cairns, in a speech in the House of Commons, called 'dodge' 'that homely but expressive term'. Nor is 'crusty', in the sense of 'peevish', so low as it was once thought. It has long been a question, whether the word 'bamboozle' should be admitted. This is also to be found in Latham's *Johnson*, though it is there entered as 'colloquial'.

But though it may be allowed to use some of these terms in familiar discourse, no one of any sense or good taste will ever think of indulging in slang language either spoken or written. It is, no doubt, a bad sign of the times, and much to be deplored, that it is so common. Some writers have calculated that there are, at least, three thousand slang terms in common use. The above are but a few examples of this widespread corruption. We may regard it, as concerns our language, in the light of a pest to society. It takes a long time to clear the atmosphere from the baneful influences of certain epidemics. Now, the language of every-day conversation is suffering from this infectious disease, and it becomes the duty of every Englishman who has a proper feeling for his language, to refrain from this evil himself, and to throw in its way every possible discouragement.

Americanisms

The recklessness with which the Americans use the English language bids fair to flood it with many new and strange terms. It is very possible that some of these terms may some day take their places as forming part of the legitimate materials of our language; and it is also possible, as the Americans themselves sometimes declare, that some of the words and phrases which are now called American, are, in reality, genuine English words which have become obsolete in the mother tongue. But, in the mean time, they certainly must be regarded as interlopers — candidates for an office to which they are not yet, if they ever will be, entitled.

One rather curious explanation has been given of the word 'guess'. It has been well known that the Americans use it in the sense of *to know for certain*. 'I guess' is equivalent, in American phraseology, to 'I know it' — 'I am sure of it'. Now, it has been argued that this is the proper meaning of the word – that it is derived from the German 'gewiss', which comes originally from 'wissen', to know. When first imported into America, in the seventeeth century, they say that it had this meaning in English — that we in England have since then altered the meaning of the word, and that the Americans have preserved its original signification. Even supposing that this could be proved, it does not follow that the American practice is the right one; nor, of course, that we should alter our present meaning of the word, and conform to the American custom. The fountain-head of the English language is in England, and in no other country; and all departures from the English use of English words must be looked upon as faults against purity of style.

Americanisms may be considered under two heads — 1st, legitimate English words used in a wrong sense; and, 2nd, words of a new invention, mutilated or distorted from some known or unknown root. In the first class we may place the adjective 'tall'. This the Americans use in a novel and unrecognised sense. In English it is properly applied only to concrete nouns; as, 'a tall man', or 'a tall tree', &c. But, in the United States, we continually hear of 'tall talk', or even 'a tall smell', &c. It is not the word that is here objected to, but the sense in which it is applied. To 'raise' is another of this class, which is constantly used for 'to educate', or 'bring up'. 'Where were you raised?' is, in America, a very common question. Again, the word 'liquor' is a perfectly good English noun; but what a strange innovation is 'to liquor'! A genuine Yankee says, 'Stranger will you "liquor?" ' 'Handsome', 'clever', and 'fix' are all three genuine English, but 'to play *handsome* on the flute' is undoubtedly bad English. We sometimes qualify persons, but never things as 'clever'. A 'clever' boy, or a 'clever' man, &c., but never, as in America, a 'clever' house or a 'clever' cargo. Again, in America a very common use of 'to fix' is 'to prepare', or 'put in order'. This is not sanctioned by English usage. But 'a fix', in the sense of a dilemma or predicament, is condemned by literary men in the United States as a vulgarism.

The other class consists of words wholly unrecognised in English in any sense — in fine, genuine Americanisms; such words as 'secesh', 'skedaddle', 'recuperate', 'rowdy', 'rile', 'stampede', &c., which can in no sense be said to belong to our language. Nor is it likely that English writers of any pretensions to good taste will ever adopt them. The Americans call the English 'Britishers'; to tease or vex anyone is, with them, 'to rile' him; to make a set speech is 'to orate'; a sudden panic and flight of soldiers is a 'stampede', &c. There are other words of this class which it would puzzle most English writers to explain; such as 'slick', 'spry', 'kedge', 'boss', 'absquatulate', &c. These are not English words, and we may pretty confidently predict that they will never become English.

There can be little doubt, however, that certain expressions now known as Americanisms were, at one time, very commonly used in English. Madame D'Arblay, as well as other writers of her time, has, over and over again, 'mighty fine', 'mighty pretty', &c. 'Mighty pretty' is exactly on a par with '*uncommon* nice'. The one is just as incorrect as the other. This is a form of expression continually used by American writers. Forty or fifty years ago the adjective 'rare' was commonly used for 'underdone' (meat). Now, though common enough in the United States, it is seldom, if ever, applied by us in that sense. Some of these peculiarities appear to be making way in English, in spite of our struggles against them. Such are 'to progress' for 'to advance', 'to effectuate' for 'to accomplish', 'right off', or 'right away' for 'at once' or 'immediately', 'laid over' for 'put off', &c.

The Americans use 'tiresome' for 'tiring'; they speak of a 'tiresome' − for a fatiguing − journey. Also a 'good' time is used for a 'pleasant' time, 'fall' for 'autumn', and to 'go ahead' for 'to prosper'. One American word which seems likely to establish itself in the English language is, 'a loafer'. This would seem to be derived from the German 'laufen', to run, though it has not that meaning in the United States, where it signifies one who lounges about lazily.

In America many new terms are the offspring of a political excitement, which is sure to occur every four years, i.e. as often as a new President is elected. On these occasions such words as 'Copperheads', 'Ring-tailed Roarers', 'Know-nothings', 'Fenians', 'Wolverines', &c., &c., are sure to make their appearance. These words may have a meaning for those who invent and use them, but to the great majority of Englishmen they are altogether a mystery.

Language, in the hands of a great poet, has been often called 'a flame of fire'. However this may be, in the hands of some American journalists it does seem, now and then, very likely to burn their own fingers. In the New York papers we meet with the verb 'to concertize', 'which may possibly mean to give a succession of concerts. We remember hearing that process once called 'going about matineeing'! And there is quite as good authority for the one as for the other of these expressions. Another unintelligible phrase, drawn from the same source, is 'an *emergent* meeting'. This word is never used, in modern English, in a concrete sense. We may say an *emergent* occasion, or *emergent* doubts, but not an *emergent* candidate or an *emergent* character. It is possible that the writer meant a meeting called together on an emergency.

The rapid communication established of late years between England and the United States has brought the two nations into a much closer connection with each other. This, in a commercial or political view, may be of advantage to both countries. But every advantage has its drawback, and it is very doubtful whether this condition of things is likely to benefit the English language. The Americans are well known to set great store by liberty, and of course we have no right whatever to interfere with their opinions concerning principles or forms of political government. But it becomes a serious matter for us when they think proper to take liberties with our language. They set up for themselves, probably by way of showing their independence, new modes of spelling; and they are perpetually introducing all sorts of meanings, words and phrases, none of which have the remotest title to be called English. In the writings of the late N.P. Willis, we meet with such terms as the following: 'An unletupable nature', 'wideawakeity', 'plumptitude', 'pocketually speaking', 'betweenity', and 'go-awayness'! In the same gentleman's writings, we occasionally come across such elegant forms of expression as 'whipping creation', 'flogging Europe', 'a heap of opinions', 'tarnation quick', &c. These and all such must be looked upon as abortions or deformations of our language; and no English writer who has any respect for his own reputation should ever think of countenancing, far less of adopting, such monstrosities.

TEXT AND SELECTED READING

The text is taken from Graham's *A Book About Words*, first published in 1869. The historical context for the piece is outlined in Hans Aarsleff, *The Study of Language in England 1780–1860* (Princeton: Princeton University Press, 1967), while Tony Crowley, *The Politics of Discourse* (London: Macmillan, 1989) examines the political use to which such work was put. The American perspective is detailed in D. Baron, *Grammar and Good Taste* (London: Yale University Press, 1982) and

D. Simpson, *The Politics of American English 1776–1850* (Oxford: Oxford University Press, 1986), and the class perspective in K.C. Phillips, *Language and Class in Victorian England* (Oxford: Blackwell, 1984). An interesting set of essays on the construction of 'The English national character' is that edited by R. Colls and P. Dodd, *Englishness* (London: Croom Helm, 1986).

13

Henry Alford

The phrase 'the Queen's English' derives in the first instance from 'the King's English' which in turn is formed by analogy with phrases such as 'the King's coin' or 'the King's standard'. 'The King's English' is recorded first in Thomas Wilson's *The Arte of Rhetorique* (1553) and was used with prescriptive intent. Referring to particular usage to which he objected, Wilson argued that it was 'counterfeiting the King's English'. Of course as Alford points out, this phrase does not mean that the language belongs to the monarch; he takes it instead to refer metaphorically to the language which is the 'common right' of all and the 'general property of our country'. However, despite his protestation about general access to the language, based upon comparison with the Queen's highway, it is clear that there is more to Alford's definition than he makes evident. For there is also the question of authority to be addressed. In combinations such as 'the King's counsel', 'the King's highway' or 'the King's peace', the definition given is: 'with the sense of belonging to, in the service of the King, as head of the state, royal'. That is to say, in such phrases there is an object (counsel, highway, peace, the English language) which is governed by a certain form of authority, that of the King as head of state. The phrase does not simply have the sense of commonality which Alford ascribes to it, but carries the sense of language which is validated and authorised by some sort of external power. It is clear in this case that it is not legal power (as it is in the cases of the King's counsel, highway or peace) but power of a different order. That power which governs the language is, it is specified, not that of 'rule and analogy' but that which counts as 'the usage of our language'. However, as Walker had pointed out in the eighteenth century, the problem with usage is that it does not declare itself and thus has to be ascertained and proclaimed, which is essentially to say that 'the

171

Queen's English' is properly that form of the language which is counted as such, and ratified, by prescriptivists and their institutional practices. To put it another way, 'the Queen's English' is 'the prescriptivists' English'; moreover, this is a form of prescriptivism which gains its force from the false analogy with legal and political processes.

Alford's text argues against this reading by declaring that 'the Queen's English' is,

> not that English which certain individuals, more or less acquainted with their subject, have chosen to tell us we ought to speak and write, but that which the nation in the secular unfolding of its will and habits, has agreed to speak and write.

The problem with this is that it once again suggests that there is a simple objective set of facts which are there to be recorded without dispute. The point is, that as with other objects of knowledge, such as 'the national character' for example, it is the viewpoint which is adopted that creates the object. As so often in these debates what we see here is prescription in the guise of description.

The example of the national character is an apt one here since Alford, like so many of the other writers presented, believes that it is in some objective way reflected, or even embodied, in the language. Thus he argues that 'the national mind is reflected in the national speech . . . every important feature in the language of a people has its origin in that people's character and history.' The importance of this is that if it were true that the national character is a given fact which is reflected in the language, then it would be crucial to protect the language. For corruption of the language would damage the mirror and so not enable us to see the nation's virtues; it might also, conceivably, even lead to the corruption of the national mind itself. And it is for this reason that Alford quotes with such approval the attack on foreign words in the *Leeds Mercury*. Foreign words, it follows from the logic, reflect the national characteristics of their foreign users and therefore will corrupt English. Indeed they are seen as invaders out to take over and ruin the English character and language. The writer in the newspaper describes the 'formidable invasion of foreign nouns, adjectives and verbs which promises ere long to transform the manly English language into a sort of mongrel international slang'. It is a process which will result in a 'wretched piece of patchwork' which is an abomination. The language then is under threat from foreigners whose aim is to emasculate it, bastardise it and lower its cultural status.

However, what is at stake here in this defence of the language against foreign words and their degenerative tendencies is not merely the status of the language itself. For what is defended here is the pure, undefiled and glorious English national character which is free of foreign influence. The point is, of course, that the argument is nonsensical; for just as there is no such thing as national purity, neither is there any such thing as linguistic purity. Historically it can be seen that the English nation has been, and is, made up of people from differing national, ethnic and cultural backgrounds, and if 'foreign' words were all ruled out as inadmissable then the English language would cease to exist. All its words are 'foreign' in one sense or another and any 'purity' is a result of motivated fictionality rather than objective fact.

THE QUEEN'S ENGLISH:
A MANUAL OF IDIOM AND USAGE

Chapter 1

This work is the re-publication of the little treatise, which, under the former of these titles, has been for some years before the public. It was considered desirable to render more generally useful the matter contained in that treatise; and hence the adoption of the slightly varied form in which it now appears.

Besides the slight alteration of arrangement, considerable alterations have been made, arising from correspondence, and observation, subsequent to the last edition of the former work.

It may be well to premise once for all, that it is my object not so much to enquire in each case what is according to strict rule and analogy, as to point out what is the usage of our language.

In many, indeed most cases, that usage will be found reasonable, and according to some assignable rule; and therefore we shall often find ourselves dealing with considerations pertaining to grammar, and referable to rule. But neither grammar nor rule governs the idiom of a people: and there will be a multitude of cases, where *Sic volo, sic jubeo* is the only measure of the tyranny of usage.

It was my intention to have arranged the contents of this new issue of 'The Queen's English' under the *parts of speech*. But the attempt at once shewed that such an arrangement would be undesirable. It would break the thread of continuity between matters naturally suggested the one by the other: and even if it had been rigidly adhered to, could hardly have been so managed as to be self-indexing.

Consequently the idea was abandoned, and the arrangement of the former work only so far modified as to clear, and bring out, and complete, the separate parts.

I ought to begin by explaining what I mean by the term, 'Queen's English'. It is one rather familiar and conventional, than strictly accurate. The Sovereign is of course no more the proprietor of the English language than any one of us. Nor does she, nor do the Lords and Commons assembled, possess one particle of right to make or unmake a word in the language. But we use the phrase, the Queen's English, in another sense; one not without example in some similar phrases. We speak of the *Queen's Highway*, not meaning that her Majesty is *possessed* of that portion of road, but that it is a high road of the land, as distinguished from by-roads and private roads: open of common right to all, and the general property of our country. And so it is with the *Queen's English*. It is, so to speak, this land's great highway of thought and speech; and seeing that the Sovereign in this realm is the person round whom all our common interests gather, the centre of our civil duties and of our civil rights, the *Queen's English* is not an unmeaning phrase, but one which may serve to teach us some profitable lessons with regard to our language, and to its use and abuse.

And it may be, and is for us, a very useful phrase as conveying another meaning. That which we treat is not the grammarian's English, nor the Dictionary-writers' English, but *the Queen's English*: not that English which certain individuals, more or less acquainted with their subject, have chosen to tell us we ought to speak and write, but that which the nation, in the secular unfolding of its will and habits, has agreed to speak and write. We shall have to say more of this by-and-by.

I called our common English tongue the highway of thought and speech; and it may not be amiss to carry on this similitude further. The Queen's Highway, now so broad and smooth, was once a mere track over an unenclosed country. It was levelled, hardened, widened, by very slow degrees. Of all this trouble, the passer-by sees no trace now. He bowls along it with ease in a vehicle, which a few centuries ago would have been broken to pieces in a deep rut, or would have come to grief in bottomless swamp. There were no Croydon baskets, in the day when Henry II and his train came to do penance from

Southampton up that narrow, hollow, rough pilgrim's road, leading over Harbledown Hill to Canterbury.

Now just so is it with our English language — our Queen's English. There was a day when it was as rough as the primitive inhabitants. Centuries have laboured at levelling, hardening, widening it. For language wants all these processes, as well as roads do. In order to become a good highway for thought and speech, it must not have great prominent awkward points, over which the mind and the tongue may stumble; its words must not be too weak to carry the weight of our thoughts, nor its limiting rules too narrow to admit of their extension. And it is by processes of this kind in the course of centuries, that our English tongue has been ever adapted more and more to our continually increasing wants. If ever it was found too rough, too unsubstantial, too limited, for the requirements of English thought, it was smoothed, strengthened, enlarged, – till it has become for us, in our days, a level, firm, broad highway, over which all thought and speech can travel evenly and safely. Along it the lawyer and the parliamentary agent propel their heavy waggons, clogged with a thousand pieces of cumbrous antiquated machinery, – and no wonder, when they charge freightage, not by the weight of the load, combined with the distance, but by the number of impediments which they can manage to offer to the progress of their vehicle. Along it the poet and the novelist drive their airy tandems, dependent for their success on the dust which they raise, and through which their varnished equipages glitter. On the same road divines, licensed and unlicensed, ply once a week or more, with omnibus or carrier's cart, promising to carry their passengers into another land than that over which the road itself extends, just as the coaches out of London used to astonish our boyish eyes by the '*Havre de Grace*' and *Paris* inscribed on them. And along this same Queen's Highway plods ever the great busy crowd of foot passengers — the talkers of the market, of society, of the family. Words, words, words; good and bad, loud and soft, long and short; millions in the hour, innumerable in the day, unimaginable in the year: what then in the life? what in the history of a nation? what in that of the world? And not one of these is ever forgotten. There is a book where they are all set down. What a history, it has been well said, is this earth's atmosphere, seeing that all words spoken, from Adam's first till now, are still vibrating on its sensitive and unresting medium.

But it is not so much of the great highway of Queen's English that I would now speak, as of some of the laws and usages of the road; the by-rules, so to speak, which hang up framed at the various stations, that all may read them. The language of a people is not trifle. The national mind is reflected in the national speech. If the way in which men express their thoughts is slipshod and mean, it will be very difficult for their thoughts themselves to escape being the same. If it is high-flown and bombastic, a character for simplicity and truthfulness, we may be sure, cannot be long maintained. That nation must be (and it has ever been so in history) not far from rapid decline, and from being degraded of its former glory. Every important feature in the language of a people has its origin in that people's character and history.

Carefulness about minute accuracies of inflexion and grammar may appear to some very contemptible. But it would be easy to give examples in refutation of this idea. Two strike me, of widely different kinds. Some years ago, a set of poems was published at Bristol, purporting to have been written in very early times by a poet named Rowley. Literary controversy ran high about them; many persons believed in their genuineness; some do even now. But the imposture, which was not easy to detect at the time, has been now completely unmasked by the aid of a little word of three letters. The writer uses '*its*' as the possessive case of the pronoun '*it*' of the neuter gender. Now this possessive '*its*' was never used in the early periods of our language; nor, indeed, as late down as Elizabeth. It never occurs in the English version of the Bible, made in its present authorised form in the reign of James I: '*his*' or '*her*' being always used instead. 'They came unto the iron gate that leadeth unto the city; which opened to them of *his* own accord' (Acts xii 10). 'Of beaten work made he the candlestick; *his* shaft, and *his* branch, *his* bowls, *his* knops, and *his* flowers were of the same' (Ex. xxxvii 17). 'The tree of life, which yielded *her* fruit every month' (Rev. xxii 2). It is said also only to occur three times in Shakespeare, and once in *Paradise Lost*. The reason, I suppose, being, that possession, indicated by the possessive case '*its*' seemed to imply a certain life or personality, which things neuter could hardly be thought of as having.

The other example is one familiar to us, of a more solemn character. When St. Peter was stoutly denying all knowledge of his suffering Master, they that stood by said to him, 'surely thou art one of them; for thou art a Galilean, and thy speech agreeth thereto.' So that the fact of a provincial pronunciation was made use of to bring about the repentance of an erring apostle. . . .

As I was sending these sheets to the press, I received a copy of the

Leeds Mercury containing a leading article under the title of 'English for the English', which touches on an abuse of language unnoticed in these pages, but thoroughly deserving of reprobation. It is so appropriate to my present subject that I shall venture to cite a large portion of it almost as it stands.

'While the Dean,' the writer says,

> took so much trouble to expose one danger with which our mother tongue is threatened, he took no notice whatever of another peril which to us seems much more serious. He dealt only with the insubordinate little adverbs and pronouns of native growth, which sometimes intrude into forbidden places, and ignored altogether the formidable invasion of foreign nouns, adjectives, and verbs which promises ere long to transform the manly English language into a sort of mongrel international slang. A class of writers has sprung up who appear to think it their special business to 'enrich' the language by dragging into it, without any attempt at assimilation, contributions from all the tongues of the earth. The result is a wretched piece of patchwork, which may have charms in the eyes of some people, but which is certainly an abomination in the eyes of the genuine student of language.
>
> We need only glance into one of the periodical representatives of fashionable literature, or into a novel of the day, to see how serious this assault on the purity of the English language has become. The chances are more than equal that we shall fall in with a writer who considers it a point of honour to choose all his most emphatic words from a French vocabulary, and who would think it a lamentable falling off in his style, did he write half a dozen sentences without employing at least half that number of foreign words. His heroes are always marked by an *air distingué*; his vile men are sure to be *blasés*; his lady friends never merely dance or dress well, they dance or dress *à merveille*; and he himself when lolling on the sofa under the spirit of laziness does not simply enjoy his rest, he luxuriates in the *dolce far niente*, and wonders when he will manage to begin his *magnum opus*. And so he carries us through his story, running off into hackneyed French, Italian, or Latin expressions, whenever he thinks he has anything to say which he thinks should be graphically or emphatically said. It really seems as if he thought the English language too meagre, or too commonplace a dress,

177

in which to clothe his thoughts. The tongue which gave a noble utterance to the thoughts of Shakespeare and Milton is altogether insufficient to express the more cosmopolitan ideas of Smith, or Tomkins, or Jenkins!

We have before us an article from the pen of a very clever writer, and, as it appears in a magazine which specially professes to represent the 'best society', it may be taken as a good specimen of the style. It describes a dancing party, and we discover for the first time how much learning is required to describe a 'hop' properly. The reader is informed that all the people at the dance belong to the *beau monde*, as may be seen at a *coup d'oeil*; the *demi-monde* is scrupulously excluded, and in fact everything about it bespeaks the *haut ton* of the whole affair. A lady who has been very happy in her hair-dresser is said to be *coiffée à ravir*. Then there is the bold man to describe. Having acquired the *savoir faire*, he is never afraid of making a *faux pas*, but no matter what kind of conversation is started plunges in at once *in media res*. Following him is the fair *debutante*, who is already on the look-out for *un bon parti*, but whose *nez retroussé* is a decided obstacle to her success. She is of course accompanied by mamma *en grande toilette*, who *entre nous*, looks rather *ridée*, even in the gaslight. Then, lest the writer should seem frivolous, he suddenly abandons the description of the dances, *vis-à-vis* and *dos-à-dos*, to tell us that Homer becomes tiresome when he sings of βοῶπις πότνια ροη twice in a page. The supper calls forth a corresponding amount of learning, and the writer concludes his article after having aired his Greek, his Latin, his French, and, in a subordinate way, his English.

Of course, this style has admirers and imitators. It is showy and pretentious, and everything that is showy and pretentious has admirers. The admixture of foreign phrases with our plain English produces a kind of Brummagem sparkle which people whose appreciation is limited to the superficial imagine to be brilliance. Those who are deficient in taste and art education not infrequently prefer a dashing picture by young Daub to a glorious cartoon by Raphael. The bright colouring of the one far more than counterbalances the lovely but unobtrusive grace of the other. In a similar way, students are attracted by the false glitter of the French-paste school of composition, and instead of forming their sentences upon the beautiful models of the great English masters, they twist them into all sorts of unnatural shapes for no other end other than that they may introduce a few inappropriate French or Latin words, the use of which they have learned to think looks smart. Of course, the penny-a-liners are amongst the most enthusiastic followers of the masters of this style. They not only think it brilliant, but they know it to be profitable, inasmuch as it adds considerably to their ability to say a great deal about nothing. The public sees a great deal in the newspapers about '*recherché* dinners' and 'sumptuous *déjeuners*' (sometimes eaten at night), and about the *éclat* with which a meeting attended by the '*élite* of the county' invariably passes off; but they get but a trifling specimen of the masses of similar rubbish which daily fall upon the unhappy editors. The consequence of all this is that the public is habituated to a vicious kind of slang utterly unworthy to be called a language. Even the best educated people find it difficult to resist the contagion of fashion in such a thing as conversation, and if some kind of stand is not made against this invasion, pure English will soon only exist in the works of our dead authors.

But it is not only on literary grounds that we think the bespanglement of our language with French and other foreign phrases is to be deprecated. Morality has something to say in the matter. It is a fact that things are said under the flimsy veil of foreign diction which could not be very well said in plain English. To talk in the presence of ladies about disreputable women by the plain English names which belong to them is not considered to display a very delicate mind, but anybody may talk about the *demi-monde* without fearing either a blush or a frown. Yet the idea conveyed is precisely the same in the one case as the other; and inasmuch as words can only be indelicate when they convey an indelicate idea, we should think that the French words ought to be under the same disabilities as the English ones. In like manner, things sacred are often made strangely familiar by the intervention of a French dictionary. Persons whose reverence for the Deity is properly shown in their English conversation by a becoming unwillingness to make a light use of His Holy Name, have no hesitation in exclaiming *Mon Dieu*! in frivolous conversation. The English name for the Father of Evil is not considered to be a very respectable noun, but its French synonym is to be heard in 'the best society'. Far more telling illustrations than these could easily be found, but we have no inclination to seek them. Ideas which no decent

179

person would ever think of expressing before a mixed company are certainly often spoken and written in French, and in our opinion they do not lose a particle of their coarseness by being dressed up in foreign clothes. We think, therefore, that the interests of morality as well as of pure taste concur in calling upon those who have an influence with the public to set their faces against this vicious style.

I need not say that with every word of this I heartily concur. It is really quite refreshing to read in a newspaper, and a provincial one too, so able and honest an exposure of one of the worst faults of our daily and weekly press.

TEXT AND SELECTED READING

The text is taken from the third edition (1870) of Alford's *The Queen's English: A Manual of Idiom and Usage*, first published in 1864. Again the historical and political contexts are given by Hans Aarsleff, *The Study of Language in England 1780–1860* (Princeton: Princeton University Press, 1967) and Tony Crowley, *The Politics of Discourse* (London: Macmillan, 1989), along with L. Dowling's essay, 'Victorian Oxford and the Science of Language', *PMLA*, 97 (1982). K. C. Phillips, *Language and Class in Victorian England* (Oxford: Blackwell, 1984) is a useful guide to related thinking in the period, and H. Cunningham's essay 'The Language of Patriotism', *History Workshop Journal*, 12 (1981), demonstrates the historical development of the discourse of patriotism and the uses to which it was put. For details of the famous Alford–Moon controversy concerning usage, see D. Baron, *Grammar and Good Taste* (London: Yale University Press, 1982).

14

Henry James

James' essay on the 'vox Americana' is not the most famous of his works but his strictures are none the less interesting in that they demonstrate a concern for language as the site of crucial social issues. His audience was the graduation class at Bryn Mawr college and both the tone and content of his talk reflect an engagement with the proper education of women of the bourgeois class in the period.

James views the education of this class of women, particularly in 'the question of culture', as a matter concerned essentially with 'good breeding'; with 'proprieties and values, perfect possessions of the educated spirit'. His specific interest, however, is with language and his claim is that it is largely ignored in these women's education. This is a dangerous omission, in his view, since 'all life therefore comes back to the question of our speech, the medium through which we all communicate with each other; for all life comes back to the question of our relations with each other.' Language is central to social life and should therefore be given due attention in education. Yet James' claim is not simply that *language* should be taught and studied:

> I am asking you to take it from me, as the very moral of these
> remarks, that the way we say a thing, or fail to say it, fail to learn
> to say it, has an importance in life that it is impossible to
> overstate — a far-reaching importance, as the very hinge of the
> relation of man to man.

The claim has narrowed here from language in general to 'the way that we say a thing'. It is thus not a philosophical or social study of language which James desires, but the study of the right and wrong ways of speaking for members of a particular class. In the same way that many of the eighteenth-century texts can be read as attempts to construct the rules of speech for the bourgeois public sphere in

Britain, James' essay can be taken as performing the same task in early twentieth-century America.

Such an attempt is not without danger as James notes, since the confident class which he is addressing no doubt considers itself already to be accomplished linguistically. There is, he says, 'a virtual consensus of the educated', that there already exists 'a common language, with its modes of employment, its usage, its authority, its beauty in working form'; a 'common language' designed to transmit a 'coherent culture'. His point, however, is that in fact no such 'common language' exists and moreover the language which is spoken in America is far from inculcating the proper values and breeding. On the contrary:

> Of the degree in which a society is civilised the vocal form, the vocal tone, the personal, social accent and sound of its inter-course, have always been held to give a direct reflection. That sound, the vocal form, the touchstone of manners, is the note, the representative note – representative of its having (in our poor, imperfect human degree) achieved civilisation. Judged in this light, it must frankly be said, our civilisation remains strikingly *una*chieved.

Or, as he later put it, 'our national use of vocal sound, in men and women alike, is slovenly − an absolutely inexpertly daub of un-applied tone.' It is the question of 'tone', by which James appears to mean a system of pronunciation, which is central to his argument. 'Tone' stands for many other qualities and is indeed an indicator of massive social importance for James:

> A care for tone is part of a care for many other things besides; for the fact, for the value of good breeding, above all, as to which tone unites with various other personal, social signs to bear testimony.

The questions then are, what does it mean to speak well or ill, and what is the missing 'tone standard'? The definitions bear all the usual precision of the Jamesian style but when unpicked are hard to evaluate. Speaking well means speaking in conformity with the 'tone standard', that 'clear criterion of the best usage and example'. To do this is, he asserts,

> but to recognise, once for all, that avoiding vulgarity, arriving at lucidity, pleasantness, charm, and contributing by the mode

and degree of utterance a colloquial, a genial value even to an inevitably limited quality of intention, or thought, is an art to be cultivated, just as much as any of the other, subtler arts of life.

Which, crudely put, seems to mean that 'speaking well' is the result of elocution lessons which teach the 'tone standard' or system of pronunciation. In fact it is often the case that the definition of speaking well is either circular (as in the definition which says it is speaking by the 'tone standard'), or so vague and general that it is difficult to disagree with it (as when he defines it as 'speaking with consideration for the forms and shades of our language'). What is perhaps of more interest is his definition of what speaking badly is, for it is here that the social prejudices are laid bare. Speaking badly means

> speaking as millions and millions of supposedly educated, supposedly civilised persons — that is the point — of both sexes, in our great country, habitually, persistently, imperturbably, and I think for the most part all unwittingly, speak.

It is the reduction of 'articulation to an easy and ignoble minimum' by the majority of the population which makes their language 'as little distinct as possible from the grunting, the squealing, the bawling or the roaring of animals'. The people who are particularly guilty of such corruption, James argues at the end of the lecture (not reprinted below), are the immigrants who feel that 'from the moment of their arrival, they have just as much propriety in our speech as we have, and just as good a right to do what they choose with it'.

The argument then is not one simply about language but about all sorts of other cultural values which are enmeshed with it. Questions of propriety, breeding, minority and majority culture, and above all, the social identity of the members of the class to which he addresses himself.

'THE SPEECH OF AMERICAN WOMEN'

I am offered the opportunity of addressing you a few observations on a subject that should content itself, to my thinking, with no secondary place among those justly commended to your attention on such a day as this, and that yet will not, I dare say have been treated before you, very often, as a matter especially inviting that attention. You will have been appealed to, at this season, and in preparation for this occasion, with admirable persuasion and admirable effect, I make no doubt, on behalf of many of the interests and ideals, scholarly, moral, social, you have here so happily pursued, many of the duties, responsibilities, opportunities you have learned, in these beautiful conditions, at the threshold of life, to see open out before you. These admonitions, taken together, will have borne, essentially, upon the question of culture, as you are expected to consider and cherish it; and some of them, naturally, will have pressed on the higher, the advanced developments of that question, those that are forever flowering above our heads and waving and rustling their branches in the blue vast of human thought. Others, meanwhile, will have lingered over the fundamentals, as we may call them, the solid, settled, seated elements of education, the things of which it is held, in general, that our need of being reminded of them must rarely be allowed to become a desperate or a feverish need. These underlying things, truths of tradition, aspiration, of discipline, of training consecrated by experience, are understood at present in any liberal course of study or scheme of character; yet they permit of a certain renewed reference and slightly ceremonial insistence, perhaps, on high days and holidays; without the fear, on the part of any one concerned, of their falling too much into the category of the commonplace. I repeat, however, that there is a prime part of education, an element of the basis itself, in regard to which I shall probably remain within the bounds of safety in declaring that no explicit, no separate, no adequate plea will be likely to have ranged itself under any one of your customary heads of commemoration. If there are proprieties and values, perfect possessions of the educated spirit, clear humanities, as the old collegiate usage beautifully named them, that may be taken absolutely for granted, taken for granted as rendering any process of training simply impossible, the indispensable preliminary I allude to, and that I am about to name, would easily indeed present itself in that light; thus confessing to its established character and its tacit intervention. A virtual consensus of the educated, of any gathered group, in regard to the *speech* that, among the idioms and articulations of the globe, they profess to make use of, may well strike us, in a given case, as a natural, and inevitable assumption. Without that consensus, to every appearance, the educative process cannot be thought of as at all even beginning; we readily perceive that without it the mere imparting of a coherent culture is a matter of communication and response — each of which branches of an understanding involves the possession of a common language, with its modes of employment, its usage, its authority, its beauty, in working form; a medium of expression, in short, organised and developed. So obvious is such a truth, that even at these periods of an especially excited consciousness of your happy approximation to the ideal, your conquest, so far as it has proceeded, of the humanities aforesaid, of the great attainable amenities, you would not think of expecting that your not having failed to master the system of mere vocal sounds that renders your fruitful association with each other a thinkable thing should be made a topic of inquiry or congratulation. You would say if you thought about the point at all:

> Why, of course we speak in happy forms; we arrive here, arrive from our convenient homes, our wonderful schools, our growing cities, our great and glorious States, speaking in those happy forms in which people speak whose speech promotes the refinements (in a word the success) of intercourse, intellectual and social — not in any manner in which people speak whose speech frustrates, or hampers, or mocks at them. That conquest is behind us, and we invite no discussion of the question of whether we are articulate, whether we are intelligibly, or completely, expressive — we expose ourselves to none; the question of whether we are heirs and mistresses of the art of making ourselves satisfactorily heard, conveniently listened to, comfortably and agreeably understood.

Such, I say, is the assumption that everything must always have ministered to your making: so much as to stamp almost with a certain indecorum, on the face of the affair, any breach of the silence surrounding these familiar securities and serenities. I can only stand before you, accordingly, as a breaker of the silence; breaking it as gently, of course, as all the pleasant proprieties of this hour demand, but making the point that there is an element of fallacy — in plain terms a measurable mistake – in the fine confidence I am thus feeling my way to impute to you. It is needless to make sure of the basis of the process of communication and intercourse when it is clear, when it is positive, that such a basis exists and flourishes; but that is a question as to which the slightest shade of doubt is disquieting, disconcerting — fatal indeed; so that an exceptional inquiry into the case is then prescribed. I shall suggest our making this inquiry altogether — after having taken it thus as exceptionally demanded; making it rapidly, in the limited way for which our present conditions allow us moments; but at least with the feeling that we are breaking ground where it had not hitherto, among us, strangely enough, been much broken, and where some measurable good may spring, for us, from our action.

If we may not then be said to be able to converse before we are able to talk (and study is essentially, above all in such a place as this, your opportunity to converse with your teachers and inspirers), so we may be said not to be able to 'talk' before we are able to speak: whereby you easily see what we thus get. We may not be said to be able to study — and *a fortiori* do any of the things we study *for* – unless we are able to speak. All life therefore comes back to the question of our speech, the medium through which we communicate with each other; for all life comes back to the question of our relations with each other. These relations are made possible, are registered, are verily constituted, by our speech, and are succesful (to repeat my word) in proportion as our speech is worthy of its great human and social function; is developed, delicate, flexible, rich — an adequate accomplished fact. The more it suggests and expresses the more we live by it — the more it promotes and enhances life. Its quality, its authenticity, its security, are hence supremely important for the general multifold opportunity, for the dignity and integrity, of our existence.

These truths, you see, are incontestable; yet though you are daughters, fortunate in many respects, of great commonwealths that have been able to render you many attentions, to surround you with most of the advantages of peace and plenty, it is none the less definite that there will have been felt to reign among you, in general, no positive mark whatever, public or private, of an effective consciousness of any of them; the consciousness, namely — a sign of societies truly possessed of light — that no civilised body of men and women has ever left so vital an interest to run wild, to shift, as we say, all for itself, to stumble and flounder, through mere adventure and accident, in the common dust of life, to pick up a living, in fine, by the wayside and the ditch. Of the degree in which a society is civilised the vocal form, the vocal tone, the personal, social accent and sound of its intercourse, have always been held to give a direct reflection. That sound, the vocal form, the touchstone of manners, is the note, the representative note — representative of its having (in our poor, imperfect human degree) achieved civilisation. Judged in this light, it must frankly be said, our civilisation remains strikingly *un*achieved: the last of the American idiosyncrasies, the last by which we can be conceived as 'represented' in the international concert of culture, would be the pretension to a tone-standard, to our wooing comparison with that of other nations. The French, the Germans, the Italians, the English perhaps in particular, and many other people, Occidental and Oriental, I surmise, not excluding the Turks and the Chinese, have for the symbol of education, of civility, a tone-standard; we alone flourish in undisturbed and – as in the sense of so many other of our connections – in something like sublime unconsciousness of any such possibility.

It is impossible, in very fact, to have a tone-standard without the definite preliminary of a *care* for tone, and against a care for tone, it would very much appear, the elements of life in this country, as at present conditioned, violently and increasingly militate. At one or two reasons for this strange but consumate conspiracy I shall in a moment ask you to glance with me, but in the meanwhile I should go any length in agreeing with you about any such perversity, on the part of parents and guardians, pastors and masters, as their expecting the generations whether of young women or young men, to arrive at such a position of such comparative superiority alone – unsupported and unguided. There is no warrant for placing on these inevitably rather light heads and hearts, on any company of you, assaulted in our vast vague order, by many pressing wonderments, the *whole* of the burden of a care for tone. A care for tone is part of a care for many other things besides; for the fact, for the value of good breeding, above all, as to which tone unites with various other personal, social signs to bear testimony. The idea of good breeding — without which intercourse fails to flower into fineness, without which human relations bear but crude and tasteless fruit — is one of the most precious conquests of civilisation, the very core of our social heritage; but in the transmission of which it becomes us much more to be active and interested than merely passive and irresponsible participants. It is an idea, the idea of good breeding (in other words simply the idea of *secure* good manners), for which, always, in every generation, there is yet more, and yet more, to be done; and no danger would be more lamentable than that of the real extinction, in our hands of so sacred a flame. Flames, however, even the most sacred, do not go on burning of themselves; they require to be kept up; handed on the torch needs to be from one group of patient and competent watchers to another. The possiblity, the preferability, of people speaking as people speak when their speech has had for them a signal importance, is a matter to be kept sharply present; from that comes support, comes example, comes authority — from that comes inspiration of those comparative beginners of life, the hurrying children of time, who are but too exposed to be worked upon, by a hundred circumstances, in a different and inferior sense. You don't speak soundly and agreeably, you don't speak neatly and consistently, unless you *know* how you speak, how you may, how you should, how you shall speak, unless you have discriminated, unless you have noticed differences and suffered from violations and vulgarities; and you have not this positive consciousness, you are incapable of any reaction of taste or sensibility worth mentioning, unless a great deal of thought of the matter has been taken *for* you.

Taking thought, in this connection, is what I mean by obtaining a tone-standard — a clear criterion of the best usage and example: which is but to recognise, once for all, that avoiding vulgarity, arriving at lucidity, pleasantness, charm, and contributing by the mode and the degree of utterance a colloquial, a genial value even to an inevitably limited quantity of intention, of thought, is an art to be acquired and cultivated, just as much as any of the other, subtler arts of life. There are plenty of influences round about us that make for an imperfect disengagement of the human side of vocal sound, that make for the confused, the ugly, the flat, the thin, the mean, the helpless, that reduce articulation to an easy and ignoble minimum, and so keep it as little distinct as possible from the grunting, the squealing, the barking or the roaring of animals. I do not mean to say that civility of utterance may not become an all but unconscious beautiful habit — I mean to say, thank goodness, that this is exactly what it *may* become. But so to succeed it must be a collective and associated habit; for the greater the number of persons speaking well, in given conditions, the more that number will tend to increase, and the smaller the number the more that number will tend to shrink and lose itself in the desert of the common. Contact and communication, a beneficent contagion, bring about the happy state — the state of sensibility to tone, the state of recognising, and responding to, certain vocal sounds *as* tone, and recognising and reacting from certain others as negations of tone: negations the more offensive as they have most enjoyed impunity. You will have, indeed, in any at all aspiring cultivation of tone, a vast mass of assured impunity, of immunity on the wrong side of the line to reckon with. There are in every quarter, in our social order, impunities of aggression and corruption in plenty; but there are none, I think, showing so unperturbed a face — wearing, I should slangily say, if slang were permitted me here, so impudent a 'mug' — as the forces assembled to make you believe that no form of speech is provably better than another, and that just this matter of 'care' is an affront to the majesty of sovereign ignorance. Oh, I don't mean to say that you will find in the least a clear field and nothing but favour! The difficulty of your case is exactly the ground of my venturing thus to appeal to you. That there is difficulty, that there is a great, blatant, blowing dragon to slay, can only constitute, as it appears to me, a call of honor for generous young minds, something of a trumpet-sound for tempers of high courage.

And now, of course, there are questions you may ask me: as to what I more intimately mean by speaking 'well', by speaking 'ill'; as to what I more definitely mean by 'tone' and by the 'negation' of tone; as to where you are to recognise the presence of the exemplary rightness I have referred you to — as to where you are to see any standard raised to the breeze; and above all, as to my reasons for referring with such emphasis to the character of the enemy you are to overcome. I am able, I think, to satisfy you all the way; but even in so doing I shall still feel our question to be interesting, as a whole, out of proportion to any fractions of an hour we may now clutch at; feel that if I could only treat it with a freer hand and more margin I might really create in you a zeal to follow it up. I mean, then, by speaking well, in the first place, speaking under the influence of *observation* – your own. I mean speaking with consideration for the forms and shades of our language, a consideration so inbred that it has become instinctive and well-nigh unconscious and automatic, as all the habitual, all the inveterate amenities of life become. By the forms and shapes of our language I mean the innumerable differentiated, discriminated units of sound and sense that lend themselves to audible production, to enunciation, to intonation: those innumerable units that have, each, an identity, a quality, an outline, a shape, a clearness, a fineness, a sweetness, a richness, that have, in a word, a value, which it is open to us, as lovers of our admirable English tradition, or as cynical traitors to it, to preserve or to destroy.

Many of these units are, for instance, our syllables, emphasized or unemphasized, our parts of words, or often the whole word itself, our parts of sentences, coming in *for* value and subject to be marked or missed, honored or dishonored — to use the term we use for checks at banks — as a note of sound. Many of them are in particular our simple vowel-notes and our consonantal, varying, shifting — shifting in relation and connection, as to value and responsibility and place — and capable of a complete absence of effect, according as a fine ear and a fine tongue, or as a coarse ear and a coarse tongue, preside at the use of them. All our employment of constituted sounds, syllables, sentences, comes back to the way we say a thing, and it is very largely by saying, all the while, that we live and play our parts. I am asking you to take it from me, as the very moral of these remarks, that the way we say a thing, or fail to say it, fail to learn to say it, has an importance in life that it is impossible to overstate — a far-reaching importance, as the very hinge of the relation of man to man. I am asking you to take that truth well home and hold it close to your hearts, setting your backs to the wall to defend it, heroically, when need may be. For need will be, among us, as I have already intimated, and as I shall proceed in a moment, though very briefly, to show you further: you must be prepared for such vociferous demonstration of the plea that the way we say things – the way we 'say' in general — has as little importance as possible. Let the demonstration proceed, let the demonstration abound, let it be as vociferous as it will, if you only meanwhile hug the closer the faith I thus commend to you; for you will very presently perceive that the more this vain contention does make itself heard, the more it insists, the sooner it shall begin to flounder waist-high in desert sands. Nothing, sayable or said, that pretends to expression, to value, to consistency, in whatever interest, but finds itself practically confronted, at once, with the tone-question: the only refuge from which is the mere making of a noise — since simple noise is the sort of sound in which tone ceases to exist. To simple toneless noise, as an argument for indifference to discriminated speech, you may certainly then listen as philosophically as your nerves shall allow.

But the term I here apply brings me meanwhile to my second answer to your three or four postulated challenges — the question of what I mean by speaking badly. I might reply to you, very synthetically, that I mean by speaking badly speaking as millions and millions of supposedly educated, supposedly civilised persons – that is the point — of both sexes, in our great country, habitually, persistently, imperturbably, and I think for the most part all unwittingly, speak: that form of satisfaction to you being good enough — isn't it? — to cover much of the ground. But I must give you a closer account of the evil against which I warn you, and I think none is so close as this: that speaking badly is speaking with that want of attention to speech that we should blush to see any other of our personal functions compromised by — any other controllable motion, or voluntary act, of our lives. Want of attention, in any act, results in a graceless and unlighted effect, an effect of accident and misadventure; and it strikes me in this connection that there is no better comprehensive description of our vocal habits as a nation, in their vast, monotonous flatness and crudity, than this aspect and air of unlightedness — which presents them as matters going on, gropingly, helplessly, empirically, almost dangerously (perilously, that is, to life and limb), in the dark. To walk in the dark, dress in the dark, eat in the dark, is to run the chance of breaking our legs, of misarranging our clothes, of besmearing our persons; and speech may figure for us either as the motion, the food, or the clothing of intercourse, as you will. To do things 'unlightedly' is accordingly to do them without neatness or completeness and to accept that doom is simply to accept the doom of the slovenly.

Our national use of vocal sound, in men and women alike, *is* slovenly — an absolutely inexpert daub of unapplied tone. It leaves us at the mercy of a medium that, as I say, is incomplete; which sufficiently accounts, as regards our whole vocal manifestation, for the effect of a want of finish. Noted sounds have their extent and their limits, their mass, however concentrated, and their edges; and what is the speech of a given society but a series, a more or less rich complexity, of noted sounds? Nothing is commoner than to see throughout our country, young persons of either sex — for the phenomenon is most marked, I think, for reasons I will touch on, in the newer generations – whose utterance can only be indicated by pronouncing it destitute of any approach to an emission of the consonant. It thus becomes a mere helpless slobber of disconnected vowel noises — the weakest and cheapest attempt at human expression that we shall easily encounter, I imagine, in any community pretending to the general instructed state. Observe, too, that the vowel sounds in themselves, at this rate, quite fail of any purity, for the reason that our consonants contribute to the drawing and modelling of our vowels — just as our vowels contribute to the coloring, to the painting, as we may call it, of our consonants, and that any frequent repetition of a vowel depending for all rounding and shaping on another vowel alone lays upon us an effort of the thorax under which we inevitably break down. Hence the undefined noises that I refer to when consonantal sound drops out; drops as it drops, for example, among those vast populations to whose lips, to whose ear, it is so rarely given to form the terminal letter of our 'Yes', or to hear it formed. The abject 'Yeh-eh' (the ugliness of the drawl is not easy to represent) which usurps the place of that interesting vocable makes its nearest approach to deviating into it decency of a final consonant when it becomes a still more questionable 'Yeh-ep'. . . .

TEXT AND SELECTED READING

The text of this essay was originally an address to the graduating class at Bryn Mawr College, Pennsylvania, delivered on June 8th 1905. It appeared in printed form in *Harper's Bazaar*, 40–1 (1905–6) and in another version in *The Question of Our Speech* (Boston: Houghton Mifflin, 1905). D. Baron, *Grammar and Good Taste* (London: Yale University Press, 1982) examines the piece and related works, while M.M. Mathews, *The Beginnings of American English* (London: University of Chicago Press, 1931) contains a number of interesting essays concerned with American English. The most comprehensive surveys are probably still G.P. Krapp, *The English Language in America* (New York: Century, 1925) and H.L. Mencken, *The American Language* (4th edn, New York: Knopf, 1936). Another literary figure who wrote on this subject was T.S. Eliot, *American Literature and the American Language* (Washington: Washington University Press, 1953).

15

Henry Newbolt

The historical context of the Newbolt Report is important in that its whole thrust is to view education as a possible means of intervening in history in order to restore harmony and peace. The aftermath of the First World War, the bitter class antagonism of the period, the rebellion in Ireland and the ongoing struggle of the suffragettes, created a tense and fragile social order. It is in relation to such an history that we can view both the liberality (with regard to educational ideals) and the illiberalism (with regard to many of the particular measures) of the Report.

The Report is the first both to assert and to achieve recognition of the principle that English language and literature should form the basis of education in England for all children. The reason for taking English as 'the only possible basis for a national education' is that it would create a form of ideological unity which would cement the various contending forces. An education which has English at its core, the Report holds,

> is the greatest benefit which could be conferred upon any citizen of a great state, and that the common right to it, the common discipline and enjoyment of it, the common possession of the tastes and associations connected with it, would form a new element of national unity, linking together the mental life of all classes.

Just as Buchanan had noted in the eighteenth century that Scotland and England were divided by language, the Report argues that different classes in England are sundered by 'a marked difference in their modes of speech'. Moreover, in the same way that Buchanan had offered 'a standard for an Elegant and Uniform pronunciation' as the means to unify the two nations, the Report takes the teaching of a

193

particular form of the language to be a possible 'bond of union between classes [which] would beget the right kind of national pride'.

The problem in the reporters' view was that the majority of people in Britain spoke an inferior language: 'amongst the vast mass of the population, it is certain that if a child is not learning good English he is learning bad English, and probably bad habits of thought.' It was a danger not to be underestimated and its significance can be noted by the moral tones with which the Report describes the teacher's task. It is 'to fight against the powerful influence of evil habits of speech contracted in home and street'; the problem is 'thus not with ignorance but with a perverted power'. It is clear what teachers and educationalists must do:

> Plainly, then, the first and chief duty of the Elementary School is to give its pupils speech — to make them articulate and civilised human beings, able to communicate themselves in speech and writing, and able to receive the communication of others. . . . Indeed, until they have been given civilised speech it is useless to speak of continuing their education, for, in a real sense, their education has not been begun.

The task is clear enough; but there is a significant slippage here around which are gathered enormous issues. For it is one thing to argue that children should be given speech, but it is quite another to argue that they should be given 'civilised speech'. The questions are: what is 'civilised speech' and where are we to find it?

'Civilised speech' is evidently 'standard English' since the schools are to provide:

> first, systematic training in the speech of standard English, to secure correct pronunciation and clear articulation: second, systematic training in the use of standard English, to secure clearness and correctness both in oral expression and in writing: third, training in reading.

'Standard English' is to be the model to which all children should aspire and it should be 'emphatically the business of the Elementary School to teach [it to] all its pupils who either speak a definite dialect or whose speech is disfigured by vulgarisms'. However, there is a problem with this description of the teacher's task since what had previously counted as 'standard English', as shown in the dictionary Proposal (see ch. 11), was the particular written form of the English language which was taken to have existed after the reformation. It was not in any sense the spoken language in the lexicographers' definition, but the national and uniform system of writing. How then could this be taught to children for oral use? The answer to this problem is evident in a shift in the meaning of the term 'standard English' which appears towards the end of the nineteenth century. For although the first definition of the term stipulates the written language which the lexicographers took as their object of study (with the illustration taken from the Proposal), the second definition and illustration are quite distinct. In the second sense the term is,

> applied to a variety of the speech of a country which, by reason of its cultural status and currency, is held to represent the best form of that speech. *Standard English*: that form of the English language which is spoken (with modifications, individual or local), by the generality of the cultured people in Great Britain.

The supporting illustration is taken from Sweet's *Sounds English* (1908), which proposed that 'standard English, like standard French, is now a class dialect more than a local dialect: it is the language of the educated all over Great Britain.'

'Standard English' in this later sense, and it is in this sense that the term is used in the Newbolt Report, refers to a class dialect: it is the spoken form of the language of a particular class. In one view this can be noted as a return to eighteenth-century formulations, as can be seen when the Report itself attempts to define 'standard English'. It is, the Report asserts, 'a much debated question, but for our present purposes it should suffice to say that it is a pronunciation free from provincialisms and vulgarisms'. This is a clear return to the metropolitan and class-based definition offered by the eighteenth-century elocutionists and as such must share the same fate. For just as Buchanan's attempt to use his standard as the means to unity fails on the grounds of its connection with a particular class, then likewise the Newbolt suggestion will fail and for the same reasons. The attempt to create national unity by means of a 'class dialect' belonging to the 'cultured and educated', in contradistinction to which other forms are considered 'vulgar', 'provincial', 'evil' and so on, is doomed to defeat. For what is intended to bring about unity here can only reinforce division.

THE TEACHING OF ENGLISH IN ENGLAND

Report of the Departmental Committee Appointed by the President of the Board Of Education To Inquire into the Position of English in the Educational System of England

Reference

To inquire into the position occupied by English (Language and Literature) in the educational system of England, and to advise how its study may best be promoted in schools of all types, including Continuation Schools, and in Universities and other Institutions of Higher Education, regard being had to –

1 the requirements of a liberal education;
2 the needs of business, the professions, and public services; and
3 the relation of English to other studies. . . .

The facts and needs of the situation as briefly outlined above did not form the starting point of our inquiry, but they forced themselves irresistibly upon our attention from the moment when we first began to consider the present position of English in the educational system of the country. From the evidence laid before us it became speedily clear that in many schools of all kinds and grades that part of the teaching which dealt directly with English was often regarded as being inferior in importance, hardly worthy of any substantial place in the curriculum, and a suitable matter to be entrusted to any member of the staff who had some free time at his disposal. It would be natural to suppose that there must be some reason for this neglect, but on the other hand one of the most obvious facts of which we have to take account is that education in English is, for all Englishmen, a matter of the most vital concern, and one which must, by its very nature, take precedence of all the other branches of learning. It is self-evident that until a child has acquired a certain command of the native language, no other educational development is even possible. If progress is not made at one time in the region of arithmetic or history or geography, the child merely remains backward in that respect, and the deficiency can be made up later. But a lack of language is a lack of the means of communication and of thought itself. Moreover, amongst the vast mass of the population, it is certain that if a child is not learning good English he is learning bad English, and probably bad habits of thought; and some of the mischief done may never afterwards be undone. Merely from this point of view English is plainly no matter of inferior importance, nor even one among the other branches of education, but the one indispensable preliminary and foundation of all the rest. . . .

We have now come to the point where the evidence forces our lines of thought to converge. On the one hand, our national education needs to be perfected by being scientifically refounded as a universal, reasonable and liberal process of development; on the other hand, we find coincidentally that for this purpose, of all the means available, there is only one which fulfils all the conditions of our problem. Education is complete in proportion as it includes within its scope a measure of knowledge in the principal sciences and a measure of skill in literature, the drama, music, song, and the plastic arts; but not all of these are equally useful in the training of the young. We recognise fully, on the one side, the moral, practical, educational value of natural science, on the other side the moral, practical, educational value of the arts and of all great literatures ancient or modern. But what we are looking for now is not merely a means of education, one chamber in the structure which we are hoping to rebuild, but the true starting-point and foundation from which all the rest must spring. For this special purpose there is but one material. We make no comparison, we state what appears to us to be an incontrovertible primary fact, that for English children no form of knowledge can take precedence of a knowledge of English, no form of literature can take precedence of English literature: and that the two are so inextricably connected as to form the only possible basis for a national education.

It will clearly be seen that by this statement we have declared the necessity of what must be, in however elementary a form, a liberal education for all English children whatever their position or occupation in life. We are glad to record not only our own strong conviction that such a scheme is, from every point of view, just, reasonable and for the national advantage, but also the fact that in the mass of opinions submitted to us nowhere find any evidence to the contrary. The judgments and experience laid before us by those who have a large experience and every right to express a judgment, support us in our belief that an education of this kind is the greatest benefit which could be conferred upon any citizen of a great state, and that the common right to it, the common discipline and enjoyment of it, the common possession of the tastes and associations connected with it, would form a new element of national unity, linking together the mental life

197

of all classes by experiences which have hitherto been the privilege of a limited section. From the same evidence and opinions, we have derived the further belief that to initiate all English children into such a fellowship, to set the feet of all upon that road of endless and unlimited advance, is an undertaking in no way impossible or visionary. The difficulties are undoubtedly great, the means available are at present very inadequate, but the difficulties and the inadequacy are largely those which are already troubling us, and would hamper almost any scheme of education at the present moment. On the other hand, we have the advantages given us by the necessity of a new departure among rapidly changing conditions, and by the opportunity of avoiding some causes of past failure.

In any case, and whatever studies may be added to it, English, we are convinced, must form the essential basis of a liberal education for all English people, and in the earlier stages of education it should be the principal functions of schools of whatever type to provide this basis.

Of this provision the component parts will be, first, systematic training in the sounded speech of standard English, to secure correct pronunciation and clear articulation: second, systematic training in the use of standard English, to secure clearness and correctness both in oral expression and in writing: third, training in reading. Under this last head will be included reading aloud with feeling and expression, the use of books as sources of information and means of study, and finally, the use of literature as we have described it, that is, as a possession and a source of delight, a personal intimacy and the gaining of personal experience, an end in itself and, at the same time, an equipment for the understanding of life.

Here, again, it may be well to deal at once with possible criticisms. It may be objected that while English is indeed a necessary condition of our education, it is one which may be taken for granted, like the air we breathe or the land on which we live. We do not need, it may be said, to be taught English; to write and read, in Dogberry's opinion, comes by nature. This view is, perhaps, not likely to be now so crudely stated, but it has long been acted upon by many who are engaged in education, and is acquiesced in by many who control it. We must, therefore, state clearly that in our judgment it is an entirely unpractical view. It is repudiated not merely by literary experts but by the numerous practical men of business whom we have consulted. It is an instance of that divorce of education from reality which we have already found to be a main cause of failure in the past. English may come by nature up to a certain point; but that point is soon reached, and thenceforward the possibility of mental development, in whatever direction, is seriously diminished for those who have not achieved some mastery of their mother tongue. What a man cannot clearly state he does not perfectly know, and, conversely, the inability to put his thought into words sets a boundary to his thought. Impressions may anticipate words, but unless expression seizes and recreates them they soon fade away, or remain but vague and indefinite to the mind which received them, and incommunicable to others. 'A haziness of intellectual vision', said Cardinal Newman, 'is the malady of all classes of men by nature . . . of all who have not had a really good education.' It is a common experience that to find fit language for our impressions not only renders them clear and definite to ourselves and to others, but in the process leads to deeper insight and fresh discoveries, at once explaining and extending our knowledge. English is not merely the medium of our thought, it is the very stuff and process of it. It is itself the English mind, the element in which we live and work. In its full sense it connotes not merely acquaintance with a certain number of terms, or the power of spelling these terms correctly and arranging them without gross mistakes. It connotes the discovery of the world by the first and most direct open way to us, and the discovery of ourselves in our native environment. And as our discoveries become successively wider, deeper, and subtler, so should our control of the instrument which shapes our thought become more complete and exquisite, up to the limit of artistic skill. For the writing of English is essentially an art, and the effect of English literature in education is the effect of an art upon the development of human character.

Here again we desire to guard against any possible misunderstanding. We find that the nature of art and its relation to human life and welfare is not sufficiently understood or appreciated in this country. The prevalence of a low view of art, and especially of the art of literature, has been a main cause of our defective conception of national education. Hitherto literature has, even more than science, suffered in the public mind both misunderstanding and degradation. Science has too often been considered as a kind of skilled labour, a mere handling of materials for profit. Literature has first been confused with the science of language, and then valued for its commercial uses, from the writing of business letters up to the production of saleable books. The word art has been reserved for the more highly coloured or the less seriously valued examples of the latter. We must repeat that a much higher view may be taken of both science and art, and that this higher view is the only one consistent with a true theory of education. Commercial enterprise may have a legitimate and desirable object in view, but that object cannot claim to be the satisfaction of any of the three great natural affections of the human spirit — the love of truth, the love of beauty, and the love of righteousness. Man loves all these by nature and for their own sake only. Taken altogether, they are, in the highest sense, his life, and no system of education can claim to be adequate if it does not help him to develop these natural and disinterested loves. But if it is to do this effectively we must discard or unlearn all mean views of art, and especially of the art of literature. We must treat literature, not as language merely, not as an ingenious set of symbols, a superficial and superfluous kind of decoration, or a graceful set of traditional gestures, but as the self-expression of great natures, the record and rekindling of spiritual experiences, and in daily life for every one of us the means by which we may, if we will, realise our own impressions and communicate them to our fellows. We reiterate, then, the two points which we desire to build upon; first, the fundamental necessity of English for the full development of the mind and character of English children, and second, the fundamental truth that the use of English does not come to all by nature, but is a fine art, and must be taught as a fine art.

We believe that such an education based on the English language and literature would have important social, as well as personal results; it would have a unifying tendency. Two causes, both accidental and conventional rather than national, at present distinguish and divide one class from another in England. The first of these is a marked difference in their modes of speech. If the teaching of the language were properly and universally provided for, the difference between educated and uneducated speech (this does not refer to dialect, for which see later), which at present causes so much prejudice and difficulty of intercourse on both sides, would gradually disappear. Good speech and great literature would not be regarded as too fine for use by the majority, nor, on the other hand, would natural gifts for self-expression be rendered ineffective by embarassing faults of diction or composition. The second cause of division amongst us is the undue narrowness of the ground on which we meet for the true purposes of social life. The associations of sport and games are widely shared by all classes in England, but with mental pleasures and mental exercises the case is very different. The old education was not similar for all but diverse. It went far to make of us not one nation, but two, neither of which shared the associations or tastes of the other. An education fundamentally English would, we believe, at any rate bridge, if not close, this chasm of separation. The English people might learn as a whole to regard their own language, first with respect, and then with a genuine feeling of pride and affection. More than any mere symbol it is actually part of England: to maltreat it or deliberately to debase it would be seen to be an outrage; and to become sensible of its significance and splendour would be to step upon a higher level. In France, we are told, this pride in the national language is strong and universal; the French artisan will often use his right to object that an expression 'is not French'. Such a feeling for our own native language would be a bond of union between classes and would beget the right kind of national pride. Even more certainly should pride and joy in the national literature serve as such a bond. This feeling, if fostered in all our schools without exception, would disclose itself far more often and furnish a common meeting ground for great numbers of men and women who might otherwise never come in touch with one another. We know from the evidence of those who are familiar with schools of every type that the love of fine style and the appreciation of what is great in human thought and feeling is already no monopoly of a certain class in England, that it is a natural and not exceptional gift, and that though easily discouraged by unfavourable circumstances it can also, by sympathetic treatment, be easily drawn out and developed. Within the school itself all scholars, though specialising perhaps on different lines, will be able to find a common interest in the literature class and the debating or dramatic society. And this common interest will be likely to persist when other less vital things have been abandoned. The purely technical or aesthetic appeal of any art will, perhaps, always be limited to a small number but, as experience of life, literature will influence all who are capable of finding recreation in something beyond mere sensation. These it will unite by a common interest in life at its best, and by the perpetual reminder that through all social differences human nature and its strongest affections are fundamentally the same. . . .

Nevertheless, it is on the literary side that children from the Elementary Schools are apt to be found most deficient. Among those who have the best opportunity for judging are teachers at Secondary Schools, where selected Elementary School children form a proportion of the pupils. There these children can be compared with others who come from a different school and home environment. When judged by the Secondary School standard they often prove, we are told, 'good at Arithmetic, but weak in English'.

This is far from being universally true but it is what might be expected under the conditions, and it is very desirable that its significance should be perceived. It does not mean that the Elementary Schools have neglected English. They give a great deal more attention to English than do schools of any other type. It means that it is far harder to teach English in an average Elementary School than to teach it anywhere else, and that this applies to English only, and not to other subjects. Where other subjects are harder to teach, it is lack of English that is the cause.

The great difficulty of teachers in Elementary Schools in many districts is that they have to fight against the powerful influence of evil habits of speech contracted in home and street. The teachers' struggle is thus not with ignorance but with a perverted power. That makes their work the harder, but it must also make their zeal the fiercer. A child with home advantages hears English used well, and grows up to use it well himself. He speaks grammatically, he acquires a wide vocabulary, he collects ideas. When he wants to read he can procure books, and can sit in comparative peace in a warm and well-lit room. The English which he has learnt at home may suffice, independently of any schoolteaching, to keep him well ahead of his class-room neighbour. The latter's English may be a negative quantity, requiring great pains on his teacher's part to cancel out before any positive progress can be made. We are not surprised to be told that some children leave school almost inarticulate so far as anything like educated English is concerned.

Plainly, then, the first and chief duty of the Elementary School is to give its pupils speech — to make them articulate and civilised human beings, able to communicate themselves in speech and writing, and able to receive the communication of others. It must be remembered that chidren, until they can readily receive such information, are entirely cut off from the life and thought and experience of the race embodied in human words. Indeed, until they have been given civilised speech it is useless to speak of continuing their education, for, in a real sense, their education has not been begun. For such children, then, English is, as we have said, not a subject of instruction, but the basis of school life; the lesson in English is not merely one occasion for the inculcation of knowledge, it is an initiation into the corporate life of man. Where this is not clearly recognised, elementary education fails in its main purpose.

We believe that, in many schools, what we desire is being done — that, in actual fact, the aim and standard of the English lessons are as high in the best Elementary Schools as in any schools in the country; we are less sure, however, that the broad view of English we have shown to be necessary is very generally taken. This is not always the fault of the teachers. There are still people in positions of influence who are inclined to regard a humane education of the lower classes as subversive of public order. We believe that view to be wrong. The fact that the majority of elementary school children will have to take up some form of manual labour, perhaps of unskilled labour, must not limit the kind of education they are to receive, for, as we have shown, education is a preparation for life, not, in the first hand, for livelihood; it is the development of the whole man, and not the mere training of a factory hand. . . .

Speech training

Speech training must be undertaken from the outset, and should be continued all through the period of schooling. Teachers of infants sometimes complain that when the children come to school, they can scarcely speak at all. They should regard this rather as an advantage. There is often a kind of race as to which should succeed in setting its stamp upon the children's speech, the influence of the teacher, or that of the street or home. But, unfortunately, the teacher often makes no serious effort to win, and turns aside to other things that might well be done later, as though winning were a matter of no consequence. The definite training of the ear and of the vocal organs is not one of the things to which tradition has paid regard. Uncouth speech has been assumed to be the natural heritage of the children for whom elementary schools were originally instituted. Actually, the accomplishment of clear and correct speech is the one definite accomplishment which the child is entitled to demand from the Infant School. But apart from some excellent pioneer work in schools and by individual teachers, speech training has been strangely neglected. We wish to emphasize its importance more strongly.

In London, it is true, a good deal has been done. Classes for teachers in phonetics and voice production have been largely attended, and the Board of Education's Divisional Inspector for London tells us that they have gone some way towards getting rid of undesirable forms in London speech. A Conference on *Speech Training in London Schools and Colleges* which reported in 1916, has made definite recommendations for the improvement of enunciation and pronunciation, involving systematic study of the way in which speech sounds are formed, and the use of some system of sound representation, based strictly on the principle of 'one sound one symbol'. But even in London speech training does not receive full attention, and outside London, with certain exceptions, there is marked indifference on the whole question. It is lamentable, in a great number of schools, to hear the children habitually mispronouncing words, or mumbling rather than pronouncing them, while their teachers, who may show great concern at inaccuracies where the written word is concerned, seem to accept a pitiably low standard of speech as a thing which must be taken for granted and scarcely calls for comment.

It is emphatically the business of the Elementary School to teach all its pupils who either speak a definite dialect or whose speech is disfigured by vulgarisms, to speak standard English, and to speak it clearly, and with expression. Our witnesses are agreed that this can be done, provided that definite and systematic teaching is given from the outset. It is not sufficient merely to correct the various errors of pronunciation as they occur, or to insist on the children 'speaking out'. They should learn to recognise every sound in standard English, should observe for themselves how sounds are produced and modified by the position of the speech organs, and should practise producing them properly. The really scientific method, of course, would be to associate each sound with a phonetic symbol. This may seem to some teachers an alarming suggestion, but the learning of the symbols will be found a very simple matter both by teachers and by children, and the teacher needs some means, which our system of spelling unfortunately does not afford, of referring to the sounds of the spoken language without actually producing them. The real difficulty will be found, our witnesses assure us, not in learning the symbols, but in combatting the causes which prevent production of the correct sounds, such as habitual lip laziness, or inability to detect the less obvious differences.

An objection sometimes made to the use of phonetic symbols is that they tend to accelerate, or at any rate to confirm, the modern tendency to slur over unaccented vowel sounds, giving to most of them the sound 'er'. It is outrageous, we are told, that such pronunciations as 'mountin' or 'pickcher' should receive any certificate of respectability. But this objection is really a protest against an alleged misuse of phonetic symbols, rather than against any use of phonetic symbols at all. They may be made to bolster up one pronunciation just as easily as another. The problem is not really one of the use of phonetic symbols, but of what standard English pronunciation is. This is a much debated question, but for our present purpose it should suffice to say that it is a pronunciation free from provincialisms and vulgarisms.

While we consider that the use of phonetic symbols is the scientific method of speech training, we realise that good results can be, and are, obtained, independently of any scientific system, by teachers who make a genuine effort to improve the children's speech. A Head Mistress writes: 'No scientific phonetic system has been employed in the school, but special attention is given to speech training, (a) by means of voice production in musical exercises, (b) by the preparatory work done in reading lessons, (c) by imitation of correct sounds, (d) by children's discussions in some English lessons, (e) by encouragement throughout the day.' A witness who has conducted a school attended mainly by children from the slum quarters of a large town said that she found it possible to train the children to speak correctly, 'speech being to a remarkable degree a matter of imitation'. Another witness stated that 'dramatisation by children had a marvellous effect on their speech'.

We do not advocate the teaching of standard English on any grounds of social 'superiority', but because it is manifestly desirable that all English people should be capable of speaking so as to be fully intelligible to each other and because inability to speak standard English is in practice a serious handicap in many ways. And we may quote the words of a witness who describes her methods 'of guiding the child to that refinement of speech which, in a subtle manner, is an index to the mind, and helps to place it beyond the reach of vulgarity of thought and action.' We do not, however, suggest that the suppression of dialect should be aimed at, but that children who speak a dialect, should, as often happens, become bi-lingual, speaking standard English too. Every dialect has, for those who have been brought up to speak it, intimate associations of its own, and side by side with standard English, dialect will probably persist and be used in the playground and the street. In many cases, indeed, it will deserve to persist, on account of its historic interest. The witnesses whom we have heard on the subject of dialect are not agreed on the likelihood of its continuance. But they agree that this is not a matter in which the schools ought deliberately to exert influence.

The position of the English language in the world affords another argument for all English children being taught English as distinct from a dialect of English. At the request of the Northern Peace Congress which met in Stockholm in 1919, the Northern Peace Union addressed an inquiry to the representatives of countries where none of the three great languages (English, German, and French) are spoken, as to which was, in their opinion, the most suitable language for universal use. Fifty-four replies were received. Of these, one was in favour of German, eight of French, one of Latin or Spanish, five of Ido or Esperanto. No less than twenty-nine, a majority of the whole were in favour of English, and the report of the inquiry concludes: 'If English is to become the international language, everybody who wishes to learn it must be given an opportunity. It must be taught in all the schools of the world — optional in Elementary Schools, and compulsory in the Higher Schools.' If this is a measure of the prestige which the English language possesses abroad, it surely merits more attention in the schools of England, if only from the point of view of a practical asset. English children, required by law to attend school, are surely entitled to be taught, in a scientific and effective way, the accepted speech of their own country.

TEXT AND SELECTED READING

The text is from the Newbolt Report, *The Teaching of English in England*, and was first published in 1921. The political context of the Report and the significance of the Report in that context is examined in Tony Crowley, *The Politics of Discourse* (London: Macmillan, 1989). The importance of the Report in the development of English studies in Britain is discussed in detail in C. Baldick, *The Social Mission of English Criticism 1848–1932* (Oxford: Clarendon, 1983), and more generally in T. Eagleton, *Literary Theory* (Oxford: Blackwell, 1983). The role of the Report in the discourse of 'Englishness' is discussed in R. Colls and P. Dodd (eds), *Englishness* (London: Croom Helm, 1986) and in more detail by Brian Doyle, *English and Englishness* (London: Routledge, 1989).

16

Henry Wyld

Wyld's argument for the superiority of 'received standard English' (RSE) can best be read in the context of the shift in meaning of the term 'standard English' from its sense of the written language to that of the form of the spoken language which, according to the *OED* definition, 'by means of its cultural status and currency, is held to represent the best form of that speech'. His argument in fact attempts to take the definition of 'standard English' one step further than that given by the dictionary in that he intends to demonstrate the *intrinsic* merit of 'standard English' by the methods of science. For Wyld it is scientificity rather than simply opinion which lends its authority to the claims made for RSE.

The question which Wyld sets out to answer is presented as a simple one. It is this: 'which among the various Regional or provincial dialects on the one hand, or which among the innumerable class dialects on the other' best exhibits the conditions of 'maximum resonance, or sonority', with 'the clearest possible differentiation of the sounds'? The question has the appearance of a scientific inquiry and appears therefore as one which can be resolved through the methods of phonetics (or 'phonology' as Wyld calls it, though this has a distinct sense in contemporary usage). The answer to the question, which Wyld renders almost immediately, is that on the grounds of sonority and distinctness, RSE is *intrinsically* superior to all other forms.

Wyld's work certainly has the tone of scientificity in its claims, as it proceeds by analysing and classifying different forms of the language. For example, rather than the simple division between 'dialect' and 'standard English' which had previously been used, Wyld devises the terms 'regional dialect', 'class dialect', 'modified standard' and 'received standard'. It is the last of these which is of interest and in particular

Wyld's definition of it. His description sounds familiar and recalls the dictionary definition as the language of the 'cultured and educated'. He asserts that it is the form 'neither provincial nor vulgar' which everybody would speak if they could, and want to if they do not. It is the language of members of 'the great Public Schools, and used by those classes in society which normally frequent these'. Yet his claim is represented as differing from others in that he does not, it is alleged, base his evaluation of RSE on the fact that it 'is spoken by those very often properly called "the best people" ', but on the grounds that 'it has two great advantages which make it intrinsically superior to every other type of English speech'. These advantages are 'the extent to which it is current throughout the country, and the marked distinctiveness and clarity in its sounds'.

The argument is presented as being concerned with intrinsic qualities. Yet if this is so then the first of his advantages cannot be counted in favour of his argument. For the fact that a particular form of the language is current throughout the country is not an intrinsic feature of that form, but an extrinsic and contingent fact. Moreover, it cannot even be said that this form is 'current throughout the country' since it is, by his own definition, 'the type spoken by members of the great Public Schools'. It is, once again, not the practice of the majority, but of an elite section of the populace. Even his claim that RSE is without variation throughout the country is scarcely confirmed by the dictionary definition of 'standard English' as spoken 'with modifications individual or local'. The first intrinsic quality then turns out not to be intrinsic at all. The second claim looks more promising and appears to be supported by scientific evidence. However, if we consider this evidence it is again not quite what it seems. What we have presented to us is indeed phonetic analysis of the distribution of various vowel sounds in the differing spoken forms of the language; but in itself that is not evidence for one form being superior to another. For example, he says that RSE is characterised by the long *a* vowel whereas in many dialects the short *a* is used in words such as path and so on. And this analysis is correct. However, where the claim goes awry is the extension which takes place whereby the distribution of such vowels is taken to argue for or against a particular form of the spoken language. It is a scientifically observable fact that long *a* appears in RSE and short *a* in certain dialects; but it is not a scientific fact that short *a* 'is neither as sonorous nor as beautiful as long *a*'. That is a matter of opinion and thus an extrinsic feature which is thrust upon a particular form. It cannot be taken as evidence of intrinsic superiority.

If the superiority of RSE is not intrinsic then, whence does its authority derive? The answer is not far removed from Campbell's definition of 'the language properly so-called' as 'current, especially in the upper and middle ranks, over the whole British empire'. Not far removed, but certainly more restrictive, since Wyld's definition is based on the 'best speakers' who have 'perfect confidence in themselves, in their speech, as in their manners'. It is like James' 'tone standard', all a question of good breeding and behaviour within 'a firm and gracious tradition'. The models for speech, indeed the paragons of social behaviour and identity, are the 'officers of the British Army': 'The utterance of these men is at once clear-cut and precise, yet free from affection; at once downright and manly, yet in the highest degree refined and urbane.'

'THE BEST ENGLISH: A CLAIM FOR THE SUPERIORITY OF RECEIVED STANDARD ENGLISH'

In the Society for Pure English Tract XXII, *The Nature of Human Speech*, by Sir Richard Paget, and in Tract XXVI, *English Vowel Sounds*, by Dr. A.W. Aikin, the acoustic properties of vowels are studied in relation to the inherent pitch or natural tone of each sound. It has long been known that every vowel sound in human speech possesses a specific musical tone which can only be recognised when the sounds are whispered, as in ordinary utterance this tone is drowned by the far louder vibrations set up by the vocal cords in the phenomenon known as 'voice' in the special phonetic sense. In 1890 Lloyd, in *Some Researches into the Nature of Vowel Sounds*, showed that this characteristic inherent pitch of a vowel depends upon the vibrations set up in two resonance cavities in the mouth, one at the back, and one further forward. It is the blending of the vibrations of these two cavities which, according to Lloyd, gives to a vowel its characteristic pitch, and it is the pitch which produces the distinguishing quality, character, and colour of a vowel sound in speech. The differentiation of one vowel from another depends upon the alteration of the relative size and shape of the two mouth cavities above referred to.

But this alteration of relations in the two cavities is brought about by the movements of the tongue, which can occupy a large number of different positions, thus changing the relative size of the one cavity to that of the other. Ultimately then, the character of the vowel sound is determined by the position of the tongue, and sometimes also by the participation of the lips.

In my analysis of certain vowel sounds, later in this article, I base my remarks, following the method of Sweet, upon the activities of the tongue and lips. This does not imply a difference of opinion with the authors of the earlier tracts in respect of their earlier observations on the pitch of the vowels which they describe. On the contrary, I assume these to be correct, though for my present purpose it is sufficient to attend to the positions of the tongue and lips, upon which the acoustic qualities of vowels in ordinary uttered speech depend, no less than their inherent pitch.

I might take as a text for this paper the words of Dr. Aikin, S.P.E. Tract XXVI, p. 184: 'It is best, from a phonological point of view, to combine the condition of maximum resonance, or sonority, with the clearest possible differentiation of the sounds.' I entirely agree. The questions for English speakers then are — which among the various Regional or provincial dialects on the one hand, or which of the innumerable Class dialects on the other, best exhibits the desired conditions; and, further, whether intrinsic superiority can really be claimed for one type of English above all others in respect of these qualities of sonority and distinctness. It is the purpose of the following observations to attempt an answer to these questions, and to give reasons for it.

I believe that the form of English which best satisfies Dr. Aikin's conditions, and also several others of hardly less weight, is that which I take leave to call *Received Standard*. A few words in explanation of this term are called for. It was suggested by me about twenty years ago to denote a type of English for which no specific and distinctive designation was current.

It was formerly customary to distinguish *Dialect*, meaning *Provincial English*, on one hand, and *Standard English* on the other, the implication apparently being that the latter type was perfectly uniform, and that it was spoken by everyone who did not speak a provincial dialect. This assumption is so remote from the truth that it is merely disingenuous to acquiesce in it, and to attempt to disguise what is the actual fact that thousands of persons speak a form of English which is neither a local dialect, nor what some would call 'good English'. For this latter type, which is neither one thing nor the other, I proposed the term *Modified Standard*. This term is intended to cover all the various types of English, many of them spoken by highly educated people, which types, while they adhere, on the whole, to the Standard, especially in accidence and syntax, are nevertheless more or less deeply affected, either by *provincialisms*, or by what none but the uncandid would hesitate to call *vulgarism*, in pronunciation. The latter is particularly characteristic of the speech of the middle classes in towns; the former is heard in country districts. These types I believe to be the result of an attempt to speak the 'best' or 'standard' English by those who have not had the advantage of hearing and speaking it from childhood up. It is indeed 'standard' gone wrong, and 'modified' either by a provincial or, as I prefer to call it, a *Regional Dialect*, or by an inferior *Class Dialect*. Hence the name *Modified Standard*. (*Class* is here used in the ordinary sense of a grade or section of society.)

With this type, or rather these types, for they are many, I contrast what, for want of a better name, I call *Received Standard* (henceforward referred to in this paper by the initials R.S.). Everyone knows that there is a type of English which is neither provincial nor vulgar, a type which most people would willingly speak if they could, and desire to speak if they do not. It is unnecessary to particularize R.S. farther than I have done in the preceding sentence, beyond saying that it is the type spoken by members of the great Public Schools, and by those classes in society which normally frequent these. I suggest that this is the best kind of English, not only because it is spoken by those often very properly called 'the best people', but because it has two great advantages that make it intrinsically superior to every other type of English speech — the extent to which it is current throughout the country, and the marked distinctiveness and clarity in its sounds.

There is no need to labour the first point. R.S. is heard in equal perfection in every part of the country among those classes who use it, and the variations in it are so slight and so few as to be negligible, because, except to the most keen-eared observer, they are imperceptible. The alternative pronunciations of the vowel in *soft*, *cough*, *froth*, *loss*, and so on, are equally tolerable, and neither of them is startling to a hearer who himself favours the other. Few persons could tell you which variety of the initial consonant in *white*, &c., was used by the latest speaker with whom they have conversed.

How different are the conditions with Modified Standard. Here all is variety. Every province, every town, nay, almost every suburb, and every class, has its own idiosyncrasies of pronunciation.

Another aspect of the matter may be urged in passing. An orator who uses some form of Modified Standard, unless indeed his audience consists entirely of persons drawn from his own province, or from precisely his own social grade, will of necessity speak a dialect which is in many respects unfamiliar to most of his hearers. These will themselves speak either R.S. or else some of the innumerable forms of Modified Standard which will certainly differ from that type employed by him who addresses them. Most people find it distressing to listen to a discourse uttered with a pronunciation unfamiliar to them. The effect is a continuous series of surprises which startle and distract the attention from the subject under consideration, and at last excite either amusement or disgust. Modified Standard may be vastly well when it is spoken in the family circle, but outside those narrow limits it is apt to be a source of irritation or mockery to others. Some time ago I listened in to a speaker, a noble lord I regret to say, broadcasting his belief that there was still a 'stight of dinejer' in the political atmosphere of Europe — or else that there was not — I am not sure which, for my attention was diverted from following his argument by the interest excited by his cockney accent. On the very night on which I write, a traveller may be heard over the wireless who referred again and again to a *railway* as a 'ryoowye' [*raiuwai*], and constantly said *due to* when he meant *on account of*, or *owing to* — 'we could not fly low *due to* the numerous high mountain peaks', and so on. But that is another story.

I pass now to deal with my main contention in this paper, namely that R.S. is superior, from the character of its vowel sounds, to any other form of English, in beauty and clarity, and is therefore, if for no other reason, the type best suited for public speaking. I have always held this view, but it has been greatly strengthened of late, by the enterprise of the B.B.C. who have brought to my hearing, as I sat in the heart of Oxfordshire, the utterances of a large number of speakers, representing many varieties of style, voice and accent. Most of these speakers had mastered the elementary arts of delivery, many were, indeed, highly accomplished public speakers. There is not the slightest doubt that, given an equally good delivery of both, R.S. is infinitely easier to hear and follow, than a type of English strongly coloured by provincial influence.

What are the qualities that tend to make a form of speech clear and distinct from the point of view of the hearer?

I think with Dr. Aikin that they are chiefly a sonorous quality in the vowels, and a marked differentiation of one vowel from another.

Sonority is also an element of beauty in a language. Vowels differ greatly in sonority, and no language contains only sonorous vowels, so that when we speak of a sonorous language, we mean one which possesses a considerable number of sonorous vowel sounds. R.S. has a fair share of such sounds, more, I fancy than any single provincial dialect.

Chief of these is the sound popularly expressed by *ah* [ā], as heard in *path, chaff, task, hard,* &c. It is surprising how rare this sound is in provincial speech. In some dialects the vowel is short, and even if nearly the same in actual quality, this short vowel lacks the solidity and dignity of the R.S. sound. In other dialects the vowel is an intermediate sound between that in *path* and that in *pad,* and thereby loses both sonority and beauty. We shall have more to say about these intermediate vowels in considering distinctiveness of sound. In many dialects, especially those of the South-West of England, *path, chaff,* &c., are pronounced with a long vowel indeed, but the sound is a lengthened form of that heard in *hat, pad,* and so on, in R.S. This sound [ǣ] is neither as sonorous nor as beautiful as [ā], one of the reasons being that there is usually a tendency to nasalize this vowel to some extent. In yet other dialects the vowel in the above words is simply the short [æ], a good enough sound in moderation, and very frequent (though not in *path,* &c.), in R.S. We must consider that a dialect which has no [ā] is under a grave disability as a sonorous form of speech.

Another long vowel [ʌ̄] (low–flat–tense), as in *bird, fir, herd,* and so on, has great merits of sonority and clearness. It occurs only in positions where the *r* once followed, and has now been lost, in pronunciation. Many provincial dialects preserve an *r*-sound, which is either trilled slightly, as in the North and in Scotland, or 'inverted' as in the South and South-West of England, in parts of the W. Midlands, and among many American speakers. If an *r* be pronounced, we lose, as a rule, both the quality and the length of the vowel of R.S., and the 'inverted' variety of *r* itself has a very rustic effect.

But this is not all. This R.S. vowel [ʌ̄] does not, I fancy, occur naturally in provincial dialects at all, though it may be imported by some speakers from R.S., and some of the provincial substitutes, besides being deficient in sonority, have a mean and vulgar quality compared with the pure long [ʌ̄]. Imagine Keats's *Thou wast not born for death, immortal bird,* with the final, rhyming word pronounced either with a trilled or 'inverted' *r,* preceded by one of the several variants of the vowel associated in provincial speech with these consonants; or with no *r,* but the vowel current in *bird* in the Modified Standard of the Liverpool area! This vowel in terms of the tongue position is the mid–flat–tense.

213

The R.S. dipthong [aɪ], popularly called 'long *i*', as in *sigh, hide,* &c., has the qualities of carrying power and dignity, and so has [au] in *loud, sound,* &c. The equivalents of these dipthongs heard in the innumerable provincial and social dialects are all vastly inferior to the standard sounds in the qualities here claimed for these.

The provincial and Modified Standard varieties of what in R.S. is [ū] (high–back–tense–round–) as in *food, brood, wound,* &c., are interesting to the phonetician, but have little to recommend them acoustically or aesthetically. Scotch speakers have as a rule not only a short vowel in these and similar words, but one which also differs totally in quality from that of R.S. Cockney speech knows several variants including a dipthong [əu]; in the dialects of the South-West we get yet other varieties, some of which suggest to the ear, at the first hearing, the French sound in *pure,* though actually quite different from this, but a sound of but slight sonority.

If it were possible to compare systematically every vowel sound in R.S., with the corresponding sound in a number of provincial and other dialects, assuming that the comparison could be made, as is only fair, between speakers who possessed equal qualities of voice, and the knowledge how to use it, I believe no unbiased listener would hesitate in preferring R.S. as the most pleasing and sonorous form, and the best suited to be the medium of poetry and oratory.

I come now to consider the claim of clearness and intelligibility which I make for R.S. These depend very largely, as has been already indicated, upon the relative distinctiveness of the vowel sounds, that is the quality of being clearly and easily apprehended by the ear for what they are, and of being well differentiated from each other in the effect which they produce upon the ear.

The merit of clearness is possessed by R.S. to a degree unapproached by any of the provincial and vulgar forms of English. The reason is that all those vowels in the former, which are not dipthongs, are definite, individual, and perfect types of their several kinds. Each R.S. vowel possesses a characteristic inherent tone, or pitch, which is perfectly distinct from that of the other vowels. We have no inter-mediate vowels, no sounds, that is, which are partly one thing, and partly something else, and therefore likely to be confused. . . .

From this brief comparative survey of some of the more important vowel sounds in R.S., and their equivalents in some of the types of Regional Dialect, it appears that the advantage is with the former in respect (a) of sonority and carrying power; (b) of greater definiteness of sound, in as much as the vowels are clear-cut, while vague intermediate shades are lacking; also the vowels are clearly distinguished from each other in quality and quantity; (c) of greater wealth and variety of vowel sounds.

If these points be conceded, then I have established the claim that R.S. is intrinsically superior to other types of English, more especially as a medium of public speaking.

Nothing is here intended to the disparagement of genuine Regional Dialect in its proper place, that is, in the area in which it grew up. It is urged, however, that to introduce provincial sounds into what is intended to be Standard English, addressed to educated people, is distressing and distracting. For the various forms of the Modified Standard of towns which reflect class influence, and are of the nature of plain vulgarisms, there is little to be said except in dispraise.

But if it is desirable, on the one hand, to eliminate the grosser forms of provincialism and vulgarism from the English of public speakers, it is no less so, on the other, to get rid of the equally offensive defects of pedantry, preciosity, foppishness, and coxcombry.

It is characteristic of R.S. that it is easy, unstudied, and natural. The 'best' speakers do not need to take thought for their utterance; they have no theories as to how their native tongue should be pronounced, nor do they reflect upon the sounds they utter. They have perfect confidence in themselves, in their speech, as in their manners. For both bearing and utterance spring from a firm and gracious tradition. 'Their fathers have told them' — that suffices. Nowhere does the best that is in English culture find a fairer expression than in R.S. speech. And under this should be included not merely pronunciation, but also the inflexions and modulations of the voice. If I were asked among what class the 'best' English is most consistently heard at its best, I think, on the whole, I should say among officers of the British regular Army. The utterance of these men is at once clear-cut and precise, yet free from affectation; at once downright and manly, yet in the highest degree refined and urbane.

With such a form of English we may contrast the various forms of Modified Standard. Of these I shall only mention two extremes – the frankly uncultivated and vulgar, and the over-refined and affected. Of the former nothing further need be said here; it is, unfortunately, but too familiar in the English of towns. Of the latter a few words of dispraise may not be out of place. First of all it should be noted that the kind of speech referred to is a tissue of affectations. Nothing is natural, everything – vowels, the cadence of the sentence, every tone of the voice – bears evidence of care, and the desire to be 'refined'.

The result is always ludicrous, and sometimes vulgar. The whole utterance is pervaded by an atmosphere of unreality, and the hearer not infrequently gets the impression that the speaker is endeavouring with the utmost care, by means of a mincing, finicky pronunciation, to avoid, or cover up some terrible natural defect. We feel, in listening to such speakers, that they are uneasy, unsure of themselves, that they have no traditional social or linguistic background, but have concocted their English upon some theory of what is 'correct' and 'refined', instead of absorbing it, and reproducing it unconsciously, from the converse of well-bred and urbane persons.

Better far than this kind of stuff is plain and downright vulgarism or provincialism.

Since writing the above I have had the advantage of studying Tract XXXVII, by Dr. Chapman, on *Oxford English*. The provocation to write this Tract came from an American gentleman, Dr. Vizetelly, who wrote what purported to be a characterisation of speech of the 'best people in England'. I have no knowledge of this gentleman's writings beyond a passage quoted by Dr. Chapman in his Tract which, indeed, is mainly a reply to this. I gather that Dr. Vizetelly identifies that form of English which he describes, not only with Standard English, but also with what he calls 'the Oxford voice'. Dr. Chapman has thought it worth while to defend Standard English against this attack of the American writer. He has done so temperately and with dignity. He deals also with the 'Oxford accent'. I have nothing to add to his main contentions with which I agree. I would only say that Dr. Vizetelly's account of standard English seems to me to be a travesty of the facts. The dialect he describes strikes me as a mixture of some of the worst types of vulgarism, and of preposterous affectations. I can admit no resemblance between this and the R.S. which I have had in mind in the account given earlier. Dr. Vizetelly seems to have been unfortunate in the speakers he selected for observation, and to have been misled into accepting as 'the best people' those who were actually something quite different.

Now a few words about 'Oxford English'. According to my classification of the existing varieties of English, the following statement I believe covers the facts. Among the large population of Oxford — over 80,000 persons — we find, as in other towns of the same size, speakers both of R.S. and of the various types of Modified Standard. The population of Oxford is complex. There are (i) the townsmen in the narrower sense, by which is meant primarily tradesmen and business people. There is (ii) a large number of persons now resident in Oxford consisting of retired military men, and of old Civil Servants, from India and elsewhere, and their families; (iii) the Cathedral officers; (iv) the military garrison with its Officers; (v) University Officers and teachers of all kinds — Fellows of Colleges, and other resident scholars; (vi) the Undergraduates who come and go.

The townsmen as a rule, especially the older generation, speak a form of Modified Standard more or less strongly tinged with the Regional Dialect of Oxfordshire. The remaining five classes might be expected to speak R.S., and so, no doubt, most of them do. This will probably appear most uniform, and least affected by Regional or Class influences in Classes ii, iii, iv, and v. Now all these contain a large proportion of persons who have graduated at the University, No. iii being exclusively graduates, and many of them, especially the Canons, being also University teachers, so that nearly all members of Class iii belong also to v. Classes v and vi, like other considerable bodies of Englishmen gathered together in a single centre, will be found to contain speakers both of R.S. and Modified Standard. This is inevitable seeing the divers parts of the country from which they come. While it is certainly true that much of the individual's home dialect, in its more marked, and, as those to whom they are foreign might say, its more extravagant features, tends to be worn off by the intimate social relations of College life, something still remains. In so far as a speaker retains traces of a London, a Scotch, a North Country, a Liverpool, a Birmingham accent, however admirable each of these may be in its own way, and in its own district, we must say that he speaks, not received, but Modified Standard. But where, it may be asked, do we find the 'Oxford Accent', and what is it? I do not use the term myself, but I presume it is applied by those who do, to a variety of English pronunciation, and in particular to a mode of using the voice, which is assuredly characteristic neither of a given Regional dialect, nor of a vulgar Class dialect, but which, nevertheless, is occasionally heard in Oxford, and probably in Cambridge also, among a few dons and a few undergraduates.

Since this kind of utterance is not, so far as I have observed, native and natural to any region, nor current among any considerable sections of society, it must be an artificial growth within restricted academic circles. But since it differs appreciably from unaffected R.S., it must be regarded as a form of Modified Standard.

The 'Oxford Accent' in this narrow sense reflects the habits rather of a clique than of a class. It is not nearly so widespread as foreigners sometimes believe. I do not recognise any of its characteristics in that strange form of English described by Dr. Vizetelly. It might be said perhaps that the 'Oxford Accent' conveys an impression of a precise and rather foppish elegance, and of deliberate artificiality. One can only conjecture that this amiable eccentricity is by some adopted from the same motives which animated the Frere in Chaucer's Prologue:–

> Somewhat he lipsed for his wantonnesse
> To make his English swete up-on his tonge.

By other speakers it may be acquired to cloak features of the native dialect deemed undesirable.

The dislike sometimes expressed for this particular kind of affected English is, I think, rather exaggerated. At the worst it sounds like a good-humoured burlesque of R.S., and after all, it is funny without being vulgar, and is frequently a source of innocent merriment.

TEXT AND SELECTED READING

The text is taken from Wyld's essay, 'The Best English' and was first published as Tract XXXIX in the *Proceedings of the Society for Pure English*, 4 (1934). Tony Crowley, *The Politics of Discourse* (London: Macmillan, 1989) has a chapter on 'Theorising the Standard: Jones and Wyld', and 'The Growth of Standard English' is examined by Raymond Williams in *The Long Revolution* (London: Chatto and Windus, 1961). The general question of prescription and authority is discussed in James and Lesley Milroy, *Authority in Language* (London: Routledge and Kegan Paul, 1985).

17

A.S.C. Ross

It has been noted in the Newbolt piece how language was intended to unite the social classes at a time of historical conflict, and in the Wyld essay how the language of one particular class is taken as the superior form, 'the best English'. In the essay by Ross we see an extension of this analysis in that he concerns himself with the function of language as the distinguishing feature of different classes in Britain. Although he can be said to overstate the case when he argues that 'it is solely by its language that the upper class is clearly marked off from the others', since classes are constructed economically and politically as well as culturally, there can be no doubt that he captured an important fact about British social life. For despite the amusing tone and nature of many of the examples he gives, there can be no doubt that sensitivity to forms of language as factors in the building of social identity is extraordinarily high. One reason for this of course is the heavily stratified class system in Britain in which petty differences are magnified and stressed as identifying features. Another reason is precisely that history of the deployment of language in the formation of various types of social and cultural identity which is traced in the previous texts. It is indeed a long and twisting history but it should come as no surprise to find that it has left the British with a legacy of extreme sensitivity to linguistic and social differences.

An earlier example of such sensitivity to these differences was given by G.M. Young, when he declared,

> The world is very evil. An unguarded look, a word, a gesture, a picture or a novel, might plant a seed of corruption in the most innocent heart and the same word or gesture might betray a lingering affinity with the class below.
>
> (*Victorian England: Portrait of An Age*, 1936)

Young was in fact describing Victorian England, but this same awareness continued to exist within British society for a long time after that. Indeed it might even be claimed that one of the central features of the British social scene after the Second World War is precisely this feeling for class differences. Across various cultural media — drama, television, novels, music – from Pinter to pop music or soaps, class has played a significant role in identification and placement and continues to do so. On many occasions of course the processes of identification have been constructed and they are often minor and relatively unimportant; they can also obscure many of the real differences. On many other occasions, however, they illustrate the processes by which loyalties, commitments and various forms of social practice are brought to life.

Ross's concern is with the linguistic demarcation of the upper class alone, though his remark that 'class-distinction is very near to the heart of the upper class' could be extended to other classes. The terms themselves are not quite clear; upper, middle and lower, for example, should not be confused with the terms working class and propertied or monied class; nor should they be confused with the terms bourgeoisie and proletariat. Upper, middle and lower class are terms whose force comes precisely from the fact that they are hard to define; and indeed many definitions come down to fairly small (though often significant) patterns of social behaviour. Be that as it may, Ross considers how 'the upper class' seeks to distinguish itself linguistically in British society. Evidently the opportunities for demarcation in the written language are fairly limited and therefore the principle area of identification is in the spoken language.

In many ways what we find in Ross's list of 'U' and 'non-U' terms is a precise articulation of many of the prejudices and evaluations of the nineteenth-century British texts set out above. What he produces is a type of linguistic version of Debrett's *Etiquette and Modern Manners*, that code book by which a certain social identity can be constructed and maintained. The list, though often merely amusing, is not without interest, however, and includes items around which enormous social conflicts have been fought. Historical analysis of the terms 'cultivated', 'cultured' and 'civilised', for example, terms which he links together in a semantic field, would facilitate the possible writing of the social history of Britain over the past five centuries. This is perhaps a grand claim for historical semantics, but it is not an exaggerated one.

One way in which the essay links with earlier texts, and in particular that of Wyld, is in its assertion that 'U-speakers' have a specific 'voice' or 'pronunciation'. Concluding that the attempt to acquire such a 'voice' in adulthood will always be doomed to failure, Ross recommends that those who wish to acquire 'U-speech' should (if young enough) be sent 'first to a preparatory school, then to a good public school'. Or to put it another way, if you are not to the linguistic manner born, then you will have to pay private school fees to acquire it. As with so many of these texts, the address is to an audience whose anxiety over their cultural identity belies their position of profound social advantage.

'LINGUISTIC CLASS-INDICATORS IN PRESENT-DAY ENGLISH'

Today, in 1953, the English class-system is essentially tripartite — there exist an upper, a middle, and a lower class. It is solely by its language that the upper class is clearly marked off from the others. In times past (e.g. in the Victorian and the Edwardian periods) this was not the case. But, today, a member of the upper class is, for instance, not necessarily better educated, cleaner, or richer than someone not of this class. Nor, in general, is he likely to play a greater part in public affairs, be supported by other trades or professions, or engage in other pursuits or pastimes than his fellow of another class. There are, it is true, still a few minor points of life which may serve to demarcate the upper class, but they are only minor ones. [In this article I use the terms *upper class* (abbreviated: U), *correct, proper, legitimate, appropriate,* (sometimes also *possible*) and similar expressions (including some containing the word *should*) to designate usages of the upper class; their antonyms *(non-U, incorrect, not proper, not legitimate,* etc.) to designate usages which are not upper class. These terms are, of course, used factually and not in reprobation (indeed I may at this point emphasise a point which is doubtless obvious, namely that this whole article is purely factual). *Normal* means common to both U and non-U. I often use expressions such as *U-speaker* to denote a member of the upper class and, also, *gentleman*, pl. *gentlemen* (for brevity, in respect of either sex – pl. *gentlefolk* is no longer U). Class-distinction is very near to the heart of the upper class and talk about it is hedged with taboo. Hence, as in sexual matters, a large number of circumlocutions is used. Forty years ago, as I understand, U-speakers made use of *lady* and *gentleman* without self-consciousness; the antonym of *gentleman* was often *cad* or *bounder*. Today, save by older people, these terms can hardly be used to indicate class-distinction, for they sound either pedantic or facetious (*you cad, sir!*). *Lady* and *gentleman* have, of course, senses quite unconnected with class-distinction, but, today, the use of these words in the sense 'man' and 'woman' between U-speakers has almost entirely vanished save when prefixed with old (*There's an old lady to see you* is different from *There's an old woman to see you*, for the former implies that the person is U, the latter that she is very non-U). *She's a nice lady* is non-U, *He's a nice gentleman* even more so (*man, woman, or girl* being the U-use here) — landladies sometimes call negroes *dark gentlemen* or, occasionally, *gentlemen of colour*. But U-speakers correctly use *lady and gentleman* to their servants as do servants to their masters. Today youngish U-speakers sometimes express class-distinction by such sentences as *X – is of good family* or, alternatively, *X — is rather ill-bred*, but they would perhaps be more likely to make use of circum-locutions such as *I should have thought X – was perfectly alright* (or even: *quite OK*); the antonymical form might be as vague as *X — is obviously awful*. In Oxford, in the late twenties, the term *not respectable* was sometimes used in this sense and intellectual Oxford of the period liked to use the German expression *rein/unrein* – this can of course only be used to U-speakers moderately acquainted with German and these are rare (a state of affairs in contradistinction to that obtaining some seventy years ago). U-speakers might stigmatise expressions or habits as non-U by calling them *low* (more rarely, *vulgar*); at least one Public School (Bradfield) uses *pleb* in this sense. The phrase *not done*, once perhaps a U-phrase, seems to be dying out, save in schools. At the beginning of the century many slang phrases were used to distinguish non-gentlemen e.g. *not off the top shelf, not out of the top drawer, not one of us, not quite the clean potato, L.M.C.* (= Lower Middle Class), *a bit hairy in the heel, showing the cloven hoof, showing* (or similar introduction) *the mark of the beast*. At this distance of time it is hard to decide which, if any, of these expressions were U (*he's a bad bred 'un* and *risen from the ranks, I suppose*? certainly were) and which belonged rather to the extensive class of non-U speakers trying to become U. As a boy I heard *not quite a gent, not (quite) the gentleman*, used by non-U speakers; today, *well-connected* is definitely non-U. *One of our great border families* is probably idiosyncratic. At one time *common* was used by U-speakers, though it is no longer, save of horses; the abbreviated *very comm* was apparently used by female U-speakers; *he's a commoner* is an arch U-use (implying that the person is very far from having a seat in the House of Lords).] The games of real tennis and piquet, an aversion to high tea, having one's cards engraved (not printed), not playing tennis in braces, and, in some cases, a dislike of certain comparatively modern inventions such as the telephone, the cinema and the wireless, are still perhaps marks of the upper class. Again, when drunk, gentlemen often become amorous or maudlin or vomit in public, but they never become truculent.

In the present article I am concerned with the linguistic demarcation of the upper class. This subject has been but little investigated, though it is much discussed, in an unscientific manner, by members of the upper class. The late Professor H.C. Wyld wrote a short article on the subject. He was well-equipped for the task, for he was both a gentleman and a philologist. Today, his views are perhaps a little old-fashioned; for instance, the dictum 'No gentleman goes on a bus', attributed to him, is one which most gentlemen have to neglect.

Both the written and the spoken language of the upper class serve to demarcate it, but the former to only a very slight extent. A piece of mathematics or a novel is not likely to differ in any way from one written by a member of another class, except in so far as the novel contains conversation. In writing, it is, in fact, only modes of address, postal addresses and habits of beginning and ending letters that serve to demarcate the class.

Before proceeding to the detail of the present study I must emphasise that I am here concerned with usages which serve to demarcate the upper class. Thus the sentence *That be worse nor Dunkirk's fall* (said of the fall of Torbruk in a small Buckinghamshire town by a speaker aged about sixty) is certainly not U, but sentences of this kind fall quite outside the scope of this article; not using them in no way indicates that the speaker is U. In fact, in seeking to delimit usages, the line of demarcation relevant to this study is, often, between, on the one hand, gentlemen and, on the other, persons who, though not gentlemen, might at first sight appear, or would wish to appear, as such. Thus, habits of speech peculiar to the lower classes find no place here. The same is, in general, true of dialect; it is only where a definite dialect feature appears in a Regional Standard — as, for instance, the use of the phoneme [a] instead of [æ] (e.g. in *cat*) in Northern Standard, that it will require notice. I may also note here that the U-demarcation is of two types:– (1) a certain U-feature has a different, non-U counterpart as non-U *wealthy*/U *rich*; (2) a certain feature is confined to U-speech and it has a counterpart which is not confined to non-U speech e.g. the pronunciations of *girl* as [gɛl], (?[gjɛl]), [gæl], [gɛəl] are U, but many (perhaps most male) U-speakers, like all non-U speakers, use the pronunciation [gəːl]. . . .

223

The Spoken Language

. . . (6) *Vocabulary*

Article 'chamber pot' is non-U; in so far as the thing survives, U-speakers use ['dӡɛri] (a school-boy term) or *pot*.

Bath. *To take a bath* is non-U against U *to have one's bath*.

Civil: this word is used by U-speakers to approve the behaviour of a non-U person in that the latter has appreciated the difference between U and non-U e.g. *The guard was certainly very civil*.

Coach 'char-a-banc' is non-U, doubtless because the thing itself is. Those U-speakers who are forced, by penury, to use them call them *buses*, thereby causing great confusion (a *coach* runs into the country, a *bus* within a town).

Non-U *corsets*/U *stays*.

Counterpane, bedspread, coverlet. Of these three synonyms, I think that the first is U, the second obsolete, the third, non-U.

Cruet. The sentence *Pass the cruet, please* is very non-U; cruets are in themselves non-U. In gentlemen's houses there are, ideally, separate containers — *salt-cellars, pepper-pots (castors, -grinders, -mills)* and *mustard-pots*, so that the corresponding U-expression will be *I wonder if you could pass the salt (pepper, mustard), please?*, or the like. Vinegar is a fourth constituent of many cruets but many uses of vinegar (e.g. poured on fish or bacon and eggs) are definitely non-U.

Crust or crumb?, used when cutting bread is (old-fashioned?) non-U.

Cultivated in *They're cultivated people* is non-U and so also is *cultured*. There really is no U-equivalent (some U-speakers use *civilised* in this sense).

Cup. How is your cup? is a non-U equivalent of *Have some more tea?*, or the like. Possibly negative non-U answers are *I'm doing nicely thank you* and *(Quite) sufficient, thank you*. There is a well-known non-U affirmative answer: *I don't mind if I do*.

Cycle is non-U against *bike, bicycle* (whether verb or noun); non-U *motorcycle*/U *motorbike, motorbicycle* is perhaps less pronouncedly so.

Dinner. U-speakers eat *lunch* in the middle of the day (*luncheon* is old-fashioned U) and *dinner* in the evening; if a U-speaker feels that what he is eating is a travesty of his dinner, he may appropriately call it *supper*. Non-U speakers (also U-children and U-dogs), on the other hand, have their *dinner* in the middle of the day. *Evening meal* is non-U.

Dress suit. This is a non-U word. A male speaker might answer the question *What shall I wear tonight?* in any one of the following ways:–
1) *Dinner jacket*; 2) *Short coat* (?old fashioned); 3) *Black tie*; 4) *Tails*;

5) *White tie*; Nos 1–3 mean German *smoking*, Nos 4–5 German *frack*. The term *evening dress* is often used on invitations but it has not a very wide currency among U-speakers (in any case, for men it is ambiguous); a sentence *Shall we wear evening dress?* would not be possible, the appropriate expression being *Are we going to change?*

Excuse my glove. This expression, used when shaking hands, is (?old-fashioned) non-U; male speakers do (used to?) remove their glove in order to shake hands but say nothing.

Greatcoat (also *topcoat*) are rather old-fashioned U, *overcoat* being normal. *Burberry* and *raincoat* are of the same genre, *macintosh* or *mac* being normal.

Greens 'vegetables' is non-U.

Home: non-U *They've a lovely home*/U *They've a very nice house*.

Horse riding is non-U against U *riding*. From the non-U point of view the expression is reasonable, for to the non-U there are other kinds of riding (cf. non-U *to go for a motor-ride*/U *to go for a drive in a motor car*). But *bicycle-ride* is normal.

Ill in *I was very ill on the boat* is non-U against U *sick*.

Jack. At cards, *jack* is non-U against U *knave*, save in *jackpot* (at poker). My son, Pilot-officer A.W.P. Ross, kindly calls my attention to the following passage from C. Dickens, *Great Expectations* :– 'He calls the knaves, Jacks, this boy! said Estella with disdain'.

La-di-da is an expression with which the non-U stigmatise a U habit, speech-habit, or person.

Lounge is a name given by the non-U to a room in their houses; for U-speakers, *hall* or *dining-room* might well be the nearest equivalent (but all speakers, of course, speak of the *lounge* of a hotel).

non-U *mental*/U *mad*.

A matter of business is non-U (as in *Say you've come to see him on a matter of business*).

Mention: *If you don't mind my mentioning it* is non-U.

Mirror (save in compounds such as *driving-*, *shaving-mirror*) is non-U against U *looking glass*.

non-U *note paper*/U *writing paper*.

Pardon! is used by the non-U in three main ways: 1) if the hearer does not hear the speaker properly; 2) as an apology (e.g. on brushing by someone in a passage; 3) after hiccuping or belching. The normal U correspondences are very curt viz. 1) *What?* 2) *Sorry!* 3) [Silence], though in the first two cases, U-parents and U-governesses are always trying to make children say something 'politer'; *What did you say?* and *I'm frightfully sorry* are certainly possible. For case 3) there are other non-U possibilities e.g. *Manners!*, *Beg Pardon!*, *Pardon me!*. Phrases containing *Pardon* are often answered with *Granted* by the non-U.

To pass a nasty remark. He passed the remark that . . . is non-U.

Pleased to meet you! This is a very frequent non-U response to the greeting *How d'you do?* U-speakers normally just repeat the greeting; to reply to the greeting (e.g. with *Quite well, thank you*) is non-U.

Posh 'smart' is essentially non-U but, recently, it has gained ground among school-boys of all classes.

non-U *preserve*/U *jam*. But *conserve* is legitimate, though rare (I imagine there to be some culinary distinction between, for instance, *conserve of quinces* and mere *quince jam*).

non-U *radio*/U *wireless* (but *radio* technically as in aircraft).

Rude meaning 'indecent' is non-U; there is no universal U-correspondent.

Non-U *serviette*/U *table-napkin*; perhaps the best known of all the linguistic class-indicators of English.

Sit in *He's sitting an exam* is non-U; *sitting for* is better but hardly U unless used very technically.

Study in *He's studying for an exam*, is definitely non-U (U: *working for*).

Teacher is essentially non-U, though *school-teacher* is used by the U to indicate a non-U teacher. The U equivalent is *master, mistress* with prefixed attribute (as *maths-mistress*). Non-U children often refer to their teachers without article (as *Teacher says* . . .).

Non-U *toilet-paper*/U *lavatory paper*.

Non-U *wealthy*/U *rich*.

Before concluding with some general remarks, there are two points that may appropriately receive mention here.

First, *slang*. There seems no doubt that, in the nineties and at least up to 1914, U-speakers (particularly young ones) were rather addicted to slang. Today, however, U-speakers use it little and regard much use of it as non-U — save, of course, in special circumstances (e.g. in the case of young boys at school). American slang is especially deprecated (save, perhaps, for O.K.). The ultimate War, like the penultimate one, brought a flood of slang into the services, some of it of a very vivid kind as, for instance, R.A.F. slang *He tore me off a strip* 'he reprimanded me very severely', *I was shot down in flames* 'I was completely overwhelmed in the argument'. Since the War, there has been an unfortunate tendency for non-Service personnel to use Service slang and it is clear that Service personnel regard such use as in very poor taste. Nevertheless, the expressions *I've had it!* (meaning, essentially, 'I have *not* had it') and *That's a bad show*, have become very frequent among all classes of speakers.

Secondly, *changing one's voice*. In England today – just as much as in the England of many years ago – the question 'Can a non-U speaker become a U speaker' is one noticeably of paramount importance for many Englishmen (and for some of their wives). The answer is that an adult can never attain complete success. Moreover, it must be remembered that, in these matters, U-speakers have ὦτα ἀκούειν, so that one single pronunciation, word or phrase will suffice to brand an apparent U-speaker as originally non-U (for U-speakers themselves never make 'mistakes'). Under these circumstances, efforts to change voice are surely better abandoned. But, in fact they continue in full force and in all strata of society. On the whole, the effect is deleterious. Thus, to take only one example: in village schools, any natural dialect that is still left to the children will have superimposed upon it the language of the primary school-teacher (a class of people entirely non-U) so that the children leave school speaking a mixture which has nothing to recommend it. In concluding this paragraph, I may mention that there is one method of effecting change of voice, provided the speaker is young enough. This is, to send him first to a preparatory school, then to a good public school. This method is one that has been approved for more than a century and, at the moment, it is almost completely effective. It is interesting to speculate upon the state of affairs which will arise when the day comes when virtually no U-speaker will be able to afford to educate his children at these kinds of schools (this day has already dawned).

TEXT AND SELECTED READING

The text is taken from Ross' essay 'Linguistic Class-Indicators In Present-Day English' in *Neuphilologische Mitteilungen*, 55 (1954) though another version is given in a collection of essays on a similar theme entitled *Noblesse Oblige*, ed. N. Mitford (London: Hamish Hamilton, 1956). A more recent collection is R. Buckle (ed.), *U and Non-U Revisited* (London: Routledge and Kegan Paul, 1983). R. Brown and A. Gilman's essay on 'The Pronouns of Power and Solidarity' in *Language and Social Context*, ed. P. Giglioli (Harmondsworth: Penguin, 1972) discusses related questions, while W. Mittins, M. Saln, M. Edminson and S. Coyne, *Attitudes to English Usage* (Oxford: Oxford University Press, 1970) is an interesting survey of recent views. Both

Tony Crowley, *The Politics of Discourse* (London: Macmillan, 1989) and J. and L. Milroy, *Authority in Language* (London: Routledge and Kegan Paul, 1985) give accounts of the prescriptive tradition in which this essay is situated.

18

Alison Assiter

The enormous significance accorded to language in feminist debates over the past twenty years or so provides the context for Alison Assiter's critical essay on the work of another feminist, Dale Spender. Yet although it has been feminists who have put language at the centre of a number of crucial debates across a variety of diciplines, it cannot be claimed that the question of women and their relation to language is a novel one. For as James' essay on 'The Speech of American Women' indicates, the construction of particular speech forms for women is a practice with a substantial history. And Swift in the *Proposal*, in a somewhat surprising gesture, even declared that women are better users of the language than men:

> Now, although I would by no Means give ladies the Trouble of advising us in the Reformation of our Language; yet I cannot help Thinking that, since they have been left out of all Meetings, except Parties at Play, or where worse Designs are carried on, our Conversation hath very much degenerated.

He adds: 'if the Choice had been left to me, I would rather have trusted the Refinement of our Language, as far as it relates to Sound, to the Judgment of the Women.' Of course the grounds upon which Swift makes this evaluation (that women 'do naturally discard the Consonants, as we [men] do the vowels') are dubious; but it is an interesting claim for women's rights in relation to language debates.

However, the recent feminist debates are much more our concern here, in particular the question of a 'man-made language'. Assiter's critique of Spender's claim for the existence of a 'man-made language' takes the form of an attack on the philosophical assumptions which lie behind it. Using the theories espoused by a number of modern philosophers, Assiter's fundamental criticism is that Spender's assertion

229

that men and women have not only different but irreconcilable meanings for the same expressions, is both unsophisticated and potentially harmful. It is unsophisticated because it does not take into account the work of philosophers or linguists (Frege, Saussure, Austin, Quine, Feyerabend and Chomsky among them) on the relationship between linguistic forms and their meanings. And it is potentially harmful because it can lead to linguistic separatism, a context in which men and women, because they do not share the same language, will not be able to communicate and therefore will not be able to bring about any change. Assiter also makes the objection that Spender over-exaggerates since her assertion that all language is man-made, and therefore sexist, obscures those instances which in Assiter's view are the points 'where sexism in language really operates'.

The problem here is that although Assiter's critique of the bases of Spender's philosophical position is well-argued, her own position is also open to question. For in arguing that there are linguistic forms which are always sexist, Assiter ties herself to the view that we can determine the meaning of those forms for once and for all. In a sense this is a return to the account of meaning given by Locke: that meaning should be determinate and knowable in advance, a condition which requires that it be stable and fixed. However, this view of the proper meaning of words has been subjected to attack and has been rejected by those who argue that words do not have meaning in advance of the contexts in which they are employed. Where then would this objection leave the question of sexist language? Would it mean that there is no such thing? Such a conclusion would be dangerous indeed and would clearly be contrary to the evidence we can cite easily enough. The answer is more complex. Rather than saying that there is a sexist, 'man-made', language (Spender's position), or that certain expressions really are sexist (Assiter's position), we can argue instead that the use of certain expressions is sexist precisely because they fit into a larger context of activities which serve to dominate, silence and exclude women. Deborah Cameron puts this well:

> If we take it that no expression has a meaning independent of its linguistic and non-linguistic context, we can plausibly explain the sexism of language by saying that all speech events in patriarchal cultures have as part of their context the power relation that holds between men and women (and indeed many other political factors as well). *This* varied and heterogeneous

context is what makes expressions and utterances liable to sexist interpretation. . . . But this is not a function of language alone; rather it depends on a whole cluster of culturally approved ways of making sense of the world.

('Sexism and Semantics', *Radical Philosophy*, 36 (1984), 15)

Signs in advance then are open and flexible, multi-accentual and pliable. It is their insertion into the context of particular sets of power relations which closes down the possibilities and produces the sexist effects. The conclusion from this argument, of course, is therefore not that we have to change our whole language, nor even that we have to change those uses which 'really are sexist', though language reform is a useful way of highlighting the effects which particular discursive practices can bring about. The conclusion is much harder than either of these choices, for what is being asserted if we follow the logic is that in order to eradicate sexism in language we have to alter radically, in theory and in practice, our 'whole cluster of culturally approved ways of making the world'.

'DID MAN MAKE LANGUAGE?'

Males, as the dominant group, have produced language, thought and reality.

This sentence appears on page 143 of Dale Spender's book *Man Made Language*. Spender believes that 'maleness' pervades language as a whole. Moreover, according to her, the reality most of us inhabit most of the time is a male one because language (male language) creates reality. I shall argue that though Dale Spender's examples are interesting, her major claims about language are sometimes unclear, and that where they are clear, they are positively *damaging* for women. I do not want to concede to the opposition, however, that there is no 'sexist' bias in the English language at all. I shall offer the outline of an alternative account of sexism in one area of language, the purportedly gender-neutral uses of the class noun 'man' and the pronoun 'he'.

Spender

In her book, *Man Made Language*, Dale Spender argues two things: (i) that language determines the limits of our world, constructs our reality . . . and (ii) that language is man-made – it is created by the males of the species and is still primarily under male control. . . . She believes that there is a 'man's language' and a 'woman's language'; there are men's and women's meanings. . . . While the former are 'authoritative', 'serious', 'direct', the latter lack all of these qualities. And she goes further. It is not surprising, she asserts, that men's and women's languages are seen to possess these various qualities – the one set perferved, strong, positive; the other weak, negative – because the very terms in which research projects are set up, the rules governing them, the kinds of questions asked, reflect a male bias. This utter and total mastery over language, Spender contends, is one means by which males have ensured their primacy. The English language is inclined towards males both in syntax and semantics. (Spender refers to English. Indeed, she argues that the supposed 'natural' gender in English as opposed to the grammatical one in German, where a wife takes the neuter gender, reflects a *greater* degree of sexist bias.)

Spender presents a formidable array of examples in support of her thesis. She points out that the meaning of some words is different when applied to females and males. For instance: 'He's a professional'; 'she's a professional'. Pairs of terms which appear to have approximately the same sense, the only difference being that the one is applied to males while the other is used for females, become non-equivalent, the female expression taking on derogatory significance: viz. 'Lord' and 'Lady'. 'Lord' preserves its original meaning whereas 'Lady' has undergone a 'process of democratic levelling' and is no longer preserved for women of high rank.

I believe, however, that Dale Spender's claims are often ambiguous and that they are problematic. She does not explicitly characterise the theory of meaning upon which she relies, nor does she make reference to a number of distinctions linguists and philosophers of language have drawn. I'll refer briefly to some of these in order to bring to light some of the ambiguities and problems in her reasoning.

Some difficulties in Spender's reasoning

One distinction philosophers have seen fit to draw is that between the 'sense' (Sinn) of a sign, and its reference (Bedeutung). Frege described the former as the 'mode of presentation' of the sign and the latter as the object it picks out − its bearer. He pointed to this difference as a way out of a puzzle about identity: the two expressions 'the morning star' and 'the evening star' are identical insofar as they pick out the same object (in reference), but they differ in sense. A philosopher from a different tradition has made a similar kind of point: Saussure's 'signified' is analogous to the Fregean 'sense'.

Spender claims that language creates reality. She would presumably concur with Frege's view, therefore, that the 'sense' of an expression determines its reference. The sense of the term 'table', for example, determines which object it picks out. Now Spender believes that language creates reality and that language is man made. The senses of all expressions in language are thus determined by the males of the species. Hence, the references, too, of every sign will have been decided upon by the males. Now, immediately, there is an ambiguity in Spender's case. In addition to the 'male' language, she believes that there is a 'woman's language'. Is it her belief that the sense, and hence the reference, of the word 'table' was originally determined by the males of the species and that the females now use the expression in a male way? Or does she think that there is a 'masculine' and a 'feminine' sense for the expression? If the latter, are we to suppose that there are masculine and feminine referents for this term? Or do we conclude that the two referents coincide in this case? And, if they do coincide, why do they and what determines when they do not? The claim that the senses of all expressions were originally determined by males is a much more plausible one than the view that all terms now still have masculine and feminine senses, but it is a weaker thesis. It lends support to the view that 'reality' is male only in an attenuated sense. To draw an analogy: a house that is designed by an architect is, in a sense, the architect's — it is his or her creation. But it probably belongs to someone else. On the present interpretation of Spender, language would be 'male' only in the sense that the house is the architect's. Perhaps an architect can make things difficult for the occupants of buildings he or she has created. He or she might have created a house with a dining room far from the kitchen, and this would have made things awkward, indefinitely, for a housewife. Similarly, the 'male' designers of language may have created difficulties for females which last as long as the language survives. But this makes language male no more than it makes the house the architect's. Certainly the man's creation here, *ex hypothesi*, makes matters difficult for women. Just as the housewife may continue, for a long period of time, blaming the architect for his inconvenient design, so may the female language user (if she were aware of the problem) criticise the men who 'produced' the language. But the housewife can neither blame subsequent architects for her architect's creation nor could she (or would she) make out that any one architect owns the house.

Similarly, female language users would be wrong to blame all men — unless they consciously continued the tradition of the language creators — for their predecessors' folly. They would be mistaken too, were they to make out that any man 'owned' language as a result of their progenitors' act.

If we are to take the other way of interpreting Spender's claim that there is a male and a female language: that there are *now* two sets of senses, we come up against another major problem. If language creates the world, and if there is a man's language (a man's set of senses), and a woman's one, and if the two do not overlap, it follows that there is a man's world and a woman's world, and ne'er the twain shall meet. The wife inhabits one world, and her husband another. So what, you may say. The point is important, however. If wife and husband live in different worlds, not only do they fail to communicate with each other (a well-known syndrome if the stories are to be believed) but they may be unable to understand each other. This cannot be put right by careful and painstaking effort on the part of both parties: it is an unalterable state of affairs. Quine and Feyerabend described this phenomenon as the 'incommensurability' of theories: if the corresponding terms in any two theories differ in sense, and sense determines reference, then the two terms pick out different objects. No two propositions — one from each theory – can contradict one another. They will simply be equivocal. I shall return to this point below.

I have mentioned some problems that present themselves with Spender's thought, if we point to one distinction philosophers and linguists have made. If we refer to a further set of distinctions, difficulties of another kind become apparent. Chomsky differentiated linguistic competence – the system of rules and norms of a language – from performance – actual speech behaviour. Chomskys pair corresponds roughly to Saussure's '*langue*' and '*parole*'. Inside the latter domain, another philosopher, J.L. Austin, distinguished among types of acts. First of all, there is the locutionary act – the act of uttering an expression with a definite sense and reference; and then there is the illocutionary act, what I may do in performing the locutionary act, e.g. I may make a promise in uttering the words 'I promise'; and finally there is the perlocutionary act – the act I may succeed in performing by means of my illocutionary act, e.g. in saying 'the door is open', I may perform the perlocutionary act of getting you to shut it. Supposing we were to take Spender's claim as relating to linguistic performance, her reasoning is ambiguous as between these three. At one point she suggests that the same linguistic behaviour is to be found in members of each gender, but that the descriptions given of the behaviours are gender-specific. For instance, Spender criticises Robin Lakoff for using a derogatory term like 'flowery' to characterise women's language. She suggests that some less denigratory term would have been applied to that very same behaviour in a male. However, if she admits that the behaviour could be the same, she may be conceding to her opponents that the language is the same. Witness the expression: 'I think that's a good idea.' Used by a male chairing a meeting, it could be interpreted as an authoritative, finalising remark; whereas the same utterance issuing from the mouth of a female from the floor might well be interpreted as expressing hesitation, diffidence. The respective illocutionary acts here may well be very different. The male may have performed the act of closing the discussion; while the act of the female may have been that of agreeing with the previous speaker. Additionally, the relative perlocutionary acts may differ from one another: perhaps the male carried out the perlocutionary act of getting the meeting to move on to the next topic; maybe the female performed the act of getting the meeting to continue the discussion along the lines suggested by the previous speaker. However, the *locutionary* acts are the same in each case. Significantly, here, it is the relative illocutionary and perlocutionary acts which appear to exhibit the sexist bias: whilst it is the locutionary acts — what is said — which deal with reality. Where Spender takes for granted the existence of a 'women's language', she is assuming its existence in the illocutionary and perlocutionary acts. But if she wishes to argue that 'male' language produces a male world, she must demonstrate that there is a gender-related difference in language-use specifically in the *locutionary* act, for it is here that reference to reality takes place.

Sense and reference; locutionary, illocutionary acts, etc., are two sorts of distinctions philosophers and linguists have drawn. By making them we have brought to light some ambiguities in Spender's reasoning. A further area which might reveal difficulties is that of speakers intentions. On one theory of meaning, the intentions of the speaker contribute to determining what the speaker meant by his or her utterance. But others disagree. They would argue that what I intend to say when I use a form of words is often no good indication at all of what I have really said.

Spender argues that males intended to construct language in such a way as to ensure their dominance. She makes the point that a male grammarian in the eighteenth century, writing mainly for a male audience, ruled that 'the male gender is *more comprehensive* than the female', meaning, Spender suggests, that one male counted for more than woman. Dale Spender contends that this event took place in order to ensure male dominance, and was designed with that purpose in view.

She tells us also that the use of the pronoun 'he' to cover both sexes was not just something that took on as custom and habit; it was deliberately enshrined in an Act of Parliament in 1850. As she points out, there were no female members of parliament to vote against this act. Now granted, the Act was passed by males, and there was no woman to vote against it. But this does not in itself prove that the men passed the act in order to ensure their dominance. That, in fact, would be a highly esoteric view of their intentions. In fact the Act did not concern the use of the pronoun 'he' generally. It was passed in order to simplify the language used in Acts of Parliament. Its title is: 'An Act for shortening the Language used in Acts of Parliament'; and it says: 'Be it enacted, That in all Acts to be hereafter made, Words importing the Masculine Gender shall be deemed and taken to include Females, and the Singular to include the Plural . . . and the word "Month" to mean Calendar Month . . . and "County" shall be held to mean also County of a Town or City.' The intention of the man introducing the Bill was to shorten the language used in Acts of Parliament, not at all to ensure male dominance. The sentence about the masculine gender occurs in a passage containing several other proposals for the abbreviation of language, none of which concerns the relations between the sexes.

Spender's way of presenting the evidence makes it look as though men have always worn dominance on their shirtsleeves, blatantly, for all, including themselves, to see. But they haven't. Though the effect of the use of 'he/man' may be to subjugate the female sex, it is ludicrous to suppose that every man who has ever used such language intended to do that by his use of it. Many men may have had every intention of *not* doing women down, yet they may still have done so, precisely because their language has an effect that is not apparent to them.

I have mentioned some problems in Spender's reasoning arising out of her failure to distinguish features of language use to which philosophers and linguists have drawn attention. But I want to argue more strongly that Spender's thesis about language is positively *damaging* for women. I believe this to be the case for four main reasons.

Spender's Thesis is Damaging for Women

First of all, on one interpretation of Spender, her thesis is just too bland to be of any value to women. Saying that all language is 'male' serves to divert attention away from those areas of language which really are sexist.

Secondly, there is the phenomenon to which I have already alluded: the fact that her thesis leads to incommensurability. This is damaging to women, I believe, for the following reason: if husband and wife can neither understand nor communicate with each other, then the wife cannot present criticism of the husband's use of language which he can come to accept. She and he will continue, whatever she says, to occupy their respective universes: he his, she hers. She cannot begin to enter his, nor he hers.

Now whether or not women will agree with me that this is damaging for them may depend on their politics. Some feminists will draw the conclusion that this state of affairs is not deleterious to the feminist cause; rather, what it entails is that women should have nothing whatever to do with men. Men inhabit their patriarchal realm; women live in a different world – and women should do their level best to ensure that the two universes don't overlap in any sense. Whatever men do, they will be revealing their oppressive natures, so women should have nothing to do with them.

Notice that Spender's picture of language leads to this separatist position. If men and women inhabit different worlds as a result of their language use, then women are unable to communicate with men. They are consequently unable to change men, and they might as well start building their own world, independently of the male oppressor. This is not a positive reason for separatism: rather separatism is an effect of a thesis about language. . . .

There is something in Spender which relates to my final criticism of separatism, and which provides further evidence of her thesis being damaging to women. There is an ambiguity in Spender's use of the phrase 'women's meanings'. This ambiguity is obscured by her view that there are two worlds — that of the male as well as the women's world. There are those women's meanings which are pejorative, derogatory, because according to her (or according to those whose research she is quoting) they are characterised that way by males; and there are those new, exciting, different meanings which women begin to discover, as they talk to one another in consciousness-raising groups and such like. In these gatherings, according to her, women begin to grasp that there are male and female worlds; they begin to be critical of the dominant (male) world, and to fashion a new one.

Referring indiscriminately to 'women's meanings' when Spender has these two, quite separate senses of the expression in view, serves to gloss over the differences between them. According to her, 'women's language' is seen by men as 'flowery', irrational, imaginative, etc. Now one possible response to this is to take the very same language but to view it positively — the women themselves may appropriate that 'language' and describe it in positive terms. Thus, to take an analogy, Hélène Cixous describes a Chinese story, which she takes from Sun Tse's manual of strategy — a handbook for the warrior. The story refers to a king, who is reputed to have asked Sun Tse to train his one hundred and eighty wives in the art of war. Instead of learning the code, however, the wives began laughing and chattering and not paying attention to the lesson. To the men, here, these ladies had failed at the art of war. According to Cixous, however, the women's behaviour is to be viewed positively by themselves. Cixous describes the phenomenon as a divergence of the two 'economies' — a masculine economy and a feminine one. The masculine economy is governed by order; by rules. The feminine one is quite different. The women's laughter and chatter is seen positively. It is part of their non-rule-governed behaviour. But to see their behaviour like this is simply to take women as we assume some men have wanted them to be, and to redescribe their behaviour. Women, therefore, will have a 'natural' way of being. Kristeva's work is an example of this same tendency. She speaks of 'feminine' discourses: poetry, irrationality, art, etc., which draw on areas the patriarchal culture represses.

It is not in women's interest, however, simply to remain as they have previously been characterised by males. Their 'natures' are not static. Women are not simply nurturant, passive, poetic and imaginative. They are not irrational. They are also active and rational creatures. Spender's picture of language — by leaving ambiguous the notion of 'women's meanings' — allows for the Kristeva reading of this expression. It allows 'women's language' to be the same as it is characterised by males, instead of being a new and exciting creation of women themselves.

Sexism and 'He/Man' Language

I believe, then, not only that there are problems with Dale Spender's thesis about language, but that her view is positively damaging for women. However, I don't want to say that language never exhibits sexism. I do believe the use of the expressions 'he' and 'man', for instance, in their purportedly gender-neutral fashion, reinforces power-relations between the sexes. Let's look at one of Spender's examples.

She tells us that, in 1746, John Kirby formulated his 'Eighty-eight grammatical Rules'. One of these, she says, stated that the 'male gender was *more comprehensive* than the female'. As she points out, in articulating this norm, Kirby did not mean that there were more males than females. What he must have been doing was reflecting the common belief, in society at the time, that males counted for more than females. Of course this common belief was actually *true*. It was the aristocracy and gentry – males – who occupied the positions of power in England: they were the politicians and doctors, and generally the educated. Women, as Rousseau said (and, of course, he meant upper-class women) were to be educated to be pleasing to men (i.e. males). And even in the working class, the man (the male) held power and authority in the family (though he did not in the workplace). So Kirby's reasoning did indeed serve to reinforce a state of affairs that was already in existence: the domination of women by men.

Kirby's rule that the male gender is more comprehensive than the female makes no sense independently of these facts about eighteenth century society. In a society where the roles of men and women were equal, no grammarian would propose that the male gender was 'more comprehensive' than the female. Kirby did not need to justify his rule, since it was quite acceptable, because it was implicit in 'common sense' assumptions of the period. In fact, if allowed to stand on its own feet, independently of the common sense assumptions which give it some sense, there are no grounds for accepting Kirby's rule. By articulating these assumptions, and giving them the authority of a grammatical rule, Kirby was surely reinforcing them. Subsequent usage of the pronoun 'he' in its supposedly gender-neutral manner has continued this process.

With reference to the Act of Parliament mentioned earlier; although, as I have remarked, I disagree with Spender as regards the *intentions* of those proposing the Bill, I do believe that it had the effect, and even the function, of preserving male dominance. Once again, if it had not been for male dominance generally, in society, there would have been no reason for proposing that 'he' should encompass 'she' rather than the other way about. It did not have to be uppermost in the minds of those introducing the Bill that they wanted to ensure male dominance, because the phenomenon was already well entrenched at the time. After all, the proposal that 'she' should encompass 'he' rather than the other way about would have fulfilled equally well their aim of simplifying the language. They would not have been keen on this suggestion. They wouldn't have liked it because they would have believed that it would have led to the subordination of males in some way. Some evidence that this would have been their reaction is provided by a parallel case recently — male nursery school teachers objected when it was proposed that 'she' should be a generic term for them. They resented the suggestion because they believed it would have implied a lowering of their status.

This latter example suggests that 'he' is not functioning as a generally neutral term at all. 'One' unlike 'man' carries no non-neutral connotations. 'Old' is sometimes used in neutral fashion, as in 'How old are you?', but it is invariably clear from the context that this is how it is intended. In the case of 'man' and 'he', however, the context does not always make it clear that the term is supposed to be being used in a neutral manner. Elaine Morgan describes the writings of evolutionists and ecologists when they say things like the following: 'it is just as hard for man to break the habit of thinking of himself as central to the species, as it was to think of himself as central to the universe. He sees himself quite unconsciously as the main line of evolution with a female satellite revolving around him.'

The sense of the noun 'man' is *ambiguous*. It is not understood whether or not the expression is to be understood in a neutral manner. The ambiguity allows for the continued subjection of the female. Evolutionists began by thinking neutrally and then, tacitly, switched to thinking only in terms of the male. Employers who advertise for a 'man' can trade on the ambiguity (a) to dissuade women from applying for the job; and (b) to appoint a male.

Here it is the confusion generated by the continued use of 'he' and 'man' in their purportedly neutral senses, I believe, which justifies the claim that continued use of this language serves to reinforce male oppression. So long as we can switch, unconsciously, from the neutral to the non-neutral senses, in one breath, we are silencing and excluding women.

There are two reasons, then, why 'he/man' language tends to reinforce unequal power relations between the sexes. First of all, the claim that there is a genuinely neutral sense of the term 'he' is, in fact, false; rather the introduction of such language presupposes unequal relations between the sexes. Its continual use reinforces oppression.

Secondly, there are often tacit switches from the supposed neutral to the non-neutral sense, slides which confirm that a greater degree of importance is often attached to the male in the neutral sense of the expression.

Use of 'he/man' language specifically, then, does seem to reinforce unequal power relations between the sexes. I would propose, however, that rather than this indicating that these expressions are part of a male language reflecting a male reality, it suggests that such discourse is *ideological* – it functions to disguise the power relations between the sexes. These relations are not presented clearly, for all to see; rather, it is because there is domination of one sex by the other that the expressions 'man' and 'he' can be used in their purportedly neutral senses. But, as we have seen, there is *really* no such thing as a neutral sense of them.

To conclude, while I strongly disagree with the 'philosophical' strands in Dale Spender's book, I believe that she presents an array of examples from English, many of which do provide incontrovertible evidence of sexism in language. Recognising that such 'he/man' language – as one case of such sexism – reinforces male supremacy is not at all to do away with that primacy. But it is a step in the right direction.

To say, as Spender does, that there are two realities – the male and the female – is not only to make criticism of the male 'reality' impossible, but it is to weaken the feminist case. Supposing that the phenomenon is ubiquitous makes it more difficult to see where sexism in language really operates.

TEXT AND SELECTED READING

The text is taken from Assiter's essay 'Did Man Make Language?' in a special issue ('Women, Gender and Philosophy') of *Radical Philosophy*, 34 (1983). Responses to her essay are Debbie Cameron's, 'Sexism and Semantics', and Anne Beezer's 'More on Man Made Language', both in *Radical Philosophy*, 36 (1984). The text with which Assiter herself takes issue is D. Spender's *Man Made Language* (London: Routledge and Kegan Paul, 1980). The best collection of texts in this area is D. Cameron (ed.), *The Feminist Critique of Language* (London: Routledge, 1990). The most useful introductions to many of the questions debated in this essay are D. Cameron, *Feminism and Linguistic Theory* (London: Macmillan, 1985) and J. Coates, *Women, Men and Language* (London: Longman, 1986), while a useful introduction to an alternative theoretical tradition is T. Moi's *Sexual/Textual Politics* (London: Methuen, 1985). For an essay which has much the same stance towards a static theory of meaning as that evinced in the above essay, see George Orwell's 'Politics and the English Language', in *The Collected Essays, Journalism and Letters of George Orwell*, vol. 3, ed. S. Orwell and I. Angus (Harmondsworth: Penguin, 1970), pp. 156–70.

19

John Marenbon

The historical context of Marenbon's pamphlet *English Our English*, published by the Tory think-tank the Centre for Policy Studies, is important to an understanding of its aims and arguments. The piece is best seen as a contribution to the new-right thinking on language and education which emerged in the 1980s. The historical situation is significant since it was a period of crisis across a number of related spheres with the cultural and political being the most important for our concerns. Over a wide range of practices the new right has sought to extend its influence by attacking the post-war consensus and attempting to foster new forms of activity and belief. Throughout this process language has been significant in two ways. First, at the level of vocabulary crucial changes have been wrought. One example of this has been the wrenching of the word 'community' from the political left. Formerly a word which suggested, at least in one sense, forms of social relationship which were not those organised by the state, it has now shifted its meaning. Over the past decade or so it has been used frequently precisely in order to refer to practices of the state which have required a favourable gloss. Instances of such use are: 'release into the community' (for mental patients); 'care in the community' (for the old and sick); 'community service' (for young offenders); and even 'the community charge' (otherwise known as the poll tax). The other way in which language has been used by the new right is once again in the fostering of forms of social and cultural identity by referring to particular forms of the language. This is, as can be noted in the extracts collected in this book, not just a return to Victorian values, but also an attempt to return to those of the eighteenth century.

It is important to be clear about the claims being made by the new right with regard to language and cultural identity but it may be useful first to challenge some of the assertions made about forms of language themselves. For example, it is claimed in this essay that creole and dialect speakers do not conform to the rules of their particular form of the language in the same way that standard English speakers follow the rules of their form. This is the case, it is argued, because for the creole speaker, 'parts of his speech will follow, not the rules of his language, but those of the standard language'. The point is, however, that the rules of speech are simply not delimited in this way; that *all* speakers switch codes, conform to different rules, follow different patterns of usage, according to the speech context. 'Standard English speakers' would be as likely to do this as other speakers; they do not ever simply speak standard English. Unless, that is, the rules of standard English already include the rules which govern all other forms of the spoken language. But this would be an absurdity.

Another odd claim is that the reason for the superiority of the standard language over the dialects is that whereas the standard changes slowly, the dialects change 'from decade to decade, from village to village, from street to street'. The first objection which must be made here is to ask for the evidence for this claim since none is provided. The second is to point to the counter evidence which shows that the vocabulary of the standard written language is undergoing extremely fast change in the face of the rapid advances which are taking place technologically and in the realm of social life. The claim here is also linked to the peculiar assertion that 'a mastery of the grammar of standard English' (is it the written or spoken language here? do they share the same grammar?) will remove 'any barrier at the level of basic understanding, to the formal writing of the past'. This amounts to arguing that a knowledge of the grammar of the contemporary written standard language (let us take it that it is this sense of the term which is being used here since it makes the argument at least easier to understand) can take away the difficulties 'at the basic level of understanding' of the reading of Chaucer, or even Shakespeare. Once again, however, this is to deny the significant changes which have taken place, and are taking place, in the language and which are of course the cause of the difficulties.

The text is full of such claims, usually without supporting evidence, propagated to serve as part of the general attack on linguistic study over the past thirty years. However, more important than these assertions are others which reveal the political intent of the writer. For what we find in these other claims is an appeal to a golden age once more; to a set of texts, the embodiment of a set of values it is argued, which can aid the construction of a bold and noble society. We find this claim for example in the argument that children should be acquainted not just with 'proper English', but with the 'literary heritage of the language'. There is not even a hint here that the constitution of the 'literary heritage' is open to question and debate; nor that there is in fact no agreed consensus on what this heritage is to include or leave out. However, what is perhaps most interesting in this respect is the method which is to be used for the teaching of literature (and thereby, according to the argument, the language). When the suggestion is examined, what it amounts to is that the aim of teaching children literature is simply to produce 'competent readers' who will read without originality, without technique and only according to already given standards and evaluations. It is a view of education as the unquestioning transmission and acceptance of a fixed set of values from one generation to another.

The underlying aim in this essay, as with so many others, is to construct a certain view of the social order and to propagate it. Thus this is a text which uses language as the site upon which political contestation can take place; and in particular the contestation of the prevailing modes of education. Its political intent slips through in the last lines in which the writer declares: 'in the future of its language there lies the future of a nation'. The irony is that this essay is based upon a rejection of the task of renewing our language in order to meet our present and future demands and needs. For what is being said in this text and others like it is this: 'in the past of our language there lies the future of our nation.'

ENGLISH OUR ENGLISH: THE NEW ORTHODOXY EXAMINED

What is wrong with the new orthodoxy

No part of this new orthodoxy, now so widespread among theorists, officials and teachers, stands up to scrutiny. Its tenets express, at best, half truths, in which a point of commonsense is exaggerated and distorted; and sometimes not even that.

'English is not just a subject'

This view has a positive aspect (English is more than a subject) and a negative one (English has no specific, definable subject-matter). The positive aspect is misguided, and the negative unnecessary. It is doubtless valuable that children should grow emotionally, that they should learn to tolerate the views of others and to engage in critical thinking. But these – and many of the other ambitious aims often proposed for English – are virtues which are slowly acquired in the course of acquiring particular intellectual skills and areas of knowledge. Time given to a vague and generalised attempt to gain such virtues is time lost to the specific and rigorous studies which alone will foster them. English could be one of these studies, were it to pursue the simple and well-defined aims of teaching children to write and speak standard English correctly, and of initiating their acquaintance with the literary heritage of the language.

'English teaching should be child-centred'

Good teachers have always recognised that effective instruction requires the active participation of the pupil: unless his efforts and attention are engaged, he will learn nothing. But the pupil's interest is merely a necessary condition for his learning: there is no good reason why it should determine what he learns. Few would contest this view with regard, for instance, to mathematics. The good mathematics teacher may well gain his pupil's interest by showing how numbers and their relations are relevant to their everyday concerns; but he will base his teaching not on the pupil's view of their own needs, but on his own, informed, view of what they need to know in order gradually to achieve a mastery of mathematical techniques. So long as English, too, is recognised as a subject, with definite aims, the same principles should guide its teachers. The grammar of English, its range of vocabulary and styles and its literary heritage exist independently of the child who is learning to use them.

'It is as important to teach the spoken as the written language'

Spoken language is as important – in some respects more important – than written language. But, whereas writing and reading are skills that require specific instruction, children learn to speak and listen just by being present at these activities. The child learns to speak and listen *better* in three main ways: first, by practice in the course of everyday life; second, by coming to understand more about all the various particular activities which can be the subjects of conversation (the more he knows about — for instance — woodwork, the more easily he can be taught to discuss it); third, by mastering the standard written language and thereby increasing his range of vocabulary, grasp of syntax and ability to choose standard forms correctly.

The fashionable emphasis on 'oracy' is in part a product of the tendency to regard English, not as a subject, but as an opportunity to acquire a haphazard collection of virtues (maturity, tolerance and so on); and in part an attempt to reduce the importance of standard English (which is the most usual form of the written language).

'Assessment should not concentrate on the pupil's errors'

No good teacher sets out to discourage and demoralise his pupils, concentrating on their mistakes to the exclusion of all else. But exponents of the new orthodoxy do not merely wish to insist on this sensible maxim. Their view, that it is 'more important to see what the child can do, rather than what he cannot', sounds tolerant and humane; but, in fact, it condemns those who speak and write badly to go on speaking and writing badly. The dire effects which it has are a simple consequence of other tenets of the new orthodoxy when they are applied to the question of assessment: the belief that English should be child-centred, and the belief that supposed mistakes in speech and writing are, at worst, examples of inappropriate use of language. If these tenets are rejected, then this view of assessment is left without support.

'Grammar is descriptive not prescriptive'

The error of this position is to assume that description must be an *alternative* to prescription. When I see in a French grammar that the imperfect of *je suis* is *j'étais*, I am reading both a description of how people speak in France and a prescription about how I must speak, if I am to speak French. By describing how a certain language is spoken or written, the grammarian prescribes usage for those who wish to speak or write that language. The case is the same for varieties of any given language. A grammar which describes standard English prescribes English usage for those who wish to speak or write it.

Whether a grammarian should phrase his discussion in descriptive or prescriptive terms depends on the purpose of his work. If, for instance, he is writing a monograph for linguists, who know well how to speak and write standard English but who are interested in how its various usages are to be analysed and classified, he will rightly use a descriptive terminology. But if he is writing so as to teach school-children how to write and speak standard English, it will be proper for him to prescribe. The prescriptive manner of old-fashioned school grammars, usually condemned by modern linguists, was entirely appropriate to their function.

Exponents of the new orthodoxy often use the statement that 'grammar is descriptive not prescriptive' as the slogan for their case against the teaching of standard English. In this way they manage to suggest that anyone who disagrees with them has simply misundersood the nature of grammar. But the misunderstanding is theirs. Grammar prescribes by describing.

'No language or dialect is inherently superior to any other'

This principle of linguistic equality can be understood in three different ways. Exponents of the new orthodoxy believe that it is true according to all these three interpretations.

It might be taken merely as a recognition that there is no intrinsic link between communicative adequacy and the particular forms of any given language. By this interpretation, the principle of linguistic equality is almost certainly true. There is no reason why one set of letters or sounds should be intrinsically better than another at standing for a certain sort of object or playing a certain role in sentences: *canis*, *chien*, *hund* and *dog* are equally good words for the same thing. Similarly there are all sorts of differences in structure between languages that cannot be described as better or worse: whether, for instance, the passive is formed by using an auxiliary, or by a change of form; or whether verbs are usually placed at the end or at the beginning of subordinate clauses; or whether adjectives precede or follow the nouns they qualify.

By another interpretation the principle of linguistic equality means that all languages are equally regular and rule-governed. This position is justified in one important way. Speech in, for instance, Cockney or West Indian Creole is sometimes described as 'ungrammatical'. The linguist is right to object to this description: although Cockney and West Indian Creole do not follow the grammar of standard English, they each have their own implicit rules, which modern grammarians have succeeded in describing. The linguist must, however, qualify this view. Whereas *all* the speech of someone who speaks standard English will tend, by and large, to bear out the rules with which linguists describe standard English, *all* the speech of a dialect or Creole-speaker is unlikely to bear out the rules which describe his dialect or Creole. Parts of his speech will follow, not the rules of his own language, but those of the standard language; and, at moments, his usage may reflect rules which belong to neither – for instance the phenomenon of 'hyperurbanism', where uneducated speakers use constructions such as 'They gave it to my mother and I' in an exaggerated effort at correctness.

By a third interpretation, the principle of linguistic equality means that every language is wholly (and therefore equally) adequate to the needs of the speakers. There is a sense in which this statement is not just true, but truistic. The only measure of a man's linguistic need in a particular area of life is the language he actually uses in that area of life – a language which will therefore be by definition fully adequate, whatever it is. But exponents of the new orthodoxy do not usually take adequacy to need in such a limited way: rather, they assume that the needs of speakers of different dialects and languages are all roughly the same, and that every language and dialect is equally capable of fulfilling them. From these premises they draw the conclusion that no one language is intrinsically more subtle, logical or precise than another; no one language, except by accidental convenience, more apt than another for any particular type of use or activity. This is a remarkable position, and a mistaken one.

Languages develop along with their users' manner of living; their capacity to fulfil functions is slowly gained as their users turn them to those functions. That languages such as standard English, French, German, Italian and Spanish can each be used equally well for such functions as telling a story, describing a scene, rousing a crowd to indignation and putting forward a logical argument is not the reflection of an equality between languages, but rather, of the similarities between English, French, German, Italian and Spanish cultures as they have developed. For an example of languages which have obviously different capacities, it is necessary merely to look at the different languages which language has been at different stages of its development. It was almost impossible to present clearly a complicated, abstract argument in the English of King Alfred's day, and Chaucer's English was still inadequate for this use; but as in the sixteenth and seventeenth centuries more and more writers tried to use English for such purposes, the language was gradually shaped to fulfil this function, so that Hume had in his native tongue an instrument perfectly adapted for the subtlest speculations. The differences in adequacy did not only lie in vocabulary, but in the possibilities of grammar and syntax. Chaucer's English allowed him to frame a narrative or a description with ease; but it could not accommodate complicated logical relations between concepts and arguments.

The differences in capacity between modern standard English and the modern dialects of English are even more striking than those between Chaucerian and modern English. When a man speaks a language, he draws on the resources of the culture which has produced that language. He enjoys the achievements of that culture and is restricted by its limitations. Standard English is the language of English culture at its highest levels as it has developed over the last centuries: the language not just of literature, philosophy and scholarship, but of government, science, commerce and industry. Dialects of English reflect the much more limited range of functions for which they have traditionally been used: the exchanges of everyday life, mainly among those unrefined by education. This does not mean that speakers of non-standard English cannot be verbally agile within certain areas of discourse, nor that topics traditionally discussed in the standard language are *entirely* barred to them. In a celebrated article, the sociolinguist William Labov recounts a conversation about God conducted with a young American Negro in his own dialect. Although Labov exaggerates the logical cogency of the young man's thought, there is no doubt that he was groping towards an interesting argument. But without the resources of Labov's own standard English this argument could not be clearly addressed and so made available for further elaboration and refinement.

Sometimes linguists suggest that, since most dialect speakers in England also know standard English, they could easily adapt their dialects to cover the range of functions performed by standard English, by borrowing from its vocabulary and syntax. But what gain can there be in using a conglomerate language, which was never before spoken or written, which no one will handle with ease and few will fully understand? And what justification for burdening school-children with the task of inventing it?

'Language-use should be judged by its appropriateness'

One of the criteria for judging the use of language is certainly appropriateness: the man who speaks to his wife as if she were a public meeting, or addresses a scientific congress in the language of the nursery, cannot be said to use language well. But exponents of the new orthodoxy are not content with this commonsensical position. Since they advocate the principle of linguistic equality, not only in its first and second, but also in its third interpretations, they believe that appropriateness is the *only* criterion for judging one language or sort of language superior to another. They conclude that, whilst one language might, as a matter of fact, happen to be more convenient or appropriate for a particular sort of occasion, there is no way in which any one language is intrinsically better than another. They allow that French is a better language than Finnish for buying bread in Paris, because most Parisian bakers understand French and few know any Finnish; and that standard English is a better language than Cockney or Scouse for writing a business letter, because most businessmen will receive a letter in standard English more favourably than one in dialect. But they deny that, in itself, any one language is more precise, logical, flexible or subtle than another. These conclusions cannot be upheld, once the third interpretation of the principle of linguistic equality is rejected.

The concept of 'appropriateness' has sometimes been used to defend the teaching of standard English in schools. Standard English, it is argued, should be taught because it happens to be the 'appropriate' sort of language for many activities. This argument is so unburdened by theorising and apparently commonsensical that advocates of standard English might be reluctant to reject it. But the position it supports — like so many which gain their appeal from their modesty — is a weak one. It lies defenceless against attacks from reformers who wish to change social patterns of language use in order to remove the pre-eminence of standard English. Those who support standard English solely on the grounds of its 'appropriateness' can have no principled objection to the substance of the reformers' recommendations. They can object, at most, only to their pace and their practicability.

The importance of standard english

At the centre of the new orthodoxy is its devaluation of standard English. From this derives its opponents' hostility to grammatical prescription: *because* they do not believe that standard English is superior to dialect, they do not believe that its grammar should be prescribed to children (a position they try to support by mistakenly insisting that grammar cannot ever prescribe); *because* they cannot accept that standard English is superior to dialect, they insist that the language schoolchildren use can be judged only by its 'appropriateness'.

Why is standard English superior to dialect? One important reason has already been suggested. Standard English has been developed over centuries to fulfil a far wider range of functions than any dialect – from technical description to philosophical argument, from analysis of information to fiction and poetry. Only by using another language (such as French) which had been developed similarly, over centuries, by a similar culture, could the speaker enjoy a similar resource.

Standard English gains another advantage over dialect by the very fact of being standard. When a linguist formulates the grammar of a dialect, he is engaged in an exercise which is to a considerable degree artificial. Dialect is always changing: from decade to decade, from village to village, from street to street. Outside the textbooks of sociolinguists, it is never clear which of the constructions that a dialect-speaker is using are grammatical and which are not, because it is never clear exactly which dialect he is speaking, or how consistently he is intending to speak it. Standard languages change too; but very, very slowly. The linguists may be quick to come forward with examples of constructions where usage within modern standard English is undecided (Do we say 'The Cabinet intends' or 'The Cabinet intend'? 'Throw me a lifebelt or I shall drown' or 'Throw me a lifebelt or I will drown'?) But for the vast majority of constructions, all who know standard English will recognise instantly not only whether they are correct or incorrect, but whether they are usual or unusual in their context. Similarly, all who know standard English can recognise the register to which a given word belongs. Such unanimity in usage makes standard English an excellent vehicle for clear communication, for conveying information and ideas without misunderstanding. It is no accident that standard English, rather than a dialect, has become an international language. Moreover, the existence of clearly recognised norms increases the expressive possibilities of a language. If, for instance, a standard English speaker inverts a construction for rhetorical effect, he can be sure that other speakers of standard English will notice what he has done and so appreciate his nuance. A speaker who attempted such linguistic subtlety in a dialect could not be sure that his intentions would be grasped, even by someone from the next street.

It is far easier to destroy a standard language than to create one. A standard language requires a body of speakers who have been trained to distinguish correct constructions from incorrect ones, usual forms from those which are unusual and carry with them special implications. Such training is neither short nor easy; and it is unrealistic to expect that English teachers can give it to their pupils if, along with teaching standard English (as one form of the language, appropriate for certain occasions), they are expected to encourage speech and writing in dialect and to attend to the multiplicity of other tasks with which modern educationalists have burdened them. By devaluing standard English, the new orthodoxy is destroying it. . . .

How English could be better taught in schools

The good English teacher's aims

A better approach to English teaching in schools would reject every tenet of the new orthodoxy. It would recognise English as a subject — no more and no less: the subject in which pupils learn to write standard English correctly and thereby speak it well, and in which they become acquainted with some of the English literary heritage. As such it would contain a distinct body of material which teachers must teach and pupils must learn. English teaching would therefore be 'child-centred' only in the very limited sense that all good teaching is child-centred — that it engages the interest and efforts of the pupils. Improvement in pupils' powers of speaking and listening would be achieved by improving their literacy.

The teacher would not hesitate to prescribe to the children on matters of grammatical correctness. He would recognise the superiority of standard English and see it as his task to make his pupils write it well and thereby gain the ability to speak it fluently. It does not follow from this that he would scorn dialects or their speakers. On the contrary, he would realise that many people use a dialect (or some dialect forms) in order to identify themselves as belonging to a particular social group. He would not expect his pupils to give up their dialect when talking to their friends or family, but he would recognise that children come to English lessons at school in order to be taught standard English. He would not, however, see it as an important part of his work to instruct his pupils in any specific sort of pronunciation of English (such as Received Pronunciation); but, just as he would try to avoid mistaking regional variations in pronunciation for errors in spoken language, so he would not try to overlook errors in spoken language by mistaking them for regional variations in pronunciation. And he would recognise that some regional accents can make their speakers' English hard to follow, especially to those from outside Britain.

A teacher who followed these tenets would set tasks and exercises for his pupils, not as some inchoate attempt to induce self-criticism, tolerance, maturity or liveliness of imagination, with the definite object of improving their use of language. He would regard the tasks and exercises proposed both by older text-books and by the newer ones critically but with an open mind. If the old-fashioned text-books and worksheets struck him as dull, he would ask himself whether their dullness was merely an unnecessary obstacle to engaging his pupils' interest or whether it was inevitable in what they sought to teach. He would recognise that the process of learning is often laborious and makes considerable demands on children's self-discipline. If the task suggested by modern books on English teaching seemed to him strange, he would nevertheless be willing to set them, so long as he was persuaded that they were the best way of making pupils learn an important aspect of correct speech or writing.

When such a teacher came to assess his pupils' work, he would be guided by the principle that, in English as surely as in Mathematics or Chemistry, there is right and wrong. Like any good teacher, he would mingle encouragement with correction; but he would not let an exaggerated concern to dwell on the pupils' successes distract him from his duty to point out, clearly and firmly, the pupils' mistakes — the instances where writing is ungrammatical, words are misspelt or misused, sentences are mispunctuated. He would know that the apparent kindness which spares children such admonishment is in fact a form of cruelty which denies them the opportunity to learn how to speak and write well.

While such a teacher would not discourage his pupils from writing their own poetry, he would tell them that verse requires both a command of the ordinary tools of language — syntax, vocabulary, punctuation — and also an ability to organise words according to their rhythm and sound. He would insist that his pupils learn to write rhymed and rhythmical regular poetry before venturing – if they wished – into freer forms of verse. And he would not pretend, to his pupils or himself, that their poetry was necessarily of great worth; but he would recognise that practice in this type of formally constrained writing can both help to promote good writing in all areas, and increases ability to read good poetry with taste and understanding.

How much should children and their teachers be taught about language?

Knowing about a language is not the same as knowing how to use language. An insistence that children learn to speak and write standard English correctly is not equivalent to an insistence that they learn about grammar. But the teacher who (disregarding the new orthodoxy) sets about making his pupils learn correct standard English, would find his task very difficult if he did not make them familiar with certain grammatical terms; terms with which he can frame rules which describe standard English. His pupils will need to learn to distinguish nouns, verbs, adjectives, adverbs, conjunctions, prepositions and exclamations; to identify subjects, objects and predicates; singulars and plurals; past, present, future; indicative, conditional and imperative; phrases, clauses and sentences. It is sometimes argued that these grammatical categories were originally devised in conjunction with Latin and Greek, and that they are therefore inappropriate for English. This objection ignores the fact that, as it has developed, standard English has been shaped by Latin usage and by the understanding of grammar involved in a classical education. The traditional, classically-based grammatical categories have themselves influenced the way educated men have spoken and written. It may be that, for the purposes of sophisticated linguistic description, some other set of categories is more precise; and that the professional linguist, writing for other professionals, does well to use them. But the terminology of traditional grammar remains the best instrument for describing the broad features of standard English, and so of prescribing usage to those learning it.

A teacher can impart all the knowledge about grammar necessary to help his children use standard English correctly without himself knowing about more than the traditional classically-based categories. Linguists are fond of saying that specialised knowledge of modern linguistics would make English teachers do their work better. It is hard to see why this should be so. No area of specialised knowledge can, in itself, fail to be of some benefit to teachers. But the demand that teachers learn modern linguistics is often no more than a hidden way of asking that they should be more thoroughly indoctrinated in the new orthodoxy about teaching the English language.

How English literature should be taught

For teachers who, following the new orthodoxy, allow casual speech and non-standard dialects to predominate in their classrooms, it can be difficult to introduce their pupils to literature. The only way open to them is to present literature in the context of the children's own attempts at creative writing; but this approach will still leave most literature other than some modern poetry and some sorts of narrative and drama irrecoverably distant from the pupils. Such difficulties will not trouble the teacher who has rejected the new orthodoxy. From the beginning he will have used literary texts (among others) to illustrate the usages of English, since these texts provide examples of English used at its best. And his pupils' mastery of the grammar of standard English will have removed any barrier, at the level of basic under-standing, to the formal writing of the past. Moreover, such a teacher will not have scorned the old-fashioned exercise of 'learning by heart'. He will have realised that, by learning to remember distinguished passages of prose and verse, children not only develop their capacity to memorise, but also lay down for themselves a valuable stock of literary examples, which they can come to know intimately and which will help to form their taste.

Basing himself on these foundations, the teacher should aim to introduce his pupils to a wide range of their literary heritage. He should not limit even thirteen or fourteen year-olds just to lyric poetry, prose fiction and drama; and he should try to introduce those who specialise in English at 'A' level to a whole range of genres — epic, pastoral, satire, dialogue, didactic poetry, discursive and admonitory prose. He should choose from those works which have been accepted by generations of readers as outstanding. Among poets, for instance, he might turn to Chaucer, Sidney, Spenser, Shakespeare, Donne, Jonson, Milton, Dryden, Pope, Wordsworth, Byron, Keats and Tennyson; among writers mainly of prose to Bacon, Swift, Gibbon, Hume, Richardson, Fielding, Hazlitt, Austen, Dickens and George Eliot. The Authorised Version of the Bible should be given a special place in English courses, since its language echoes through the writing of literature in succeeding centuries.

It is not among the teacher's tasks to make his pupils (even the most advanced ones) into literary historians; but, just in order to become competent readers of literature, they must learn how words change their meaning over the centuries; how literary forms are altered and elaborated; and how works written in times long past, when readers' ideas and expectations were very different from those of anyone today, are vivid and accessible to those familiar with the literary tradition of which these old books have come to be members.

Children learn to read literature as literature only by reading the literary works which are recognised as outstanding, and talking to those who are already competent readers of literature. Beyond care, patience and precision in reading, there are no techniques which can be taught for reading literature. The teacher must try to impart his own competence as a reader of literature by example, and beware of allowing his pupils to substitute for competence in reading an ability to manipulate a critical jargon and produce seemingly impressive essays. He should be sceptical of originality in response to literature because it is most likely to betray a failure of understanding. The competent reader of literature reads a work of literature much as other competent readers read it. His response is 'personal' only in that it is his; his view of the work, just as much as his judgment of it, rightly aspires to receive universal assent.

It may seem to follow from this that examinations in literature are inappropriate. This is indeed the case if they are regarded as ways of testing the competence of candidates as readers of literature. But they are useful for testing whether children have fulfilled the necessary *preconditions* for becoming competent literary readers: that they have read a wide range of outstanding literary works with care and attention to detail. Questions in literature examinations should therefore be simple, designed to test range and precision of reading; they should not – as most questions in 'A' level do now – ask candidates to write literary critical essays.

English and other subjects

There is a chapter in the Bullock Report called 'Language Across the Curriculum'. It suggests that all sorts of other subjects beside English provide opportunities for the teaching of language-use-opportunities which schools should not neglect. 'Language across the curriculum' has now become a slogan of the new orthodoxy, influencing teaching in many subjects in many schools, though not yet so universally as Her Majesty's Inspectorate (HMI) would like. There is no evidence that this policy has succeeded in making children more literate, and its effects on the study of subjects other than English are often regrettable. Pupils are distracted from the business of learning about, for instance, history or mathematics by the teacher's anxiety to develop their linguistic powers. Of course, it is necessary to speak and write well in history and mathematics. But an English course, properly regarded as a training in good English, will provide pupils with the techniques they need to discuss a mathematical problem or compose an historical essay. English is combined and confused with other subjects to its, and their, detriment.

However, there is one subject which, whilst quite distinct from English, has a special connection with it: Latin. The teaching of Latin in schools benefits the English both of those pupils who study it, and those who do not. Standard English has been formed through the centuries by its contact with Latin; and without some knowledge of Latin an Englishman will always remain, to an extent, a stranger to his own culture. But even those children not fortunate enough to be taught Latin, gain by the fact that Latin is taught in schools; or — to put it in the form which present circumstances make more pertinent — will lose if Latin continues to vanish from the school syllabus. That Latin is taught, not just as a specialist discipline like Sanskrit or Japanese, but widely at school-level, affirms that grammatical and lexical correctness are still valued; and, more practically, it ensures a supply of English teachers whose grasp of Latin will make their command of English and its grammar firmer and more explicit.

Conclusion: English, politicians and officials

The preceding sections have put forward certain arguments about how English should, and should not be taught in schools. They have suggested that it should be regarded as a subject, no more and no less, with two aims: to teach children to speak and write standard English well, and to initiate their acquaintance with the literary heritage of the language. But they have also suggested a conclusion of a different sort. They have shown how a certain set of ideas about English teaching (the 'new orthodoxy'), developed by theorists in the 1960s, have come to be adopted as principles by official bodies, such as the Bullock Commission, HMI and the APU. This conclusion should disturb even those who reject many of the other arguments proposed here.

There is a common tendency for government to look to experts for guidance about specialised matters. It is questionable whether such expert advice can ever be free from fashionable or political bias, even if the subject is apparently scientific or technical. To look in this way to experts for advice about the teaching of a subject such as English is unquestionably to invite confusion. The experts can merely provide theories, and information collected and interpreted in the light of those theories. *They* are not to be blamed for following the theories which have happened to be prevalent in learned circles (although their partiality to every fashionable folly should not, perhaps, go without remark or censure); but rather those who have endorsed their recommendations as if they were readily observable fact or indisputable scientific knowledge.

It is in this context that the activities of the HMI are particularly worrying. When the Inspectorate reports on pupil numbers, successes in examinations or the organisation of teaching in particular schools, its evidence is rightly regarded as authoritative. But recently — and especially with regard to English — HMI has made reports of quite another sort. Both in its general discussions and in its reports on individual schools, it has recommended how English and other subjects *should* be taught; what should be their aims, and what methods should be used to achieve them. Their recommendations largely reflect the tenets of the new orthodoxy; but they have been accepted as authoritative even by politicians whose own explicit, ideological convictions are the opposite of those on which the new orthodoxy is founded. Ministers of government, preoccupied with the external politics of education, have repeatedly been defeated in the more important internal politics of what is taught and how: defeated by an enemy they do not recognise, in a battle they do not know they are fighting.

It is now being proposed that a national curriculum be established to guide the content of teaching at school. And a committee has already been appointed by the Secretary of State for Education to recommend aims and methods for teaching how the English language works. The motive behind the proposal for a national curriculum is a worthy one: not a desire for uniformity, but an attempt to ensure that no child is denied a solid grounding by the whims of teachers and local authorities beguiled by modish subjects and syllabuses. But the record of official involvement in the English curriculum over the past two decades is not encouraging. In English, at least, there is every danger that a national curriculum will have the very opposite of its intended effect, and that it will succeed only in enforcing principles and practices which its political proponents would be the first to repudiate, if they understood their basis and their implications. It need not be so, if politicians and committees keep strong in their common sense, distrustful of experts, and chaste towards fashion.

May God grant them sharpness of mind and firmness of resolve, for in the future of its language there lies the future of a nation!

TEXT AND SELECTED READING

The text is taken from *English Our English: The New Orthodoxy Examined*, published by a Conservative think-tank, the Centre for Policy Studies (London: Centre for Policy Studies, 1987). Another example of such new-right thought on language and education is John Honey's *The Language Trap* (Middlesex: National Council for Educational Standards, 1983). The classic text with which both Marenbon and Honey take issue is W. Labov's, 'The Logic of Non-Standard English' in *Language in the Inner City* (Philadelphia: University of Pennsylvania Press, 1972). Tony Crowley, *The Politics of Discourse* (London: Macmillan, 1989), ch. 7, explores the political and educational implications of the new-right thought on language, as do D. Cameron and J. Bourne in 'No Common Ground: Kingman, Grammar and the Nation', *Language and Education*, 2(3) (1988). An excellent study and critique of the construction of a national identity on the lines laid down in the essay above is Paul Gilroy's *There Ain't No Black in the Union Jack* (London: Hutchinson, 1987).

Select bibliography

Aarsleff, Hans (1962) 'The Early History of the Oxford English Dictionary', *Bulletin of the New York Public Library*, 66.

Aarsleff, Hans (1967) *The Study of Language in England 1780–1860*, Princeton: Princeton University Press.

Aarsleff, Hans (1983) *From Locke to Saussure: Essays in the Study of Language and Intellectual History*, London: Athlone Press.

Alford, H. (1864) *The Queen's English: A Manual of Idiom and Usage*, London: Longman and Green.

Andresen, J.T. (1990) *Linguistics in America 1769–1924: A Critical History*, London: Routledge.

Ashcroft, B., Griffiths, G. and Tiffin, H. (1989) *The Empire Writes Back: Theory and Practice in Post-Colonial Literatures*, London: Routledge.

Assiter, A. (1983) 'Did Man Make Language?', *Radical Philosophy*, 34.

Attridge, D. (1988) 'Language as History/History as Language: Saussure and the Romance of Etymology' in *Peculiar Language: Literature as Difference from the Renaissance to James Joyce*, London: Methuen.

Baldick, C. (1983) *The Social Mission of English Criticism 1848–1932*, Oxford: Clarendon.

Baron, D. (1982) *Grammar and Good Taste: Reforming the American Language*, London: Yale University Press.

Barrell, J. (1983) 'The Language Properly So-Called' in *English Literature in History 1730–80. An Equal Wide Survey*, London: Hutchinson.

Beezer, A. (1984) 'More on Man Made Language', *Radical Philosophy*, 36.

Benzie, W. (1972) *The Dublin Orator: Thomas Sheridan's Influence on Eighteenth Century Rhetoric and Belles Lettres*, Leeds: Leeds University Press.

Bhabha, Homi K. (ed.) (1990) *Nation and Narration*, London: Routledge.

Brown, R. and Gilman, A. (1972) 'The Pronouns of Power and Solidarity' in *Language and Social Context*, ed. P. Giglioli, Harmondsworth: Penguin.

Buchanan, James (1764) *An Essay Towards Establishing A Standard For An Elegant and Uniform Pronunciation Of the English Language . . .*, London: Edward and Charles Dilly.

Buckle, R. (1983) *U and Non-U Revisited*, London: Routledge and Kegan Paul.

Burke, P. and Porter, R. (eds) (1987) *The Social History of Language*, Cambridge: Cambridge University Press.

Burrow, J. (1967) 'The Uses of Philology in Victorian Britain' in *Ideas and Institutions of Victorian Britain*, ed. R. Robson, New York: Barnes and Noble.

Bynack, V.P. (1984) 'Noah Webster's Linguistic Thought and the Idea of an American National Culture', *Journal of the History of Ideas*, 45.

Cameron, D. (1984) 'Sexism and Semantics', *Radical Philosophy*, 36.

Cameron, D. (1985) *Feminism and Linguistic Theory*, London: Macmillan.

Cameron, D. (1990) *The Feminist Critique of Language: A Reader*, London: Routledge.

Cameron, D. and Bourne, J. (1988) 'No Common Ground: Kingman, Grammar and the Nation', *Language and Education*, 2, 3.

Cassirer, E. (1953) *The Philosophy of Symbolic Forms, Vol. 1: Language*, London: Yale University Press.

Coates, J. (1986) *Women, Men and Language*, London: Longman.

Cohen, M. (1977) *Sensible Words: Linguistic Practice in England 1640–1785*, Baltimore: Johns Hopkins University Press.

Colls, R. and Dodd, P. (eds) (1986) *Englishness: Politics and Culture 1880–1920*, London: Croom Helm.

Crowley, T. (1989) 'Bakhtin and the History of the Language' in *Bakhtin and Cultural Theory*, ed. D. Shepherd and K. Hirschkop, Manchester: Manchester University Press.

Crowley, T. (1989) *The Politics of Discourse: The Standard Language Question in British Cultural Debates*, London: Macmillan.

Crowley, T. (1990) 'That Obscure Object of Desire: A Science of Language' in *Ideologies of Language*, ed. J.E. Joseph and T.J. Taylor, London: Routledge.

Crowley, T. (1991) 'The Return of the Repressed: Swift and Saussure on Language and History' in *New Departures in Linguistics*, ed. G. Woolf, New York: Garland.

Cunningham, H. (1981) 'The Language of Patriotism', *History Workshop Journal*, 12.

Davies, T. (1978) 'Education, Ideology and Literature', *Red Letters*, 7.

Dowling, L. (1982) 'Victorian Oxford and the Science of Language', *PMLA*, 97.

Doyle, B. (1989) *English and Englishness*, London: Routledge.

Eagleton, T. (1984) *The Function of Criticism*, London: Verso.

Eliot, T.S. (1953) *American Literature and the American Language*, Washington: Washington University Press.

Emsley, B. (1933) 'James Buchanan and the Eighteenth-Century Regulation of English Usage', *PMLA*, 48.

Fanon, F. (1967) *Black Skin, White Masks*, London: Grove Press.

Formigari, L. (1974) 'Language and Society in the Late Eighteenth-Century', *Journal of the History of Ideas*, 35.

Friend, J. (1967) *The Development of American Lexicography*, The Hague: Mouton.

Gilroy, P. (1987) *There Ain't No Black in the Union Jack: The Cultural Politics of Race and Nation*, London: Hutchinson.

Graham, G.F. (1869) *A Book About Words*, London: Longman and Green.

Harris, R. and Taylor, T.J. (1989) *Landmarks in Linguistic Thought: The Western Tradition from Socrates to Saussure*, London: Routledge.

History Workshop Journal (1989) 'Special Feature: Language and History', 27.

Honey, J. (1983) *The Language Trap: Race, Class and the 'Standard English' Issue in British Schools*, Middlesex: National Council for Educational Standards.

Howatt, A.P.R. (1984) *A History of English Language Teaching*, Oxford: Oxford University Press.

James, H. (1905–6) 'The Speech of American Women', *Harper's Bazaar*, 40–1.

Johnson, S. (1747) *The Plan of A Dictionary Of the English Language*, London.

Joseph, J.E. and Taylor, T.J. (eds) (1990) *Ideologies of Language*, London: Routledge.

Kelly, A.C. (1988) *Swift and the English Language*, Philadelphia: University of Pennsylvania Press.

Krapp, G.P. (1925) *The English Language in America*, New York: Century.

Labov, W. (1972) 'The Logic of Non-Standard English' in *Language in the Inner City*, Philadelphia: University of Pennsylvania Press.

Land, S.K. (1974) *From Signs to Propositions: The Concept of Form in Eighteenth Century Semantic Theory*, London: Longman.

Land, S.K. (1986) *The Philosophy of Language in Britain*, New York: AMS Press.

Locke, John (1690) *An Essay Concerning Human Understanding*, London: Awnsham and John Churchill.

Marenbon, J. (1987) *English Our English: The New Orthodoxy Examined*, London: Centre for Policy Studies.

Mathews, M.M. (1931) *The Beginnings of American English*, London: University of Chicago Press.

Mencken, H.L. (1936) *The American Language*, 4th edn, New York: Knopf.

Milroy, J. and Milroy, L. (1985) *Authority in Language*, London: Routledge and Kegan Paul.

Mittins, W., Saln, M., Edminson, M. and Coyne, S. (1970) *Attitudes to English Usage*, Oxford: Oxford University Press.

Moi, T. (1985) *Sexual/Textual Politics*, London: Methuen.

Murray, K.M.E. (1979) *Caught in the Web of Words: James A.H. Murray and 'The Oxford English Dictionary'* Oxford: Clarendon.

Newbolt, H. (1921) *The Teaching of English in England*, London: HMSO.

Ngugi Wa Thiongo (1986) *Decolonising the Mind: The Politics of Language in African Literature*, London: James Currey.

Orwell, G. (1946) 'Politics and the English Language' in *The Collected Essays, Journalism and Letters of George Orwell*, vol. 3, ed. S. Orwell and I. Angus, 1970, Harmondsworth: Penguin.

Paulin, T. (1984) 'A New Look at the Language Question' in *Ireland and the English Crisis*, Newcastle: Bloodaxe.

Pedersen, H. (1931) *The Discovery of Language: Linguistic Science in the Nineteenth Century*, trans. J.W. Spargo, 1959, Bloomington: Indiana University Press.

Phillips, K.C. (1984) *Language and Class in Victorian England*, Oxford: Blackwell.

Pickering, J. (1816) *A Vocabulary or Collection of Words and Phrases Which Have Been Supposed to be Peculiar To the United States of America*, Boston.

Proposal for the Publication of A New English Dictionary By The Philological Society, 1858, London: The Philological Society.

Rollins, R. (1976) 'Words as Social Control: Noah Webster and the Creation of the American Dictionary', *American Quarterly*, 28.

Ross, A.S.C. (1954) 'Linguistic Class-Indicators In Present-Day English', *Neuphilologische Mitteilungen*, 55.

Saussure, F. de (1916) *Course in General Linguistics*, trans. R. Harris, 1983, London: Duckworth.

Sheridan, Thomas (1762) *A Course of Lectures on Elocution*, London.

Simpson, D. (1986) *The Politics of American English 1776–1850*, Oxford: Oxford University Press.

Sledd, J. and Kolb, G. (1955) *Dr Johnson's Dictionary: Essays in the Biography of a Book*, Chicago: Chicago University Press.

Smith, O. (1984) *The Politics of Language 1791–1819*, Oxford: Oxford University Press.

Spender, D. (1980) *Man Made Language*, London: Routledge and Kegan Paul.

Swift, J. (1712) *A Proposal For Correcting, Improving and Ascertaining The English Language*, London: Benjamin Tooke.

Trench, R.C. (1851) *On the Study of Words*, London: Parker.

Walker, J. (1791) *A Critical Pronouncing Dictionary And Expositor Of the English Language*, London.

Watts, T. (1850) 'On the Probable Future Position Of the English Language', *Proceedings of the Philological Society*, 4.

Weber, S. (1976) 'Saussure and the Apparition of Language: The Critical Perspective', *Modern Language Notes*, 91.

Webster, N. (1789) *Dissertations on the English Language*, Boston.

Williams, R. (1961) *The Long Revolution*, London: Chatto and Windus.

Wood, N. (1983) *The Politics of Locke's Philosophy: A Social Study of 'An Essay Concerning Human Understanding'* Berkeley: University of California Press.

Woolf, G. (ed.) (1991) *New Departures in Linguistics*, New York: Garland.

Wyld, H. (1934) 'The Best English: A Claim for the Superiority of Received Standard English', *Proceedings of the Society for Pure English*, 4.

Index

Aarsleff, Hans 27, 135, 148, 158, 169, 180
abuse: of language *see* language
academy: American 113, 119; French 43, 44, 47
accent 72, 99–100, 104–6, 108–9, 212, 253–4
Addison, Joseph 54, 56, 59, 113, 117, 121
Alford, Henry 171–80
American English 83–93, 111–22, 131–4, 161, 166–9, 181–91, 213; Americanisms 167–8
analogy 36, 43, 52–3, 96–101 *passim*, 161
Andresen, Julie 93, 122
Armstrong, Ursula 1
Ashcroft, Bill 135
Assiter, Alison 229–42
Attridge, Derek 11
Austin, J. L. 234–5
authority: in language *see* language

Baldick, Chris 206
Baron, Denis 93, 122, 169, 180, 192
Barrell, John 41, 62, 72, 79
Beattie, James 118
Beezer, Anne 241
Benzie, William 72
Bhabha, Homi 11
Bible 9, 38, 155, 160, 256
Blair, Hugh 121
Book of Common Prayer 9, 38
Brown, R. 227
Buchanan, James 73–9, 81, 193, 195

Buckle, R. 227
Burke, Peter 12
Burrow, John 149
Bynack, V. P. 93

Cameron, Deborah 230, 241, 260
Campbell, George 95, 108–9, 118–19, 209
cant 33, 52, 160
Cassirer, Ernst 27
Caxton, William 64
change: in language *see* language
Chaucer, Geoffrey 89, 218, 244, 249–50, 256
Chomsky, Noam 234
Cicero 121, 130, 147
citizenship: and language *see* language
civilisation: and language *see* language
Cixous, Hélène 238
class: and language *see* language
Coates, Jennifer 241
cockney pronunciation 68, 70, 106–9, 212, 248
Cohen, Murray 62, 71, 72, 79, 110
Colls, Robert 11, 170, 206
colonialism 5, 7, 8, 124–5, 131–4
common tie of society: language as *see* language
communicational scepticism 14
consonant 36, 37, 104–6, 191
corruption: of language *see* language
Craik, G. L. 159
creole 248–9

265

Crowley, Tony 11, 12, 135, 148, 158, 169, 180, 218, 227, 260
cultural identity: role of language in formation of 1–11, 196–206, 243–4
culture: language as carrier of *see* language
Cunningham, Hugh 180
custom 49, 57, 71, 94, 100–3

Davies, Tony 158
Defoe, Daniel 11
dialect 52, 61, 64, 68–9, 74, 75, 78, 95, 106, 108–9, 113, 114, 134, 152, 194, 195, 204–5, 207–18 *passim*, 223, 244, 248–59 *passim*; as mark of disgrace 68–71, 74, 106–9
dictionary 25, 26, 33, 45–61, 69, 70, 75–7, 86, 90, 94, 96–109, 150–8, 174; delimitation of language in 46–8, 150–8
Dowling, Linda 148, 180
Doyle, Brian 11, 206
Dryden, John 59, 121, 256

Eagleton, Terry 62, 206
Eliot, T. S. 192
elocution 62–72, 73–9, 94–109, 203–5, 227; *see also* pronunciation
empiricism 13; *see also* Locke
Emsley, Bert 80
etymology 35, 48, 49, 51–2, 89–90, 139–48, 150–1, 154–5

Fanon, Frantz 135
feminism: and language 229–42
Fielding, Henry 63
Formigari, Lia 72
Franklin, Benjamin 81, 92, 118–21 *passim*
Frege, G. 232–3
Friend, J. 122

gender: and language *see* language
genius 36, 44; of the nation recorded in language 137
Gilroy, Paul 11, 260
golden age: of language 9, 28, 29, 33–4, 58, 244–5

Graham, G. F. 159–69
grammar 25, 31, 37, 43, 53, 54, 59, 60, 78, 96, 98, 105, 173–5 *passim*, 231, 244–59 *passim*

Harris, James 137
Harris, Roy 27
Herder, J. G. 123, 136–7
history: and language *see* language
history of the language 2, 7
HRH The Prince of Wales 9
Hobbes, Thomas 123
Honey, John 260
Horace 94, 102, 131
Howatt, A. P. R. 41, 62, 79, 110
Hume, David 126, 131, 249, 256

ideas *see* Locke
imperfections: of language *see* language
imperialism 124–51
institutions: and language *see* language
interpretation: of words in dictionary 55–6, 154–7
Irish pronunciation 69, 95, 103–6, 117

James, Henry 181–91, 209, 229
jargon 34, 50
Johnson, Samuel 3, 42–61, 63, 89, 91–2, 94, 96, 98–9, 103, 112, 121, 130–1, 150, 151, 166
Jonson, Ben 161, 256
Joseph, J. E. 11
Junius 89, 90

Kelly, A. C. 41
Kirby, John 239
Krapp, G. P. 122, 192

Labov, William 250, 260
Land, S. K. 27, 41
language: abuse of 13–27, 35, 85; authority in 37, 42, 43–4, 59–60, 119, 161, 167, 171–2; change in 28, 29, 33, 37–8, 40, 42, 49, 53, 60, 84–9, 101, 111, 114–29 *passim*, 231; and citizenship 43; civilisation

and 182, 186, 194, 202; class
  and 8, 44, 63, 67, 87, 95–6,
  108–9, 118, 160–9, 181–91,
  193–206 *passim*, 207–8, 219–27
  passim; common tie of society 14,
  19, 197–8; corruption of 31–3,
  50, 89, 111, 115–20 *passim*,
  162–9, 172–3, 177; culture and
  182, 184–91, 220; and gender 8,
  183–91, 229–42; and history
  3–9, 28–30, 31–4, 126–7,
  136–49 *passim*, 150, 193–5,
  243–5; imperfections of 19–27,
  31, 53, 101; institutions and 5,
  7, 171–2, 174–5; and morality
  138–48 *passim*, 179–80, 194,
  202; and nation 5, 7, 10, 43, 44,
  79, 81–93 *passim*, 111–22 *passim*,
  123–4, 136–49 *passim*, 150,
  172–3, 174–6, 197–200, 245,
  260; purity of 31, 33, 46, 50, 60,
  101, 113–20 *passim*, 159–69,
  177–80; and race 5, 7, 10, 29;
  reform of 28–9, 37, 83–93;
  sexism in 8, 229–42; women and
  36–7, 183–91, 229–42
lexicography 45, 46, 58, 139,
  150–9, 195
linguistics: 4, 255; external
  linguistics 6, 159; internal
  linguistics 6
literature: repository of standard
  language 150–1, 153–8; as
  standard of excellence for
  language 34–5, 38, 43–4, 60,
  119, 122
Locke, John 8, 13–27, 63, 65–7,
  123, 230; remedies for the
  imperfection of language
  19–27; theory of knowledge
  13–15; theory of signification
  15–27, 63, 65
Lowth, Robert 94, 96, 107

'man made language' 232–41
Marenbon, John 243–60
Mathews, M. M. 122, 192
Mencken, H. L. 192
metaphor 47, 55

Milroy, L. and J. 218, 227
Milton, John 47, 48, 50, 57, 60,
  113, 130, 132, 155, 256
Mittins, W. 227
Moi, Toril 242
morality: language and *see* language
Murray, K. M. E. 158

Nares, T. 97, 98
nation: language and *see* language
nationalism 2, 10; role of language in
  123–4, 151, 172–3, 193–5,
  197–201
Newbolt, Henry 193–206, 219
'new orthodoxy' 245–59
Ngugi wa Thiongo 135

orthoepy 97, 108
orthography 35–6, 42, 49–50, 76–7,
  83–93, 99–100, 107
Orwell, George 242
'Oxford English' 216–18

Paulin, Tom 93
Pedersen, H. 149
Pickering, John 111–22
Phillips, K. C. 170, 180
philological society 135, 150–8
philology 58
Pope, Alexander 44, 51, 56, 59, 60,
  113, 256
prescriptivism 3, 7, 11, 28, 172,
  247–8, 251
Priestley, J. 3
pronunciation 35, 42, 49, 50–1,
  67–72, 73–9, 83–93, 94–109, 181,
  183–91, 199–200, 203–5, 207–18,
  219–27; careless 162–3; colloquial
  98–9; 'received pronunciation'
  253
proper English 1, 2, 7, 8, 43; as
  construction of linguistic and
  cultural identity 28, 64, 73, 75, 77,
  161
proposal for the publication of a new
  English dictionary 150–8
propriety of speech 23, 34, 59, 66,
  102–3, 209–18 *passim*, 221–7

proscriptivism 7, 11
provincialisms 68, 108–9, 117, 195, 207, 210–11
public sphere 28, 181
purity: of language *see* language
Puttenham, George 73

Queen's English 170–80
Quintilian 53, 94–5, 121

race: and language *see* language
reform: of language *see* language
Rollins, R. 93
Ross, A. S. C. 219–27
rustic pronunciation 68, 70–1

Saussure, Ferdinand de ii, 4–7, 159–60, 230, 233–4; *Course in General Linguistics* 4–7
Scottish usage 214; Scotticisms 214
sexism: in language *see* language
Shakespeare 48, 56, 109, 132, 156, 161, 176, 244, 256
Shepherd, David 11
Sheridan, Richard 63
Sheridan, Thomas 63–72, 97–8, 103–6
signification 56, 89; Frege's theory of 231–2; Locke's theory of *see* Locke
Simpson, David 93, 110, 122, 170
slang 160–6, 179, 226
Sledd, J. 62
Smith, Olivia 79, 110
social unity: engendered by language 14, 19, 74, 79, 193–5, 196–206 *passim*
Society for Pure English 218
spelling *see* orthography; spelling reform 81–93
Spender, Dale 229–41
Spenser, Edmund 32, 256
standard: of linguistic usage 26, 33, 34, 38, 72, 73, 114–21 *passim*, 223; of pronunciation 72–9 *passim*, 115, 204–5, 207–18

standard English (*see also* standard language) 198, 204–5, 207–18, 244–59; received standard English 207–18
standard language: as form of spoken English 194–5, 198, 204, 207–18, 244–59; as literary language 152, 154, 195, 198, 244–59
style 1, 33, 38, 57, 58, 61, 118–19, 122, 153, 164, 167–8
Sweet, Henry 195, 210
Swift, Jonathan 3, 28–41, 51, 111–13, 117, 121, 130, 166, 229, 256
syntax 53–4, 250, 254

Taylor, T. J. 27
tone 182, 186–91 *passim*; tone standard 182–3, 186–91
Trench, R. C. 136–49, 150

'U and non-U' 220–7
universal language 123, 125, 206

vowels 37, 104–6, 191, 208–10, 212–15
vulgarism 109, 118, 160, 164–7 *passim*, 182, 188, 194, 204, 205, 208–11, 222

Walker, John 94–109
Waller, Edmund 29, 130
Wallis, John 28
Watts, Thomas 123–35
Weber, Samuel 11
Webster, Noah 81–93, 111–13, 119
Wilkins, John 123
Williams, Raymond 1, 8, 218
Wilson, Thomas 171
Wither, George 141
Witherspoon, J. 118, 120
women: and language *see* language
Wood, N. 27
Wyld, Henry 207–18, 219, 223

Young, G. M. 219